NCERT SOLUTIONS

with Chapterwise **Study Notes**

SCIENCE 10th

NCERT SOLUTIONS

with Chapterwise **Study Notes**

SCIENCE 10th

Author

Sushant Batra
Tarnija Midha
Nidhi Sehgal

Including Selected Questions of **DIKSHA**

arihant
SUCCESS AND NOTHING LESS

ARIHANT PRAKASHAN (Series), MEERUT

卐 **Administrative & Production Offices**

Regd. Office

'Ramchhaya' 4577/15, Agarwal Road, Darya Ganj, New Delhi -110002
Tele: 011- 47630600, 43518550

卐 **Head Office**

Kalindi, TP Nagar, Meerut (UP) - 250002
Tel: 0121-7156203, 7156204

卐 **Sales & Support Offices**

Agra, Ahmedabad, Bengaluru, Bareilly, Chennai, Delhi, Guwahati, Hyderabad, Jaipur, Jhansi, Kolkata, Lucknow, Nagpur & Pune.

卐 **PRICE** ₹255.00

卐 PO No. : TXT-59-T065424-06-25

Published by Arihant Publications (India) Ltd.

For further information about the books published by Arihant, log on to www.arihantbooks.com or e-mail at info@arihantbooks.com

Follow us on

Preface

Feeling the immense importance and value of NCERT books, we are presenting this book, having the **NCERT Exercises Solutions**. For the overall benefit of the students we have made this book unique in such a way that it presents not only solutions but also detailed explanations. Through these detailed and through explanations, students can learn the concepts which will enhance their thinking and learning abilities.

We have introduced some Additional Features with the solutions which are given below:

- **Explanatory Solutions** Along with the solutions to questions we have given all the points that tell how to approach to solve a problem. Here we have tried to cover all those loopholes which may lead to confusion. All formulae and hints are discussed in full detail.
- Also included **Thinking Process** and **Mistake Alert** to understanding 'How to solve question' and points of mistakes.
- **Note** We have provided notes also to solutions in which special points are mentioned which are of great value for the students.

Apart from all those who helped in the compilation of this book a special note of thanks to all. With the hope that this book will be of great help to the students, we wish great success to our readers.

Sushant Batra
Tarnija Midha
Nidhi Sehgal

Contents

Chemical Reactions and Equations

CHAPTER 01

Important Points

01 A chemical reaction may result in

- change in state
- change in colour
- evolution of a gas
- change in temperature

02 The method of representing a chemical reaction with the help of symbols and formulae of the substances involved in it, is known as **chemical equation.**

03 The process of making the number of atoms of each element equal on both the sides of an equation is called **balancing of an equation.**

e.g., $H_2 + Cl_2 \longrightarrow 2HCl$

04 To make a chemical equation more informative, the physical states of the reactants and products should be mentioned along with their chemical formulae.

05 A chemical reaction in which two or more substances combine to form a single substance is called a **combination reaction.**

e.g.,
$$\underset{\text{Carbon}}{C} + \underset{\text{Oxygen}}{O_2} \longrightarrow \underset{\text{Carbon dioxide}}{CO_2}$$

06 A reaction in which a substance breaks down into two or more substances is called **decomposition reaction.**

e.g.,
$$\underset{\text{Sodium chloride}}{2\,NaCl(s)} \xrightarrow[\text{current}]{\text{Electric}} \underset{\text{Sodium}}{2Na(s)} + \underset{\text{Chlorine}}{Cl_2(g)}$$

$$2\,AgCl(s) \xrightarrow{\text{Sunlight}} 2Ag(s) + Cl_2(g)$$

07 A chemical reaction in which a more reactive metal displaces a less reactive metal from its salt solution is called **displacement reaction.**

e.g., $Zn\,(s) + CuSO_4(aq) \longrightarrow ZnSO_4(aq) + Cu(s)$

08 In **double displacement** reaction, two different atoms or group of atoms are exchanged.

e.g., $BaCl_2 + Na_2SO_4 \longrightarrow BaSO_4 + 2NaCl$

09 Some double displacement reactions are also called **precipitation reactions** as during the reaction insoluble salts are produced, which are known as precipitate.

10 During some reactions, heat is given out and they are called **exothermic reactions,** while in some reactions heat is absorbed and they are called **endothermic reactions.**

11 The process of addition of oxygen or removal of hydrogen is known as **oxidation**, whereas removal of oxygen or addition of hydrogen is known as **reduction**.

12 A reaction in which oxidation and reduction both takes place simultaneously, is known as **redox reaction.**

13 Decay or decomposition of metal surfaces in presence of moisture, acids, etc., is known as **corrosion.** In case of iron, it is known as **rusting.**

14 When fats and oils are oxidised, their smell and taste changes and they become **rancid** (old and stale). This process is known as **rancidity.**

Intext Questions

On Page 6

Question 1 Why should a magnesium ribbon be cleaned before burning in air?

Sol. Magnesium ribbon reacts with oxygen present in air to form MgO (magnesium oxide). The MgO layer does not burn or slows down the burning process and thus should be removed.

Question 2 Write the balanced equation for the following chemical reactions.

(i) Hydrogen + Chlorine $\longrightarrow$ Hydrogen chloride

(ii) Barium chloride + Aluminium sulphate $\longrightarrow$ Barium sulphate + Aluminium chloride

(iii) Sodium + Water $\longrightarrow$ Sodium hydroxide + Hydrogen

◎ ***Thinking Process*** The number of atoms of each element remains the same on both sides of the balanced chemical equation.

Sol. (i) The symbol/formulae of hydrogen, chlorine and hydrogen cholride are H_2, Cl_2 and HCl respectively.

Thus, the simplest equation is $\underset{\text{Reactant}}{H_2 + Cl_2} \longrightarrow \underset{\text{Product}}{HCl}$

Now the balancing is done in following steps.

Step I Count the number of atoms of each elements on the reactant and product side of the equation.

Elements	LHS	RHS
H	2	1
Cl	2	1

Step II In order to equate the number of H atoms, write 2 in the equation before HCl. Now the equation becomes.

$$H_2 + Cl_2 \longrightarrow 2HCl$$

Step III Count further the number of atoms of each element on both sides.

At LHS		At	
No. of H atoms	No. of Cl atoms	No. of H atoms	No. of Cl atoms
2	2	2	2

Now the number of atoms of each element are equal on both the sides. Thus, $H_2(g) + Cl_2(g) \longrightarrow 2HCl(g)$ is the balanced equation for the given reaction (Where, (g) represents the gaseous state).

(ii) Formula of barium chloride, aluminium sulphate, barium sulphate and aluminium chloride is $BaCl_2$, $Al_2(SO_4)_3$, $BaSO_4$, $AlCl_3$ respectively. So, the unbalanced equation is

$$BaCl_2 + Al_2(SO_4)_3 \longrightarrow BaSO_4 + AlCl_3$$

On balancing the above equation [by the similar method as shown for (i)] we get

$$3BaCl_2(aq) + Al_2(SO_4)_3(aq) \longrightarrow 3BaSO_4(s) + 2AlCl_3(s)$$

(iii) Similary balanced equation for the give reaction is

$$2Na(s) + 2H_2O(l) \longrightarrow 2NaOH(aq) + H_2(g)$$

Mistake Alert One can make a mistake of not writing the physical states of reactants and products in a balanced chemical equation.

Question 3 Write a balanced chemical equation with state symbols for the following reactions.

(i) Solutions of barium chloride and sodium sulphate in water react to give insoluble barium sulphate and the solution of sodium chloride.

(ii) Sodium hydroxide solution (in water) reacts with hydrochloric acid solution (in water) to form sodium chloride solution and water.

Sol. (i) In this reaction, reactants are barium chloride ($BaCl_2$) and sodium sulphate (Na_2SO_4) and products are barium sulphate ($BaSO_4$) and sodium chloride (NaCl). So the balanced equation is:

$$\underset{\text{Barium chloride}}{BaCl_2(aq)} + \underset{\text{Sodium sulphate}}{Na_2SO_4(aq)} \longrightarrow \underset{\text{Barium sulphate}}{BaSO_4(s)} + \underset{\text{Sodium chloride}}{2NaCl(aq)}$$

(ii) In this reaction, sodium hydroxide (NaOH) and hydrogen chloride (HCl) are reactants and sodium chloride (NaCl) and water (H_2O) are the products so, the balanced equation for this reaction is:

$$\underset{\text{Sodium hydroxide}}{NaOH(aq)} + \underset{\text{Hydrogen chloride}}{HCl(aq)} \longrightarrow \underset{\text{Sodium chloride}}{NaCl(aq)} + \underset{\text{Water}}{H_2O(l)}$$

This reaction is known as **neutralisation reaction.**

On Page 10

Question 1 A solution of substance 'X' is used for white washing.

(i) Name the substance 'X' and write its formula.

(ii) Write the reaction of substance 'X' named in (i) above with water.

Sol. (i) We use quicklime solution for white washing. Hence, X is quicklime (CaO).

(ii) Quicklime + water $\longrightarrow$ slaked lime + Heat

$$\underset{(X)}{CaO(s)} + H_2O(l) \longrightarrow Ca(OH)_2(aq) + \text{Heat}$$

The reaction is highly exothermic and a lot of heat is produced.

Question 2 Why is the amount of gas collected in one of the test tubes in activity 1.7 double of the amount collected in another? Name this gas.

◎ ***Thinking Process*** Electrolysis of water is a decomposition reaction in which water breaks down to give simple products like hydrogen and oxygen gases.

Sol. The activity 1.7 of NCERT book is electrolysis of water. During electrolysis of water, water decomposes to form hydrogen and oxygen gases.

$$2\ H_2O\,(l) \xrightarrow{\text{Electrolysis}} 2H_2(g) + O_2(g)$$

The balanced equation shows clearly that the water decomposes during electrolysis to form hydrogen and oxygen gases in the ratio 2 : 1 by volume. Hence, the amount of hydrogen gas collected is twice or double the amount of oxygen collected. Thus, the name of the gas is hydrogen.

On Page 13

Question 1 Why does the colour of copper sulphate solution change when an iron nail is dipped in it?

Sol.

$$\underset{\text{(Blue)}}{CuSO_4\,(aq)} + Fe\,(s) \longrightarrow \underset{\text{(Green)}}{FeSO_4\,(aq)} + Cu\,(s)$$

The above equation clearly shows that the colour of solution changes from blue to green. This is actually a displacement reaction in which a more reactive element displaces a less reactive element from its salt solution. Iron being more reactive than copper displaces copper from $CuSO_4$ solution (blue) to form $FeSO_4$ (green). Hence, change in colour is observed.

Question 2 Give an example of double displacement reaction other than the one given in Activity 1.10.

◎ ***Thinking Process*** Double displacement reactions are reactions in which there is an exchange of ions between the reactants to form products.

Sol.

$$\underset{\text{Silver nitrate}}{AgNO_3\,(aq)} + \underset{\text{Sodium chloride}}{NaCl\,(aq)} \longrightarrow \underset{\text{Silver chloride (white ppt.)}}{AgCl\,(s)} + \underset{\text{Sodium nitrate}}{NaNO_3\,(aq)}$$

Question 3 Identify the substances that are oxidised and substances that are reduced in the following reactions.

(i) $4Na(s) + O_2(g) \longrightarrow 2Na_2O(s)$

(ii) $CuO(s) + H_2(g) \longrightarrow Cu(s) + H_2O(l)$

◎ *Thinking Process*

- If a substance grains oxygen during a reaction, it is said to be oxidised.
- If a substance loses oxygen during a reaction, it is said to be reduced.

Sol. (i) $4Na(s) + O_2(g) \longrightarrow 2Na_2O(s)$

In this reaction, Na has gained oxygen so Na is oxidised to Na_2O. Whereas, O_2 is being reduced to Na_2O as it has lost an oxygen.

Reduced (O_2)

$$4Na(s) + O_2(g) \longrightarrow 2Na_2O(s)$$

Oxidised (Na)

Oxidised (H_2)

(ii) $CuO(s) + H_2(g) \longrightarrow Cu(s) + H_2O(l)$

Reduced (CuO)

CuO is losing oxygen to form Cu (s), so it is getting reduced whereas, $H_2(g)$ is gaining this oxygen to form $H_2O(l)$, so it is getting oxidised.

Exercises

Question 1 Which of the statements about the reaction below are incorrect?

$$2PbO(s) + C(s) \longrightarrow 2Pb(s) + CO_2(g)$$

(a) Lead is getting reduced.

(b) Carbon dioxide is getting oxidised.

(c) Carbon is getting oxidised.

(d) Lead oxide is getting reduced.

(i) (a) and (b) (ii) (a) and (c)

(iii) (a), (b) and (c) (iv) all

Sol. (i) (a) and (b) are incorrect. In the given reaction, oxygen is removed from PbO, so lead oxide is getting reduced. Oxygen is added to carbon so carbon is getting oxidised.

Question 2 $Fe_2O_3 + 2Al \longrightarrow Al_2O_3 + 2Fe$

The above reaction is an example of a

(a) combination reaction
(b) double displacement reaction
(c) decomposition reaction
(d) displacement reaction

Sol. (d) In the above reaction, since Al is more reactive than Fe, so it displaces Fe from Fe_2O_3 to form Al_2O_3. Hence, it is a displacement reaction.

Question 3 What happens when dilute hydrocloric acid is added to iron fillings? Tick the correct answer.

(a) Hydrogen gas and iron chloride are produced
(b) Chlorine gas and iron hydroxide are produced
(c) No reaction takes place
(d) Iron salt and water are produced

Sol. (a) Iron being more reactive than hyrogen, displaces hydrogen from dilute HCl. Thus, hydrogen gas and iron chloride are formed.

$$Fe\,(s) + 2HCl\,(aq) \longrightarrow FeCl_2\,(aq) + H_2(g)$$

Mistake Alert In a displacement reaction, only a more reactive element can displace the lesser reactive element from its salt solution and not *vice-versa.*

Question 4 What is a balanced chemical equation? Why should chemical equations be balanced?

Sol. A chemical change is represented by a **chemical equation.** When the number of atoms of different elements on reactant and product side are equal then the chemical equation is called a balanced **chemical equation.**

It is important to balance a chemical equation because

1. a chemical reaction should obey the **law of conservation of mass** which states that the mass of reactants should be equal to the mass of the products and the total mass of a system is thus conserved.

   This law holds true only if number of atoms of reactants reacting together is equal to number of product atoms formed.
2. a balanced chemical equation tells us about the physical states and of the reactants and products whether they are in solid (*s*), liquid (*l*), gas (*g*) or aqueous (*aq*) states.
3. it tells us about heat changes that can take place in a chemical reaction.

   (Δ is the symbol of heat). Hence, if the reaction is endothermic or exothermic can be deduced from a balanced chemical equations.

Question 5 Translate the following statements into chemical equation and then balance them.

(a) Hydrogen gas combines with nitrogen to form ammonia.

(b) Hydrogen sulphide gas burns in air to give water and sulphur dioxide.

(c) Barium chloride reacts with aluminium sulphate to give aluminium chloride and a precipitate of barium sulphate.

(d) Potassium metal reacts with water to give potassium hydroxide and hydrogen gas.

Sol. (a) The symbol equation for the reaction is

$$H_2 + N_2 \longrightarrow NH_3$$

The balancing of equation is done in the following steps

Step I Let us count the number of atoms of all the elements of the reactants and the products on both sides of the equation.

Elements	No. of atoms of reactants (LHS)	No. of atoms of products (RHS)
H	2	3
N	2	1

A simple look at the equation reveals that the number of H and N atoms are not equal on both side of the equation.

Step II In order to equate the number of H atoms on both sides, put coefficient 3 before H_2 on the reactant side and coefficient 2 before NH_3 on the product side.

$$3H_2 + N_2 \longrightarrow 2NH_3$$

Step III On counting, the number of N atoms on both sides of the equation, they are also the same (2). This means that equation is balanced and can be written as:

$$3H_2(g) + N_2(g) \longrightarrow 2NH_3(g)$$

(b) The symbol equation for the reaction is

$$H_2S + O_2 \longrightarrow H_2O + SO_2$$

The balancing of equation is done in the following steps:

Step I Let us count the number of atoms of all the elements on both sides of the equation.

Elements	No. of atoms of reactants (LHS)	No. of atoms of products (RHS)
H	2	2
S	1	1
O	2	3

A simple look at the equation reveals that the number of H and S atoms are equal on both the sides. At the same time, the number of O atoms are not equal.

Step II In order to equate the number of O atoms, put coefficient 3 before O_2 on the reactant side and coefficient 2 before SO_2 on the product side.

$$H_2S + 3O_2 \longrightarrow H_2O + 2SO_2$$

Step III O atoms are still not balanced. To achieve this, put coefficient 2 before H_2O on the product side.

$$H_2S + 3O_2 \longrightarrow 2H_2O + 2SO_2$$

Step IV To balance S atoms put coefficient 2 before H_2S on the reactant side.

$$2H_2S + 3O_2 \longrightarrow 2H_2O + 2SO_2$$

Step V On inspection, the number of atoms of all the elements in both side of the equation are equal. Therefore, the equation is balanced and can be written as:

$$2H_2S(g) + 3O_2(g) \longrightarrow 2SO_2(g) + 2H_2O(l)$$

(c) The symbol equation for the reaction is

$$BaCl_2 + Al_2(SO_4)_3 \longrightarrow AlCl_3 + BaSO_4$$

The balancing of equation is done in the following steps.

Step I Let us count the number of atoms of all the elements on both sides of the equation.

Elements	No. of atoms of reactants (LHS)	No. of atoms of products (RHS)
Ba	1	1
Al	2	1
Cl	2	3
S	3	1
O	12	4

A simple look at the equation reveals that only Ba atoms are equal on both the sides. The rest of the atoms are to be balanced. It is done as follows

Step II In order to equate the number of Al atoms, put coefficient 2 before $AlCl_3$ on the product side.

$$BaCl_2 + Al_2(SO_4)_3 \longrightarrow 2AlCl_3 + BaSO_4$$

Step III In order to balance Cl atoms, put coefficient 3 before $BaCl_2$ on the reactant side.

$$3BaCl_2 + Al_2(SO_4)_3 \longrightarrow 2AlCl_3 + BaSO_4$$

Step IV To balance Ba atoms, put cofficient 3 before $BaSO_4$ on the product side.

$$3BaCl_2 + Al_2(SO_4)_3 \longrightarrow 2AlCl_3 + 3BaSO_4$$

Step V On inspection, the number S and O atoms on both sides of the equation are also found to be equal. Thus, the equation is in balanced form and can be written as:

$$3BaCl_2(aq) + Al_2(SO_4)_3(aq) \longrightarrow 2AlCl_3(aq) + 3BaSO_4(s)$$

(d) The symbol equation for the reaction is $K + H_2O \longrightarrow KOH + H_2$

The balancing of the equation is done in the following steps :

Step I Let us count the number of atoms of all the elements on both sides.

Elements	No. of atoms of reactants (LHS)	No. of atoms of products (RHS)
K	1	1
H	2	3
O	1	1

A simple look at the equation reveals that the number of K and O atoms on both sides of the equation are equal. At the same time, the number of H atoms are not equal.

Step II To balance the number of H atoms, put coefficient 2 before KOH on the product side and 2 before H_2O on the reactant side.

$$K + 2H_2O \longrightarrow 2KOH + H_2$$

Step III To balance the number of K atoms in the above equation, put coefficient 2 before K atom on the reactant side.

$$2K + 2H_2O \longrightarrow 2KOH + H_2$$

Step IV On inspection, the number of atoms of all the elements are found to be equal on both sides of the equation. The equation is finally balanced and can be written as:

$$2K(s) + 2H_2O(l) \longrightarrow 2KOH(aq) + H_2(g)$$

Question 6 Balance the following chemical equations.

(a) $HNO_3 + Ca(OH)_2 \longrightarrow Ca(NO_3)_2 + H_2O$

(b) $NaOH + H_2SO_4 \longrightarrow Na_2SO_4 + H_2O$

(c) $NaCl + AgNO_3 \longrightarrow AgCl + NaNO_3$

(d) $BaCl_2 + H_2SO_4 \longrightarrow BaSO_4 + HCl$

Sol. (a) The symbol equation as given for the reaction is

$$HNO_3 + Ca(OH)_2 \longrightarrow Ca(NO_3)_2 + H_2O$$

The balancing of the equation is done in the following steps.

Step I Let us count the number of atoms of all the elements on both the sides of the equation.

Elements	No. of atoms of reactants (LHS)	No. of atoms of products (RHS)
H	3	2
O	5	7
N	1	2
Ca	1	1

A simple look at the equation reveals that the number of Ca atoms are equal on both sides. But, the rest of the atoms are to be balanced.

Step II In order to equate the number of N atoms, put coefficient 2 before HNO_3 on the reactant side.

$$2HNO_3 + Ca(OH)_2 \longrightarrow Ca(NO_3)_2 + H_2O$$

Step III In order to equate the number of H atoms, put coefficient 2 before H_2O on the product side.

$$2HNO_3 + Ca(OH)_2 \longrightarrow Ca(NO_3)_2 + 2H_2O$$

Step IV On inspection the number of O atoms on both sides of the equation is the same, *i.e.*, 8. Therefore, the equation is balanced and can be written as:

$$2HNO_3(aq) + Ca(OH)_2(aq) \longrightarrow Ca(NO_3)_2(aq) + 2H_2O(l)$$

(b) The symbol equation as given for the reaction is

$$NaOH + H_2SO_4 \longrightarrow Na_2SO_4 + H_2O$$

Step I Let us count the number of atoms of all the elements on both sides of the equation.

Elements	No. of atoms of reactants (LHS)	No. of atoms of products (RHS)
H	3	2
O	5	5
Na	1	2
S	1	1

A simple look at the equation reveals that the number of O and S atoms are equal on both sides. But, the number of H and Na are not equal.

Step II In order to equate the number of Na atoms, put coefficient 2 before NaOH on the reactant side.

$$2NaOH + H_2SO_4 \longrightarrow Na_2SO_4 + H_2O$$

Step III In order to equate the number of H atoms, put coefficient 2 before H_2O on the product side.

$$2NaOH + H_2SO_4 \longrightarrow Na_2SO_4 + 2H_2O$$

Step IV On inspection, the number of O atoms on both sides of the equation is the same *i.e.* 6. Therefore, the equation is balanced and can be written as:

$$2NaOH\,(aq) + H_2SO_4(aq) \longrightarrow Na_2SO_4(aq) + 2H_2O(l)$$

(c) The symbol equation as given for the reaction is already balanced.

$$NaCl(aq) + AgNO_3(aq) \longrightarrow AgCl(s) + NaNO_3(aq)$$

(d) The symbol equation as given for the reaction is

$$BaCl_2 + H_2SO_4 \longrightarrow BaSO_4 + HCl$$

Step I Let us count the number of atoms of all the elements on both sides of the equation.

Elements	No. of atoms of reactants (LHS)	No. of atoms of products (RHS)
Ba	1	1
H	2	1
O	4	4
S	1	1
Cl	2	1

A simple look at the equation reveals that the number of Ba, S and O atoms are equal on both the sides. But the number of H and Cl atoms are not equal.

Step II In order to equate the number of Cl atoms, put coefficient 2 before HCl on the product side.

$$BaCl_2 + H_2SO_4 \longrightarrow BaSO_4 + 2HCl$$

Step III On inspection the number of H atoms on both sides of the equation is the same *i.e.* 2. Therefore, the equation is balanced and can be written as:

$$BaCl_2(aq) + H_2SO_4(aq) \longrightarrow BaSO_4(s) + 2HCl(aq)$$

Question 7 Write the balanced chemical equation for the following reactions.

(a) Calcium hydroxide + Carbon dioxide $\longrightarrow$ Calcium carbonate + Water

(b) Zinc + Silver nitrate $\longrightarrow$ Zinc nitrate + Silver

(c) Aluminium + Copper chloride $\rightarrow$ Aluminium chloride + Copper

(d) Barium chloride + Potassium sulphate $\longrightarrow$ Barium sulphate + potassium chloride

Sol. (a) $Ca(OH)_2(aq) + CO_2(g) \longrightarrow CaCO_3(s) + H_2O(l)$

(b) $Zn(s) + 2AgNO_3(aq) \longrightarrow Zn(NO_3)_2(aq) + 2Ag(s)$

(c) $2Al(s) + 3CuCl_2(aq) \longrightarrow 2AlCl_3(aq) + 3Cu(s)$

(d) $BaCl_2(aq) + K_2SO_4(aq) \longrightarrow BaSO_4(s) + 2KCl(aq)$

Question 8 Write the balanced chemical equation for the following and identify the type of reaction in each case.

(a) Potassium bromide (*aq*) + Barium iodide (*aq*) $\longrightarrow$ Potassium iodide (*aq*) + Barium bromide (*s*).

(b) Zinc carbonate (*s*) $\rightarrow$ Zinc oxide (*s*) + Carbon dioxide (*g*)

(c) Hydrogen (*g*) + Chlorine (*g*) $\longrightarrow$ Hydrogen chloride (*g*)

(d) Magnesium (*s*) + Hydrochloric acid(*aq*) $\longrightarrow$ Magnesium chloride (*aq*) + Hydrogen (*g*)

Sol. (a) $2KBr\ (aq) + BaI_2(aq) \longrightarrow 2KI\ (aq) + BaBr_2(s)$

This is a double displacement reaction because Br is replaced by I and I is replaced by Br in KBr and BaI_2, respectively.

(b) $ZnCO_3\ (s) \longrightarrow ZnO(s) + CO_2(g)$

This is a decomposition reaction because one compound splits into two compounds.

(c) $H_2(g) + Cl_2\ (g) \longrightarrow 2HCl(g)$

This is a combination reaction because two reactants combine to form a single product.

(d) $Mg(s) + 2HCl\ (aq) \longrightarrow MgCl_2\ (aq) + H_2(g)$

This is a displacement reaction because H is replaced by Mg.

Question 9 What does one mean by exothermic and endothermic reactions? Give examples.

Sol. On the basis of heat changes that take place during a chemical reaction we have two types of reactions–exothermic and endothermic.

Chemical reactions on the basis of heat changes

• heat is **absorbed**	• heat is **released**
• + **heat**	• – heat
• **endothermic**	• **exothermic**

⇒ In exothermic reactions, energy of reactants is greater than energy of products.

Example $CH_4 + 2O_2 \longrightarrow CO_2 + 2H_2O + Heat$
Methane Oxygen

$C + O_2 \longrightarrow CO_2 + Heat$

⇒ In endothermic reactions, energy of products is greater than the energy of reactants.

Example $2HgO(s) + Heat \longrightarrow 2Hg(l) + O_2(g)$

$N_2(g) + O_2(g) + Heat \longrightarrow 2NO(g)$

Note We can write + Heat with products in exothermic reactions and –Heat with products in endothermic reactions.

Question 10 Why is respiration considered an exothermic reaction? Explain.

Sol. We need energy to stay alive, which we get from the food we eat. When we eat food we are actually consuming different nutrients like fats, proteins and carbohydrates. When the process of digestion begins in the body these complex nutrients are broken down into simpler forms like glucose, due to the action of various enzymes. This reaction releases heat. During respiration, the air we breathe oxidises the glucose formed due to digestion and CO_2 and H_2O are released with heat. Since, heat is released therefore respiration is considered an exothermic reaction.

$$\underset{\text{Glucose}}{C_6H_{12}O_6} + \underset{\text{(from air)}}{6O_2} \longrightarrow 6CO_2 + 6H_2O + \underset{\text{energy}}{\text{Heat}}$$

Question 11 Why are decomposition reactions called the opposite of combination reactions? Write equations for these reactions.

Sol. When two or more substances combine together to form a new substance, it is called a combination reaction.

e.g.,
$$CaO + CO_2 \longrightarrow CaCO_3$$
$$2H_2 + O_2 \longrightarrow 2H_2O$$

In decomposition reactions, just the opposite happens. One substance splits to give two or more simpler substances. Hence, it is the opposite of combination reaction.

$$CaCO_3 \xrightarrow{\Delta} CaO + CO_2$$
$$2FeSO_4 \xrightarrow{\Delta} Fe_2O_3 + SO_2 + SO_3$$

Question 12 Write one equation each for decomposition reaction where energy is supplied in the form of heat, light or electricity?

Sol. (i) $CaCO_3\,(s) \xrightarrow{\Delta} CaO\,(s) + CO_2(g)$

(ii) $2AgBr\,(s) \xrightarrow{\text{Light}} 2Ag\,(s) + Br_2\,(g)$

(iii) $2H_2O\,(l) \xrightarrow{\text{Electricity}} 2H_2\,(g) + O_2\,(g)$

Question 13 What is the difference between displacement and double displacement reactions ? Write equation for these reactions.

Sol. I. Displacement reaction

$$\underset{\text{(Blue)}}{CuSO_4(aq)} + Fe(s) \longrightarrow \underset{\text{(Green)}}{FeSO_4(aq)} + Cu(s)$$

In this reaction, since Fe is more reactive than Cu so it displaces Cu from $CuSO_4$ to form $FeSO_4$ and sets Cu free. Hence, colour of solution changes from blue to green. This is single displacement reaction.

II. Double displacement reaction

e.g., $AgNO_3(aq) + NaCl\,(aq) \longrightarrow AgCl\,(s)\downarrow + NaNO_3(aq)$

In this reaction, displacement occurs twice and mutual exchange of ions takes place between $AgNO_3$ and NaCl, and hence it is a double displacement reaction.

$$AgNO_3(aq) + NaCl(aq) \longrightarrow AgCl(s) + NaNO_3(aq)$$

Question 14 In the refining of silver, the recovery of silver from silver nitrate solution involved displacement by copper metal. Write down the reaction involved.

Sol. The chemical equation of the displacement reaction is

$$\underset{\text{Copper}}{Cu\,(s)} + \underset{\text{Silver nitrate}}{2AgNO_3(aq)} \longrightarrow \underset{\text{Copper nitrate}}{Cu(NO_3)_2(aq)} + \underset{\text{Silver}}{2Ag\,(s)}$$

Question 15 What do you mean by precipitation reaction? Explain by giving examples.

Sol. An insoluble product formed during a chemical reaction is called a **precipitate.** Those reactions in which reactants react to form a product which is insoluble and separates out in the form of a precipitate is called a **precipitation reaction.**

e.g., $AgNO_3(aq) + NaCl(aq) \longrightarrow AgCl\,(s) + NaNO_3(aq)$

$Na_2SO_4(aq) + BaCl_2(aq) \longrightarrow BaSO_4(s) + 2NaCl\,(aq)$

Question 16 Explain the following in terms of gain or loss of oxygen with two examples each.

(a) Oxidation (b) Reduction

Sol. When oxygen is gained by a chemical substance, it is called **oxidation.**

e.g., $C(s) + O_2(g) \longrightarrow CO_2(g)$ (C is oxidised to CO_2)

$2Mg(s) + O_2(g) \longrightarrow 2MgO(s)$ (Mg is oxidised to MgO)

When oxygen is lost by a chemical substance, it is called **reduction.**

e.g., $ZnO(s) + C\,(s) \longrightarrow Zn\,(s) + CO\,(g)$ (ZnO is reduced to Zn)

$PbO(s) + C(s) \longrightarrow Pb(s) + CO(g)$ (PbO is reduced to Pb)

Question 17 A shiny brown coloured element 'X' on heating in air becomes black in colour. Name the element 'X' and the black coloured compound formed.

Sol. A Shiny brown coloured substance is copper. It turns black on heating due to the formation of black coloured copper oxide.

$$2Cu(s) + O_2(g) \xrightarrow{\Delta} \underset{\substack{\text{Copper (II) oxide} \\ \text{(black)}}}{2CuO(s)}$$

Hence, *X* = copper and compound formed is CuO (copper (II) oxide).

Question 18 Why do we apply paint on iron articles?

◎ ***Thinking Process***

- The corrosion of iron is called rusting.
- Rusting occurs when iron is in contact with moisture and air.

Sol. We apply paint on iron articles to prevent their damage from rusting. By doing this, the surface of the articles do not come in contact with air and moisture, and gets protected against rusting.

Question 19 Oil and fat containing food items are flushed with nitrogen. Why?

Sol. Oil and fat containing food items when exposed to oxygen (or air), gets oxidised to form compounds that change the taste and smell of these food stuffs, making them **rancid.**

Flushing these food items with nitrogen, which is an inert gas protects the food items from getting rancid.

The 'Lays' chips that you eat has nitrogen gas flushed in it to prevent rancidity.

Question 20 Explain the following terms with one example each.

(a) Corrosion (b) Rancidity

Sol. (a) **Corrosion** The process of slow degradation or eating up of metals when exposed to moist air is called corrosion.

When a metal is attacked by substances around it such as moisture, acids, etc., it is said to corrode and the process is called **corrosion.**

The black coating on silver and the green coating on copper are some examples of corrosion.

e.g., **Silver** develops black coat due to hydrogen sulphide of air.

$$2Ag + H_2S \longrightarrow \underset{\text{(black)}}{Ag_2S} + H_2$$

(b) **Rancidity** When fats and oils are oxidised, they become rancid and their smell and taste gets changed. This process is known as rancidity. Usually substances which prevent oxidation (antioxidants) are added to foods containing fats and oils. Keeping food in air tight containers and in refrigerators also helps to slow down oxidation. Chips which we eat are usually flushed with nitrogen gas to prevent rancidity.

Mistake Alert One can make a mistake of using the terms, corrosion and rusting interchangibly, which is not correct. Rusting is only the process of corrosion of iron and not other metals like silver, copper, etc. Whereas, corrosion is a common process of degradation of any metal with moisture, acid, etc.

DIKSHA APP Questions

☐ Multiple Choice Questions

Q.1 The following reaction is an example of a

$Mg + CuSO_4 \longrightarrow MgSO_4 + Cu$

(a) Combination reaction
(b) Decomposition reaction
(c) Displacement reaction
(d) Double Displacement reaction

Sol. (c) $Mg + CuSO_4 \longrightarrow MgSO_4 + Cu$

- Reaction is an example of a Displacement reaction.
- Displacement reactions are chemical reactions in which an element displaces another element in a compound.

Note Here Mg is oxidised (addition of oxygen) and $CuSO_4$ is reduced (removal of oxygen) so it is also a redox reaction.

Q.2 Which of the following gas can be used for storage of fried potato chips in packets for a long time?

(a) Carbon dioxide
(b) Nitrogen
(c) Oxygen
(d) Hydrogen

◎ ***Thinking Process*** The oxidative deterioration of oil is known as rancidity.

Sol. (b)
- Nitrogen (N_2) gas can be used for storage of fried potato chips in packets for a long time.
- Helium and Nitrogen are unreactive gases. They provide an inert atmosphere and prevent the oxidation of the oil (or rancidty).

Q.3 Which of the following is a double displacement reaction?

(a) $Pb + CuCl_2 \longrightarrow PbCl_2 + Cu$
(b) $H_2 + Cl_2 \longrightarrow 2HCl$
(c) $BaCl_2 + K_2SO_4 \longrightarrow BaSO_4 + 2KCl$
(d) $Zn + AgNO_3 \longrightarrow ZnNO_3 + Ag$

Sol. (c) $BaCl_2 + K_2SO_4 \longrightarrow BaSO_4 + 2KCl$ is a double displacement reaction.

- A double displacement reaction is a reaction where the ions of the reactants exchange between one another to form products.
- K^+ ion form K_2SO_4 combine with Cl^- ion of $BaCl_2$ and SO_4^{2-} ion combines with Ba^{2+} ion to form two new compounds as potassium chloride (KCl) and barium sulphate ($BaSO_4$) respectively.

Q.4 Which of the following statements about the given reaction are correct?

$$CuO + H_2 \longrightarrow Cu + H_2O$$

(a) Copper metal is getting oxidised.
(b) Water is getting reduced.
(c) Water is acting as reducing agent.
(d) Copper oxide is acting as oxidising agent.

Thinking Process

- Oxidising agent is a substance that helps another substance to undergo oxidation and itself gets reduced.
- Reducing agent helps another substance to undergo reduction and itself gets oxidised.

Sol. (d) Option (d) statement, copper oxide is acting as oxidising agent is correct.

$$CuO + H_2 \longrightarrow Cu + H_2O$$

During this reaction, copper (II) oxide is losing oxygen and is being reduced. Whereas, the hydrogen is gaining oxygen and is being oxidised.

So, CuO acts as oxidising agent and H_2 acts as reducing agent.

Q.5 Which of the following is an exothermic process?

(a) Electrolysis of molten sodium chloride.
(b) Dilution of an acid.
(c) Sublimation of Naphthalene balls.
(d) Evaporation of acetone.

Sol. (b) Dilution of an acid is an exothermic process. An exothermic process is a reaction that releases heat energy.

Q.6 When a magnesium ribbon is burnt in air, the ash formed is

(a) black
(b) pink
(c) yellow
(d) white

Sol. (d)
- When a magnesium ribbon is burnt in air, the ash formed is white.
- The chemical name of white ash is magnesium oxide.

$$2Mg(s) + O_2(g) \longrightarrow \underset{\text{(White ash)}}{2MgO(s)}$$

Q.7 Which information is not conveyed by a balanced chemical equation?

(a) Physical states of reactants and products.

(b) Symbols and formulae of all the substances involved in a particular reaction.

(c) Number of atoms/molecules of the reactants and products formed.

(d) Whether a particular reaction is actually feasible or not.

Sol. (d) Whether a particular reaction is actually feasible or not, is not conveyed by a balanced chemical equation.

A balanced equation does convey the physical state of both the reactants and products and the formula and symbol for all the substances involved. It also conveys the number of atoms and molecules in a reaction.

Q.8 Dilute hydrochloric acid is added to granulated zinc taken in a test tube. The following observations are recorded. Point out the correct observation.

(a) The surface of metal becomes shining.

(b) The reaction mixture turns milky.

(c) Odour of a pungent smelling gas is recorded.

(d) A colourless and odourless gas is evolved.

Sol. (d) When dilute hydrochloric acid is added to granulated zinc placed in a test tube, colourless and odourless gas is evolved with bubbles.

The reaction is

$$Zn(aq) + 2HCl(aq) \longrightarrow ZnCl_2(l) + H_2(g)$$

In the reaction, we can see that zinc being more reactive than H displaces H from HCl to form $ZnCl_2$ and H_2 gas is evolved.

Q.9 When carbon dioxide is passed through lime water

(a) calcium hydroxide is formed.

(b) white precipitate of CaO is formed.

(c) colour of lime water disappears.

(d) lime water turns milky.

Sol. (d) When carbon dioxide is passed through lime water, it turns milky due to the formation of a white precipitate of calcium carbonate ($CaCO_3$).

Reaction for the formation of Calcium Carbonate is

$$Ca(OH)_2(aq) + CO_2(g) \longrightarrow CaCO_3(s) + H_2O(l)$$

The white precipitate of calcium carbonate will settle down at the bottom if left undisturbed for some time.

Q.10 Both CO_2 and H_2 gases are

(a) heavier than air. (b) colourless.
(c) soluble in water. (d) acidic in nature.

Sol. (b) • Both CO_2 and H_2 gases are colourless in nature because of their distinct properties. Being colourless is the only common property when it comes to CO_2 and H_2 whereas all the other properties are completely opposite.

- CO_2 is heavier than air, whereas H_2 is lighter than air.
- CO_2 is soluble in water (to form H_2CO_3, carbonic acid), but H_2 is only slightly soluble in water.
- CO_2 is acidic in nature, as it forms carbonic acid (H_2CO_3) when dissolved in water. However, H_2 is neutral and does not form an acidic solution.

Q.11 In double displacement reaction between aqueous potassium iodide and lead nitrate, a yellow precipitate of lead iodide is formed. While performing activity, if lead nitrate is not available which one of following can be used

(a) Lead sulphate (b) Lead acetate
(c) Ammonium acetate (d) Potassium sulphate

Sol. (a) In a double displacement reaction between potassium iodide (KI) and lead (II) nitrate ($Pb(NO_3)_2$), lead iodide (PbI_2) forms as a yellow precipitate. If lead nitrate is unavailable, lead acetate ($Pb(CH_3COO)_2$) can be used instead, as it will react with potassium iodide to form the same yellow precipitate of lead iodide (PbI_2).

- Lead sulphate ($PbSO_4$) is already insoluble in water, and it does not react with potassium iodide to form lead iodide. Therefore, it cannot be used to produce the yellow precipitate of lead iodide.
- Ammonium acetate and potassium sulphate does not contain lead, so they cannot participate in the reaction to form lead iodide.

Q.12 Anu heated some lead nitrate crystals in a boiling tube. She recorded the evolution of

(a) colourless gas (b) odourless gas (c) brown gas (d) violet gas

Sol. (c) When lead nitrate ($Pb(NO_3)_2$) is heated, it undergoes a decomposition reaction. The heat causes the lead nitrate to break down into lead oxide (PbO), nitrogen dioxide (NO_2) gas, and oxygen (O_2) gas. The brown gas that is released is nitrogen dioxide (NO_2), which has a characteristic brown colour.

$$2Pb(NO_3)_2(s) \xrightarrow{\text{heat}} 2PbO(s) + 4NO_2(g) + O_2(g)$$

Q.13 Silver chloride turns grey on exposure to sunlight for a long duration due to

(a) the formation of silver by decomposition of silver chloride.
(b) sublimation of silver chloride.
(c) formation of chlorine gas from silver chloride.
(d) oxidation of silver chloride.

Sol. (a) White silver chloride undergoes decomposition of silver chloride into silver and chlorine by light. The silver (Ag) formed in the reaction is in its metallic form, which is grey in colour and this causes the silver chloride (AgCl) to turn grey upon exposure to sunlight.

Q.14 What is the chemical name for rust?

(a) Ferric sulphate (b) Ferric oxide
(c) Hydrated ferric oxide (d) Ferric chloride

Sol. (c) Rust is the common name for the corrosion product formed when iron (Fe) reacts with oxygen (O_2) and water (H_2O) over time. The chemical name for rust is hydrated ferric oxide and its formula is often represented as $Fe_2O_3 \cdot xH_2O$, where x represents the number of water molecules associated with the iron oxide.

Mistake Alert One can make a mistake in considering the chemical name of rust as ferric oxide, instead of hydrated ferric oxide.

☐ Very Short Answer Type

Q.1 Identify the combination reactions out of the two:

(i) $Cl_2 + 2KI \rightarrow 2KCl + I_2$ (ii) $2K + Cl_2 \rightarrow 2KCl$

Thinking Process When two or more substances (elements or compounds) combine to form a single product, the reactions are called combination reactions.

Sol. (ii) $2K + Cl_2 \rightarrow 2KCl$ is the combination reaction.

Q.2 Identify the reducing agents in the following reactions:

(a) $CH_4 + 2O_2 \rightarrow CO_2 + 2H_2O$
(b) $3Fe + 4H_2O \rightarrow Fe_3O_4 + 4H_2$

Sol. (a) Methane (CH_4) is the reducing agent because it undergoes oxidation (addition of oxygen) to form CO_2 and it removes oxygen from O_2 and causes its reduction to form H_2O.

(b) Iron (Fe) is the reducing agent because it undergoes oxidation (addition of oxygen) to form Fe_3O_4 and it removes oxygen from H_2O and causes its reduction to form H_2.

Q.3 Give one example of exothermic reaction.

◎ *Thinking Process* Reactions in which heat is released along with the formation of products are called exothermic chemical reactions.

Sol. One example of exothermic reaction is burning of natural gas.

$$CH_4(g) + 2O_2(g) \longrightarrow CO_2(g) + 2H_2O\,(g) + \text{Heat}$$

Q.4 Give two examaples of oxidation from day to day life.

Sol. Two examples of oxidation from day to day life are:

(i) Rusting of iron (ii) Burning of coal or natural gas

Q.5 Write the type of reaction in the following

(i) The reaction between an acid and a base (ii) Rusting of iron

Sol. (i) Neutralisation reaction

(ii) Oxidation reaction

☐ Short Answer Type

Q.1 One should not store copper sulphate in an iron vessel. Give reason.

Sol. One should not store copper sulphate ($CuSO_4$) in an iron vessel because of a displacement reaction between copper sulphate and iron. Iron (Fe) displaces copper (Cu) from copper sulphate ($CuSO_4$) because iron is more reactive than copper. This results in the formation of iron sulphate ($FeSO_4$) and copper metal (Cu). This means that iron will corrode and copper metal will form in the solution.

$$Fe\,(s) + CuSO_4(aq) \longrightarrow FeSO_4(aq) + Cu\,(s)$$

Q.2 Copper articles generally get coated with green layer when kept in the open for a few days.

(a) Why do copper articles generally get coated with green layer when kept open for a few days? Name the phenomenon involved.

(b) Name the green substance formed.

Sol. (a) Copper articles develop a green layer when exposed to air for a few days because of a chemical process called corrosion. Copper reacts with oxygen in the air to form copper oxide. Copper oxide then combines with carbon dioxide and water to form copper carbonate and copper hydroxide, which gives the copper a green colour.

(b) The green substance that forms is a mixture of copper carbonate and copper hydroxide, also known as basic copper carbonate [$CuCO_3.Cu(OH)_2$].

Q.3 Silver bromide should be stored in brown bottles. Explain why.

Sol. Silver bromide (AgBr) should be stored in brown bottles to protect it from light. It is light-sensitive and undergoes photodecomposition when exposed to light. The silver (Ag) formed from this decomposition can tarnish and alter the quality of the silver bromide. Bromine gas (Br_2) is also released Suring the photodecomposition of AgBr, which is volatile and can be harmful.

$$2AgBr(s) \xrightarrow{\text{Sunlight}} 2Ag(s) + Br_2(g)$$

Q.4 2 g of ferrous sulphate crystals are heated in a dry boiling tube.

(i) List any two observations.

(ii) Name the type of chemical reaction that takes place.

(iii) Write the chemical equation for the reaction.

Sol. (i) Smell of burning sulphur and reddish brown solid of ferric oxide is formed during the heating of ferrous sulphate crystals.

(ii) This is a type of decomposition reaction.

(iii) $$\underset{\text{(Ferrous Sulphate)}}{2FeSO_4(s)} \xrightarrow{\text{Heat}} \underset{\text{(Ferric oxide)}}{Fe_2O_3(s)} + SO_2(g) + SO_3(g)$$

Q.5 Varun carried out the chemical reaction between aqueous solutions of barium chloride and sodium sulphate. Write any one prominent observation that Varun would have recorded. Name the type of chemical reaction that has occurred and define it. Write a balanced chemical equation to explain above reaction.

Sol. Varun would have observed that a white substance, which is insoluble in water, is formed. It is a type of double displacement reaction, in which there is an exchange of ions between the reactants to form products.

$$\underset{\text{(Sodium sulphate)}}{Na_2SO_4(aq)} + \underset{\text{(Barium chloride)}}{BaCl_2(aq)} \longrightarrow \underset{\text{(Barium sulphate)}}{BaSO_4(s)} + \underset{\text{(Sodium chloride)}}{2NaCl(aq)}$$

It can also be considered as a precipitation reaction as it results in the formation of a precipitate or an insoluble substance.

☐ Long Answer Type

Q.1 Write an example of each reaction which is characterized by

(a) change in colour (b) evolution of heat

(c) formation of precipitate (d) evolution of a gas

Sol. (a) Change in colour

$$\underset{}{Fe(s)} + \underset{\text{(Blue)}}{CuSO_4(aq)} \longrightarrow \underset{\text{(Green)}}{FeSO_4(aq)} + Cu(s)$$

(b) Evolution of heat

$$CaO(s) + H_2O(l) \longrightarrow Ca(OH)_2(aq) + \text{Heat}$$

(c) Formation of precipitate

$$\underset{\text{(Sodium sulphate)}}{Na_2SO_4(aq)} + \underset{\text{(Barium chloride)}}{BaCl_2(aq)} \longrightarrow \underset{\text{(Barium sulphate)}}{BaSO_4(s)} + \underset{\text{(Sodium chloride)}}{2NaCl(aq)}$$

(d) Evolution of a gas

$$2Na(s) + 2H_2O(l) \longrightarrow 2NaOH\,(aq) + H_2(g)$$

Q.2 On heating blue coloured powder of copper nitrate in a boiling tube, copper oxide oxygen gas and a brown gas X is formed.

(a) Write a balanced chemical equation of the reaction.

(b) Identify the brown gas X evolved.

(c) Identify the type of reaction.

(d) What could be the pH range of the aqueous solution of the gas X?

Sol. (a) The decomposition reaction of copper nitrate ($Cu(NO_3)_2$) when heated is as follows

$$2Cu(NO_3)_2(s) \xrightarrow{\text{heat}} 2CuO(s) + 4NO_2(g) + O_2(g)$$

(b) The brown gas is nitrogen dioxide gas.

(c) It is a decomposition reaction.

(d) NO_2 is an oxide of non-metal, so it is an acidic oxide. On dissolving it in water, it will produce an acidic solution, thus, the pH of the solution will be less than 7.

Acids, Bases and Salts

CHAPTER 02

Important Points

01 Acids are sour in taste and change the colour of blue litmus to red, whereas, bases are bitter in taste and change the colour of the red litmus to blue.

02 Acid-Base indicators like litmus, turmeric, phenolphthalein, etc., are the substances that indicates the presence of an acid or a base in solution.

03 Some indicators tell us whether a substance is acidic or basic by changing colour. *e.g.*, phenolpthalein, litmus, turmeric, etc.

04 Some substances changes odour in acidic or basic media, and these are called olfactory indicators. Examples of olfactory indicators are : vanilla, onion and clove. All these three retain their smell in acidic solutions, but loses their smell in basic solutions.

05 Acids are the compounds which contain one or more hydrogen atoms and when dissolved in water they produce hydronium ions (H_3O^+). H^+ ions from acids cannot exist alone, so they combine with water molecules to form hydronium ions.

$$H^+ + H_2O \longrightarrow H_3O^+$$

06 Acids are classified as organic and mineral acids on the basis of their sources.

07 Acids are classified as strong and weak acids on the basis of their strength.

08 Acidic oxides (non-metallic oxides) dissolve in water to give acids.

09 Active metals react with acids to produce metallic salts and hydrogen.

10 Acids react with bases to give salt and water and the reaction is called neutralisation reaction.

11 When an acid reacts with a metal carbonate or metal hydrogen carbonate, it gives the corresponding salt, carbon dioxide gas and water.

12 Base is either a metallic oxide or a metallic hydroxide which reacts with hydronium ions of an acid to form salt and water only.

13 Formation of hydroxyl (OH^-) ions in the solution is responsible for the basic nature of a substance.

14 An alkali is a base soluble in water. **Examples :** NaOH, KOH, etc.

15 Mixing of an acid or a base with water results in decrease in the concentration of ions $\left(\frac{H_3O^+}{OH^-}\right)$ per unit volume. Such a process is called dilution and the acid or base is said to be diluted.

16 The pH of a solution is the logarithm of the reciprocal of its hydrogen ion concentration. Higher is the hydronium ion concentration, lower is the pH value.

17 The pH of water is 7. Hence, it is neutral.

18 An acidic solution has a pH less than 7 and a basic solution has a pH more than 7.

19 Generally, paper impregnated with the universal indicator is used for measuring pH.

20 Living beings carry out their metabolic activities within an optimum pH range.

21 pH is important in daily life as :

(a) When pH of rain water is less than 5.6, it is called acid rain. It affects the survival of aquatic life in rivers.

(b) Plants require a specific pH range for their healthy growth.

(c) Our stomach produces HCl which helps in digestion of food. During indigestion, excess of this acid is produced in the stomach, which can be neutralised by antacids (like milk of magnesia) .

(d) When pH of the mouth gets lower than 5.5, then tooth decaying starts. This can be prevented by using toothpastes, which are generally basic in nature.

(e) Bee-sting and stinging hair of nettle leaves inject formic acid (or methanoic acid), which causes burning pain and irritation. This can be relieved by using a mild base like baking soda on the stung area.

22 Some naturally occurring acids and their sources are :

Natural source	Acid	Natural source	Acid
Vinegar	Acetic acid	Sour milk (Curd)	Lactic acid
Orange	Citric acid	Lemon	Citric acid
Tamarind	Tartaric acid	Ant sting	Methanoic acid
Tomato	Oxalic acid	Nettle sting	Methanoic acid

23 Acidic and basic solutions in water conduct electricity because they furnish hydrogen and hydroxide ions respectively.

24 Some salts have a fixed number of water molecules, chemically attached to each formula unit of the salt in its crystalline form and is known as water of crystallisation.

25
- Salts of a strong acid and a strong base are neutral with a pH value of 7.
- Salts of a strong acid and a weak base are acidic with a pH value less than 7.
- Salts of a strong base and a weak acid are basic with a pH value more than 7.

26 Common salt (NaCl) is an important raw material for various chemicals like sodium hydroxide, baking soda, washing soda, bleaching powder, etc.

27 For the detection of acids in laboratory sodium carbonate (Na_2CO_3) or sodium bicarbonate ($NaHCO_3$) is used, because they releases CO_2 gas.

28 Baking powder is a mixture of baking soda and a mild edible acid such as tartaric acid. When baking powder is heated or mixed in water, it produces carbon dioxide gas, which causes the bread or cake to rise, making them spongy and soft.

$$\underbrace{NaHCO_3 + \underset{\text{(From acid)}}{H^+}}_{\text{Baking powder}} \xrightarrow{\Delta} CO_2\uparrow + H_2O + \text{Sodium salt of acid}$$

29

Important salts	Chemical name	Chemical formula	Preparation	Uses
Common salt	Sodium chloride	$NaCl$	By combination reaction of sodium hydroxide and hydrochloric acid $NaOH(aq) + HCl(aq) \rightarrow NaCl(aq) + H_2O(aq)$	(i) As raw material for making many chemicals such as sodium hydroxide baking soda, washing soda, bleaching powder, etc. (ii) In edible food.
Caustic soda	Sodium hydroxide	$NaOH$	By passing electricity through aqueous sodium chloride (brine) solution. This process is known as chlor-alkali process. $2NaCl\,(aq) + 2H_2O(aq) \rightarrow 2NaOH(aq) + Cl_2(g) + H_2(g)$	(i) In detergents and soaps (ii) In paper making (iii) In bleach manufacture (iv) In bauxite purification to extract aluminum
Bleaching powder	Calcium oxy-chloride	$CaOCl_2$	By passing chlorine gas over dry slaked lime. $Ca(OH)_2 + Cl_2 \rightarrow CaOCl_2 + H_2O$	(i) For bleaching cotton and linen, wood pulp in paper factories and washed clothes in laundary textile. (ii) For disinfecting drinking water. (iii) As an oxidising agent in chemical industry.

Baking soda	Sodium hydrogen carbonate	$NaHCO_3$	On reacting cold concentrated sodium chloride (brine) solution with ammonia and carbon dioxide $NaCl + NH_3 + CO_2 + H_2O \rightarrow NaHCO_3 + NH_4Cl$	(i) Preparing baking powder. (ii) As an antacid in medicine (iii) In soda-acid fire extinguisher.
Washing soda	Sodium carbonate deca-hydrate	Na_2CO_3 $10H_2O$	By recrystallisation of sodium carbonate in water $Na_2CO_3 + 10H_2O \rightarrow Na_2CO_3.10H_2O$	(i) In glass, soap and paper industries. (ii) Cleaning agent for domestic purposes (iii) Softing hard and water
Plaster of Paris	Calcium sulphate hemi-hydrate	$CaSO_4 \cdot \frac{1}{2}H_2O$	By heating gypsum at 373 K $CaSO_4 \cdot 2H_2O \xrightarrow{\Delta} CaSO_4 \cdot \frac{1}{2}H_2O + \frac{3}{2}H_2O$	(i) For making casts of statues, models toys etc. (ii) For making fire proof materials. (iii) For setting fractured bones.

Intext Questions

On Page 18

Question 1 You have been provided with three test tubes. One of them contains distilled water and the others two contain an acidic solution and a basic solution, respectively. If you are given only red litmus paper, how will you identify the contents of each test tube?

◎ *Thinking Process*

- In acidic solutions, blue litmus paper turns red.
- In basic or alkaline solutions, red litmus paper turns blue.
- In neutral solutions, no change in either blue or red litmus paper is observed.

Sol. We first dip the red litmus paper in each of the 3 test tubes. The tube in which it turns blue, will indicate that the solution is basic.

Now this blue litmus paper formed above is dipped in remaining two tubes. That tube in which it again changes back to red, indicates, that the solution is acidic. The last test tube in which neither red litmus turned blue, nor blue litmus turned red contains distilled water.

On Page 22

Question 1 Why should curd and sour substances not be kept in brass and copper vessels?

◎ *Thinking Process* Acids are sour in taste and they are very reactive towards brass and copper.

Sol. Curd and sour substances are acidic in nature. The acid present in curd and sour substances react with metal surface of brass and copper vessels to produce toxic compounds, which are not fit for consumption. Thus, curd and sour substances should not be kept in brass and copper vessels.

Question 2 Which gas is usually liberated when an acid reacts with a metal? Illustrate with an example. How will you test for the presence of this gas?

Sol. Reaction between a metal and an acid is :

$$\text{Acid} + \text{Metal} \longrightarrow \text{Metal salt} + H_2(g)$$

When metals react with acids, they release H_2 gas. *e.g.*, Magnesium metal reacts with sulphuric acid to give magnesium sulphate. Hydrogen gas is released in this process.

$$Mg(s) + H_2SO_4(aq) \xrightarrow{\Delta} MgSO_4(aq) + H_2(g)\uparrow$$

We can test for the presence of this gas by passing it through the soap solution and then bringing a burning candle near a gas filled bubble. The soap bubbles bursts and the H_2 (gas) burns with a 'pop' sound.

Question 3 Metal compound *A* reacts with dilute hydrochloric acid to produce effervescence. The gas evolved extinguishes a burning candle. Write a balanced chemical equation for the reaction if one of the compounds formed is calcium chloride.

Sol. According to question,

$$A + \text{HCl (dil.)} \longrightarrow \text{effervescence (gas)}$$
$$\longrightarrow \text{extinguishes a burning candle (so it may be } CO_2)$$

We know CO_2 extinguishes fire and when metal carbonates and bicarbonates react with dil. acids, CO_2 is produced with brisk effervescence. So, the equation will be :

$$\underset{[A]}{MCO_3} + \text{2dil. HCl } (aq) \longrightarrow MCl_2 + CO_2\uparrow + H_2O \quad (\text{where, } M = \text{Metal})$$

If one of the compunds formed is calcium chloride, then the balanced chemical equation is :

$$CaCO_3(s) + 2 \text{ dil. } HCl(aq) \longrightarrow CaCl_2\ (aq) + H_2O(l) + CO_2(g)\uparrow$$

Hence, *A* is calcium carbonate ($CaCO_3$).

On Page 25

Question 1 Why do HCl, HNO_3, etc., show acidic characters in aqueous solutions while solutions of compounds like alcohol and glucose do not show acidic character?

◎ ***Thinking Process*** H^+ or H_3O^+ ions in aqueous solution are responsible for acidic character of solutions of compounds.

Sol. Acids like HCl and HNO_3, ionise in water (aqueous solutions) completely to form hydronium ions. Due to this reason, they show acidic behaviour in aqueous solutions.

$$H|Cl + H_2O \longrightarrow \underset{\text{Hydronium ion}}{H_3O^+} + Cl^-$$

On the other hand, the compounds like glucose ($C_6H_{12}O_6$) and ethanol (C_2H_5OH) do not ionise in the aqueous solution to give hydronium ions. Hence, they do not show acidic character.

Question 2 Why does an aqueous solution of an acid conduct electricity?

◎ *Thinking Process* The movement of ions in an aqueous solution is responsible for the ability of the solution to conduct electricity.

Sol. A solution of a compund in water is called an aqueous solution *e.g.*, when an acid is added to water, we get its aqueous solution. Acid completely ionises in its aqueous solution to form positively charged cation (H_3O^+) and negatively charged anion. These ions move towards opposite electrodes and this movement of ions conducts electricity in aqueous medium.

$$HCl + H_2O \longrightarrow H_3O^+ + Cl^-$$
$$HNO_3 + H_2O \longrightarrow H_3O^+ + NO_3^-$$

Question 3 Why does dry HCl gas not change the colour of the dry litmus paper?

Sol. Dry HCl gas cannot ionise to give H_3O^+ ions. For any reaction to take place, the dry HCl gas has to first form ions. HCl ionises in aqueous medium to form (H_3O^+) ions. Therefore, dry HCl gas does not change the colour of dry litmus paper, and to show its acidic behaviour it needs wet litmus paper.

Mistake Alert Dry litmus paper only works in solutions of acids and bases.

Question 4 While diluting an acid, why is it recommended that the acid should be added to water and not water to the acid?

◎ *Thinking Process* Concentrated acids are corrosive in nature and dilution of such acids is a highly exothermic reaction.

Sol. Dilution of a concentrated acid is a highly exothermic reaction and a lot of heat is generated. Care must be taken while mixing concentrated acid with water. The acid must always be added slowly to water with constant stirring. If water is added to the concentrated acid, the heat generated may cause the mixture to splash out and cause burns. The glass container may also break due to excessive local heating.

Question 5 How is the concentration of hydronium ions (H_3O^+) affected when a solution of an acid is diluted?

◎ *Thinking Process* Dilution is a process of mixing of an acid or a base with water.

Sol. An acid dissociates into hydronium ions (H_3O^+) and anions when dissolved in water. When a solution is diluted, the volume of the solution increases but the number of ions remains the same, so concentration of hydronium ions (H_3O^+) per unit volume decreases.

Question 6 How is concentration of hydroxide ions (OH^-) affected when excess base is dissolved in a solution of sodium hydroxide?

Sol. The concentration of OH^- ions **increases** when excess base is dissolved in a solution of NaOH.

On Page 28

Question 1 You have two solutions, *A* and *B*. The pH of solution *A* is 6 and pH of solution *B* is 8. Which solution has more hydrogen ion concentration? Which of these is acidic and which one is basic?

Thinking Process pH is inversely related to the concentration of H^+ ions.

Sol. Solution *A* is acidic in nature because its pH is less than 7 and solution *B* is basic in nature because its pH is more than 7. Also, higher the pH of a solution lesser is the concentration of H^+ ions. So, solution *A* will have more H^+ ions concentration.

Mistake Alert One can make a mistake in considering that concentration of H^+ ions increases, if the pH of the solution increases.

Question 2 What effect does the concentration of $H^+(aq)$ ions have on the nature of the solution?

Sol. More the concentration of H^+ ions in a solution, more acidic is the solution. The concentration of hydrogen ions is directly proportional to the acidic strength of the solution.

Question 3 Do basic solutions also have $H^+(aq)$ ions? If yes, then why are these basic?

Sol. Yes, basic solutions also have $H^+(aq)$ ions in addition to $OH^-(aq)$, but the concentration of $OH^-(aq)$ will be much higher than that of $H^+(aq)$ since it is a basic solution.

Question 4 Under what soil condition do you think a farmer would treat the soil of his fields with quicklime (calcium oxide) or slaked lime (calcium hydroxide) or chalk (calcium carbonate)?

Sol. Slaked lime, quicklime and chalk are all basic in nature. Thus, if the soil is acidic, the farmer will add these basic substances so that the pH of the soil becomes neutral (pH = 7). This value of pH is very essential for healthy growth of plants.

On Page 33

Question 1 What is the common name of compound $CaOCl_2$?

Sol. Bleaching powder is the common name of compound $CaOCl_2$.

Question 2 Name the substance which on treatment with chlorine yields bleaching powder.

Sol. Dry slaked lime [$Ca(OH)_2$] on treatment with chlorine yields bleaching powder.

Question 3 Name the sodium compound which is used for softening hard water.

Sol. Washing soda (sodium carbonate) is used in softening hard water.

Question 4 What will happen if a solution of sodium hydrogen carbonate is heated? Give the equation of the reaction involved.

Sol. On heating $NaHCO_3$, it will decompose to give carbon dioxide, water and sodium carbonate (Na_2CO_3). The reaction involved is shown below.

$$2\,NaHCO_3 \xrightarrow{\Delta} Na_2CO_3 + CO_2 \uparrow + H_2O$$

Question 5 Write an equation to show the reaction between Plaster of Paris and water.

Sol. Plaster of Paris reacts with water to give gypsum as shown below:

$$\underset{\text{(Plaster of Paris)}}{CaSO_4 \cdot \frac{1}{2}H_2O} + 1\frac{1}{2}H_2O \longrightarrow \underset{\text{(Gypsum)}}{CaSO_4 \cdot 2H_2O}$$

Exercises

Question 1 A solution turns red litmus blue, its pH is likely to be

(a) 1 (b) 4 (c) 5 (d) 10

◎ ***Thinking Process***

- Acidic solution ; pH < 7
- Basic solution ; pH > 7
- Neutral solution ; pH = 7

Sol. (d) The solution turns red litmus blue if it is basic in nature. The pH of basic solution is greater than 7.

Question 2 A solution reacts with crushed egg-shells to give a gas that turns lime water milky. The solution contains

(a) NaCl (b) HCl (c) LiCl (d) KCl

Sol. (b) The crushed egg shells consist of layer of calcium carbonate which reacts with dil. HCl to evolve $CO_2(g)$. This gas turns lime water milky.

$$CaCO_3 + 2HCl \longrightarrow CaCl_2 + H_2O + CO_2 \uparrow$$

$$CO_2 \uparrow + \underset{\text{(lime water)}}{Ca(OH)_2} \longrightarrow \underset{\text{(milkiness)}}{CaCO_3 \downarrow} + H_2O$$

Question 3 10 mL of a solution of NaOH is found to be completely neutralised by 8 mL of a given solution of HCl. If we take 20 mL of the same solution of NaOH, the amount of HCl solution (the same solution as before) required to neutralise it would be

(a) 4 mL (b) 8 mL (c) 12 mL (d) 16 mL

Sol. (d) Since both the solutions have same strength and only the amount of base is doubled. So, 20 mL of NaOH requires 16 mL [(2 × 8) mL] of HCl.

Question 4 Which one of the following types of medicines is used for treating indigestion?

(a) Antibiotic (b) Analgesic (c) Antacid (d) Antiseptic

Sol. (c) Indigestion is caused due to the excess acid produced in the stomach. Antacid is alkaline in nature and it neutralises the excess acid in the stomoach and provides relief from indigestion.

Question 5 Write word equations and then balanced equations for the reaction taking place when

(a) dilute sulphuric acid reacts with zinc granules
(b) dilute hydrochloric acid reacts with magnesium ribbon
(c) dilute sulphuric acid react with aluminium powder
(d) dilute hydrochloric acid reacts with iron filings

Sol. (a) Zinc + dil. sulphuric acid $\longrightarrow$ zinc sulphate + hydrogen

$$Zn\,(s) + H_2SO_4\,(aq) \longrightarrow ZnSO_4(aq) + H_2(g)$$

(b) Magnesium + dil. hydrochloric acid $\longrightarrow$ magnesium chloride + hydrogen

$$Mg\,(s) + 2\,HCl(aq) \longrightarrow MgCl_2(aq) + H_2(g)$$

(c) Aluminium + dil. sulphuric acid $\longrightarrow$ aluminium sulphate + hydrogen

$$2\,Al\,(s) + 3H_2SO_4(aq) \longrightarrow Al_2(SO_4)_3(aq) + 3\,H_2(g)$$

(d) Iron + hydrochloric acid $\longrightarrow$ iron (II) chloride + hydrogen.

$$Fe\,(s) + 2HCl\,(aq) \longrightarrow FeCl_2(aq) + H_2(g)$$

Mistake Alert It is important to mention physical state of reactants and products in a balanced chemical equation.

Question 6 Compounds such as alcohols and glucose also contain hydrogen but are not categorised as acids. Describe an activity to prove it.

Sol. Alcohols and glucose contain hydrogen but are not categorised as acids because they do not ionise in the solution to produce $H^+(aq)$ ions and hence can not conduct electricity.

Activity Set the apparatus as shown below and test for the solutions of HCl, alcohol and glucose. Insert two nails into the rubber cork and place it in a beaker. Connect the iron nails to a bulb, a 6-volt battery and a wire connected to the switch. Pour the solutions in the beaker, so as to dip the nails in it. Turn the switch on and observe if the bulb glows or not.

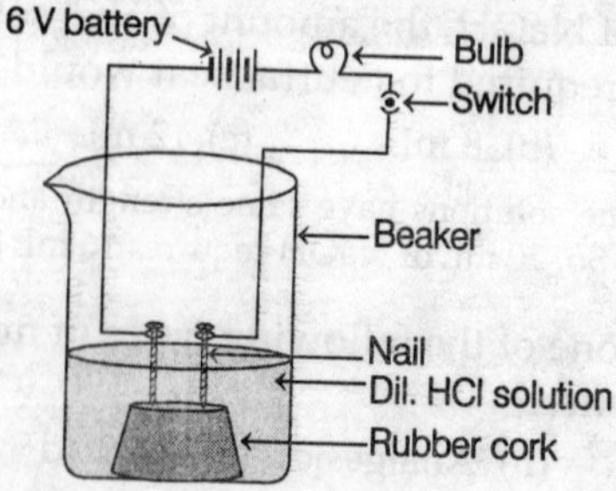

Observation

(a) The bulb glows when dil. HCl was added to beaker.

(b) The bulb did not glow when alcohol and glucose solution was added to the beaker.

Conclusion

(a) Alcohol and glucose cannot form ions in solution and hence, they can not conduct electricity.

(b) Dil. HCl solution forms $H^+(aq)$ ions and hence, can conduct electricity, suggesting that electric current is carried through the solution by ions formed by them.

Question 7 Why does distilled water not conduct electricity, whereas rain water does?

Sol. Distilled water is free from dissolved ions and hence, cannot conduct electricity.

Rain water on the other hand has dissolved atmospheric gases like CO_2, SO_2, NO_2, etc., which forms acids like H_2CO_3, H_2SO_4 and HNO_3. The amount of these acids is very low, but still rain water can conduct electricity as these acids can easily dissociate into ions.

Question 8 Why do acids not show acidic behaviour in the absence of water?

◎ ***Thinking Process*** Acidic behaviour of an acid is due to its ability to ionise and form H_3O^+ ions.

Sol. For acids to show acidic behaviour, they need to ionise and for the ionisation of acids, water is needed. Only in the presence of water, acids dissociate to form ions and hence, show acidic behaviour.

$$HCl + H_2O \longrightarrow H_3O^+ + Cl^-$$

Question 9 Five solutions *A, B, C, D* and *E* when tested with universal indicator showed pH as 4, 1, 11, 7 and 9 respectively. Which solution is

(a) neutral? (b) strongly alkaline?
(c) strongly acidic? (d) weakly acidic?
(e) weakly alkaline?

Arrange the pH in increasing order of hydrogen ion concentration.

◎ ***Thinking Process*** pH scale ranges from 0 (strongly acidic) to 14 (strongly alkaline), and solution having pH = 7 is called a neutral solution.

Sol.

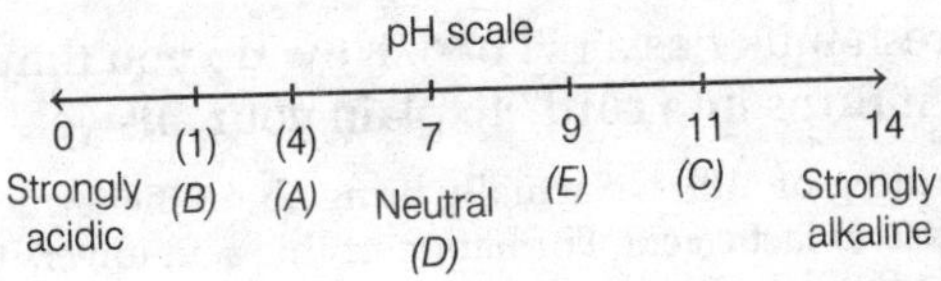

For acidic solution, pH is less than 7. For basic solution, pH is greater than 7. For neutral solution, pH = 7.

Thus, we see

(a) *D* is neutral because pH = 7.
(b) *C* is strongly alkaline because pH = 11.
(c) *B* is strongly acidic because pH = 1.
(d) *A* is weakly acidic because pH = 4.
(e) *E* is weakly alkaline because pH – 9.

H^+ ion concentration varies inversely with pH, thus,

$$C < E < D < A < B$$

is the increasing order of H^+ ion concentration.

Question 10 Equal lengths of magnesium ribbons are taken in the test tubes *A* and *B*. Hydrochloric acid is added to test tube *A*, while acetic acid (CH_3COOH) is added to test tube *B*. Amount and concentration taken for both the acids are same. In which test tube will the fizzing occur more vigorously and why?

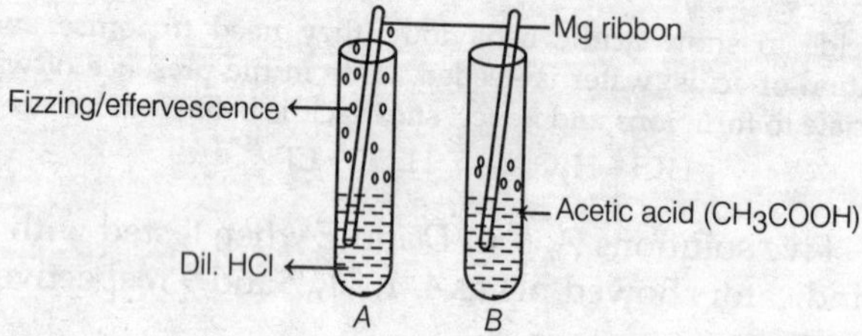

Sol. Fizzing occurs more vigorously in test tube *A* with magnesium ribbon and HCl. This is because HCl is a more stronger acid than acetic acid. Being stronger, it produces more number of $H^+(aq)$ ions and hence, rapid and faster release of H_2 gas takes place which is responsible for fizzing.

$$Mg + 2\,HCl \longrightarrow MgCl_2 + H_2 \uparrow \text{ (rapid fizzing)}$$

$$Mg + 2CH_3COOH \longrightarrow \underset{\text{Magnesium acetate}}{Mg(CH_3COO)_2} + H_2 \uparrow \text{ (slow reaction)}$$

Question 11 Fresh milk has a pH of 6. How do you think the pH will change as it turns into curd? Explain your answer.

Sol. During curdling of milk we actually bring about the fermentation of milk sugar, lactose to lactic acid. Formation of this acid lowers the pH of curd. Thus, curd is acidic and has pH less than 6 (milk).

Question 12 A milkman adds a very small amount of baking soda to fresh milk.

(a) Why does he shift the pH of the fresh milk from 6 to slightly alkaline?

(b) Why does this milk take a longer time to set as curd?

Sol. (a) Milk sours easily at lower pH and gets curdled and spoiled. So to prevent the spoilage of milk, the milkman adds a very small amount of baking soda (alkaline in nature).

(b) In curd formation process, lactose is converted to lactic acid by fermentation and an acidic pH is needed for this. But, when baking soda is added to the milk, it turns alkaline in nature. So, lactic acid produced to set curd has to first neutralise the base present in this milk. Therefore, it takes a longer time for the curd to set.

Question 13 Plaster of Paris should be stored in a moisture proof container. Explain why?

Sol. Plaster of Paris (POP) is chemically calcium sulphate hemihydrate. $CaSO_4 \cdot \frac{1}{2}H_2O$. When it comes in contact with water it sets into a hard solid mass, called gypsum ($CaSO_4 \cdot 2H_2O$).

$$\underset{\text{Plaster of Paris}}{CaSO_4 \cdot \frac{1}{2}H_2O} + \underset{\text{(from moisture)}}{1\frac{1}{2}H_2O} \longrightarrow \underset{\text{(Gypsum)}}{CaSO_4 \cdot 2H_2O}$$

To prevent this reaction, POP must be stored in moisture-proof container.

Question 14 What is a neutralisation reaction? Give two examples.

Sol. The reaction between an acid and a base is called neutralisation reaction. In this reaction, water and salt is formed. It is a highly exothermic reaction.

$$\text{Acid} + \text{Base} \longrightarrow \text{Salt} + \text{Water}$$

$$H{-}X + MOH \longrightarrow MX + H_2O$$

e.g.,

$$NaOH + HCl \longrightarrow NaCl + H_2O$$

$$2KOH + H_2SO_4 \longrightarrow \underset{\text{(Potassium sulphate)}}{K_2SO_4} + 2H_2O$$

Question 15 Give two important uses of washing soda and baking soda.

Sol. **Washing soda** ($Na_2CO_3 \cdot 10H_2O$)

1. Used for removing permanent hardness of water.
2. Used as a cleaning agent for domestic purposes.

Baking soda ($NaHCO_3$)

1. Used in soda-acid fire extinguishers.
2. Used as an ingredient in antacids, since it neutralises excess acid in the stomach.

DIKSHA APP Questions

☐ Multiple Choice Questions

Q.1 Which among the following is not a base?

(a) KOH (b) C_2H_5OH (c) $Ca(OH)_2$ (d) $Mg(OH)_2$

Sol. (b) C_2H_5OH is not a base. C_2H_5OH, also known as ethanol or ethyl alcohol, is an organic compound and is acidic in nature. It does not dissociate and produce OH^- ions in the slightly solution like other bases mentioned.

Q.2 Which of the following is a hydrated salt?

(a) Bleaching powder (b) Washing soda
(c) Caustic soda (d) Baking soda

Sol. (b) Washing soda is a hydrated salt of sodium carbonate and its chemical formula is $Na_2CO_3 \cdot 10H_2O$. Washing soda is prepared by adding 10 molecules of water of crystallization to sodium carbonate.

$$\underset{\text{(Sodium carbonate)}}{Na_2CO_3} + 10H_2O \longrightarrow \underset{\text{(Washing soda)}}{Na_2CO_3 \cdot 10H_2O}$$

Q.3 Which one of the following solutions will turn red litmus blue?

(a) Lemon juice (b) Distilled water
(c) Baking soda solution (d) Aerated drinks

Sol. (c) Baking soda solution will turn red litmus blue. Baking soda is a base and when it comes into contact with red litmus paper, the paper will turn blue. Baking soda is also known as sodium hydrogen carbonate and has a pH value of around 8.3.

Q.4 Doctors advise us to brush our teeth regularly to prevent tooth decay. The nature of the tooth paste commonly used is

(a) acidic (b) basic (c) neutral (d) amphoteric

◎ ***Thinking Process*** Tooth decay starts when the pH of the mouth is lower than 5.5. Tooth enamel is made up of calcium hydroxy apatite , which gets corroded when pH of the mouth is below 5.5.

Sol. (b) Doctors advise us to brush our teeth regularly to prevent tooth decay. The nature of the tooth paste commonly used is basic which neutralises acid produced by bacteria present in mouth. This prevents deterioration of tooth enamel.

Q.5 Potassium carbonate is a basic salt because it is a salt of

(a) weak acid and strong base. (b) strong acid and weak base.
(c) strong acid and strong base. (d) weak acid and weak base.

Sol. (a) Potassium carbonate (K_2CO_3) is a basic salt because it is a salt of weak acid and strong base. It is formed by the reaction of carbonic acid and potassium hydroxide. Carbonic acid is a weak acid and potassium hydroxide is a strong base.

Q.6 A dry blue litmus paper is brought in contact with the following. In which case will the colour of the litmus paper turn red?

(i) Dry hydrogen chloride gas
(ii) Aqueous solution of hydrochloric acid
(iii) Dry vapours of sulphuric acid

(a) Only (i) (b) Both (ii) and (iii)
(c) Both (i) and (ii) (d) Only (ii)

Sol. (d) Aqueous solution of hydrochloric acid will turn the colour of the litmus paper turn red. An aqueous solution hydrochloric acid dissociates completely and produces H^+ ion that turn blue litmus paper red.

Q.7 Harsh is using phenolphthalein indicator to test the nature of a solution. He added some drops of this indicator to the soution. Which of the following statements can he conclude with certainity?

Statement I If the solution turns pink, it is basic.
Statement II If the solution remains colourless, it is acidic.
Statement III If the solution turns pink, it is acidic.

(a) Both II and III (b) Only II (c) Both I and II (d) Only I

Sol. (c) Both I and II statements are correct.
Phenolphthalein is an acid-base indicator which is colourless in acidic solution, but it turns pink if the solution is basic in nature.

Q.8 Which of the following salts does not contain water molecules of crystallisation and it is also used as a reactant in Soda Acid fire extinguisher?

(a) Washing soda (b) Plaster of Paris (c) Copper sulphate (d) Baking soda

◎ ***Thinking Process*** Water of crystallisation is the fixed number of water molecules present in one formula unit of a salt.

Sol. (d) Baking soda salt does not contain water molecules of crystallisation. Its chemical formula is $NaHCO_3$. It is also used as a reactant in soda-acid fire extinguisher.

Q.9 In a very polluted city, water from the first rain in monsoon season is collected in a beaker. Which of the following changes will it have on a litmus paper?

(a) Turn red litmus blue.

(b) It will have no effect on the litmus paper.

(c) Both (a) and (b).

(d) Turn blue litmus red.

Sol. (d) The correct option is (d) because first rain is acidic in nature which turns blue litmus red. Acid rain forms when compounds like sulphur dioxide and nitrogen oxides are released into the air and they are mixed with rain water.

Q.10 Ammonium chloride is an acidic salt because it is a salt of

(a) strong acid and strong base. (b) weak acid and weak base.

(c) strong base and weak acid. (d) weak base and strong acid.

Sol. (d) Ammonium chloride (NH_4Cl) an acidic salt because it is a salt of strong acid and a weak base. Ammonium chloride is formed by hydrochloric acid (HCl) and NH_4OH (ammonium hydroxide).

$$\underset{\text{Strong acid}}{HCl\,(aq)} + \underset{\text{Weak base}}{NH_4OH\,(aq)} \longrightarrow \underset{\text{Ammonium Chloride (Salt)}}{NH_4Cl(aq) + H_2O\,(l)}$$

☐ Very Short Answer Type

Q.1 Why do we feel pain when a bee stings? How do we get relief?

Sol. We feel pain when a bee stings because bee injects formic acid in our body. We can get relief by rubbing a mild base like baking soda on the stung area.

Q.2 A chemical substance is used to set the fractured bones in the right position. Give the chemical name and formula of this substance.

Sol. Plaster of Paris is a chemical substance which is used to set the fractured bones in the right position. Its chemical name and formula is calcium sulphate hemihydrate and $CaSO_4.\frac{1}{2}H_2O$.

Q.3 Give two examples of olfactory indicators.

◎ ***Thinking Process*** Olfactory indicators are some substances whose odour changes in acidic or basic medium.

Sol. Two examples of olfactory indicators are onion extract and vanilla essence.

Q.4 Name the acids present in vinegar and curd.

Sol. The acids present in vinegar and curd are acetic acid and lactic acid, respectively.

Q.5 What will be the effect of the following substances on methyl orange? Aerated drink and baking soda solution

◎ *Thinking Process* Methyl orange is an orange-coloured dye that turns red in acidic solutions and yellow in basic solutions.

Sol. Aerated drink turns methyl orange red as it contains an acid (carbonic acid). Whereas, baking soda solution turns methyl orange yellow as it contains a base.

☐ Short Answer Type

Q.1 An element '*X*' on reaction with dilute acid evolves a gas that burns with a pop sound, while a compound '*Y*' on reaction with dilute acid evolves a gas that turns lime water milky. Identify *X* and *Y*.

Sol. *X* is a metal, as it reacts with dilute acid to form salt and hydrogen gas. This hydrogen gas evolved burns with a pop sound.

$$\underset{(X)}{\text{Metal}} + \text{dil. Acid} \longrightarrow \text{Salt} + \text{Hydrogen gas}$$

Y is a metal carbonate or bicarbonate, as it reacts with dilute acid to form salt, carbon dioxide gas and water. This carbon dioxide gas evolved turns lime water milky.

$$\underset{(Y)}{\text{Metal carbonate or bicarbonate}} + \text{dil. Acid} \rightarrow \text{Salt} + \text{Carbon dioxide gas} + \text{Water}$$

$$CO_2 + \underset{\text{(Lime water)}}{Ca(OH)_2} \longrightarrow \underset{\text{(Milkiness)}}{CaCO_3 \downarrow} + H_2O$$

Q.2 Why are liquid droplets seen on the inner upper side of the test tube during the heating process of ferrous sulphate crystals?

Sol. Ferrous sulphate is a hydrated salt ($FeSO_4.7H_2O$), which loses water of crystallisation as vapour on heating. This steam condenses on the inner upper side of the test tube and forms water droplets.

Q.3 You are given three solutions *A*, *B* and *C* with pH values 2, 8 and 13 respectively. Which solution has more hydrogen ion concentration among the three and state the nature of each solution.

Sol. Solution *A* has more hydrogen ion concentration as pH is inversely proportional to the hydrogen ion concentration. Lesser the pH value, larger is the concentration of hydrogen ions and stronger is the acid.

- Solution A is strongly acidic in nature as it has pH = 2.
- Solution B is weakly basic in nature as it has pH = 8.
- Solution C is strongly basic in nature as it has pH = 13.

Q.4 Why do we feel a burning sensation in the stomach when we overeat? What type of medicines are used to treat such situation? Write two examples.

Sol. When we overeat, the stomach produces excess hydrochloric acid to aid the digestion process. This excess acid can irritate the stomach lining, leading to a burning sensation commonly referred to as **acid reflux** or **heartburn.**

Antacids are used to treat such situation because these are mild bases which can neutralise the excess stomach acid. For example- Milk of Magnesia and sodium bicarbonate.

Q.5 Identify the compound of calcium which is a yellowish powder and is used for disinfecting drinking water. Write its chemical name and chemical formula. How is it prepared? Write the chemical reaction involved. Also, list two other uses of the compound.

Sol. The compound of calcium which is a yellowish powder, used for disinfecting drinking water is **bleaching powder.**
Its chemical name is calcium oxychloride and its chemical formula is $CaOCl_2$.
It is prepared by the action of chlorine on dry slaked lime $[Ca(OH)_2]$.

$$Ca(OH)_2 + Cl_2 \longrightarrow CaOCl_2 + H_2O$$

The two other uses of bleaching powder are:

(i) For bleaching cotton and linen in the textile industry, for bleaching wood pulp in paper factories and for bleaching washed clothes in laundry.

(ii) As an oxidising agent in many chemical industries.

□ Long Answer Type

Q.1 What is chlor-alkali process?What are the gases given off at the anode and the cathode respectively in chlor-alkali process? Write the chemical equation involved.

Sol. When electricity is passed through an aqueous solution of sodium chloride (called brine), it decomposes to form sodium hydroxide. This process is called the chlor-alkali process.

$$2NaCl\,(aq) + 2H_2O\ (l) \longrightarrow 2NaOH(aq) + Cl_2(g) + H_2\,(g)$$

Chlorine gas is given off at the anode, and hydrogen gas at the cathode. Sodium hydroxide solution is formed near the cathode.

Q.2 For making cake, baking powder is taken. If at home you use baking soda instead of baking powder in cake,

(a) how will it affect the taste of the cake and why?

(b) how can baking soda be converted into baking powder?

(c) how does baking soda make cake fluffy?

(d) what is the role of tartaric acid added to baking soda?

Sol. (a) Cake becomes bitter due to the formation of sodium carbonate, produced during heating of baking soda.

$$\underset{\text{(Sodium hydrogencarbonate)}}{2NaHCO_3} \xrightarrow{\text{Heat}} \underset{\text{(Sodium carbonate)}}{Na_2CO_3} + H_2O + CO_2$$

(b) Baking soda can be converted into baking powder by adding a mild edible acid such as tartaric acid.

(c) Baking soda on heating produces carbon dioxide gas which makes a cake fluffy.

(d) Tartaric acid neutralises sodium carbonate produced during the heating of baking soda, to give sodium salt of acid.

$$NaHCO_3 + \underset{\text{(From any acid)}}{H^+} \longrightarrow CO_2 + H_2O + \text{Sodium salt of acid}$$

Q.3 (a) Salt *A* (commonly used in making bread or cakes), on heating gets converted into another salt *B* (used in paper industries and in the making of glass and soap) and a gas *C* is evolved.

(b) The gas *C* when passed through lime water, turns it milky. What would happen if the gas released is passed in excess in lime water. Identify *A*, *B* and *C*.

(c) Write all the reactions involved with explanation.

Sol. (a) Salt *A* is baking soda or sodium bicarbonate as it is used in making breads or cakes. Sodium bicarbonate on heating gives carbon dioxide gas (gas C) and sodium carbonate salt (salt *B*), which is used in paper industries and in making of glass and soap.

(b) The gas *C* *i.e.*, carbon dioxide gas when passed through lime water, turns it milky. If the gas is passed in excess in lime water, milkiness disappears and a colourless solution of calcium bicarbonate ($Ca(HCO_3)_2$) is formed.

(c)
$$\underset{\substack{\text{(Sodium hydrogencarbonate)}\\\text{(Salt }A\text{)}}}{2NaHCO_3} \xrightarrow{\text{Heat}} \underset{\substack{\text{(Sodium carbonate)}\\\text{(Salt }B\text{)}}}{Na_2CO_3} + H_2O + \underset{\text{(Gas C)}}{CO_2}$$

$$\underset{\text{(Gas C)}}{CO_2(g)} + \underset{\text{(Lime water)}}{Ca(OH)_2(aq)} \longrightarrow \underset{\text{(Milkiness)}}{CaCO_3(s)} + H_2O(l)$$

$$CaCO_3(s) + \underset{\text{(Excess)}}{CO_2(g)} + H_2O(l) \longrightarrow \underset{\text{(Milkiness disappears)}}{Ca(HCO_3)_2(aq)}$$

Metals and Non-Metals

CHAPTER 03

Important Points

01 **Elements** are classified as metals and non-metals on the basis of their properties.

02 **Metals** are mostly solids, lustrous (have a shiny surface), hard, have high density, good conductor of heat and electricity, malleable, ductile, sonorous and have high melting points.

03 Mercury is a liquid metal. Metals like gallium and caesium have very low melting points.

04 Silver and copper are best conductors of heat, whereas, silver and copper are comparatively poor conductors of heat.

05 Alkali metals (lithium, sodium, potassium) are so soft that they can be cut with a knife.

06 Metals lose electrons to form cations.

07 Metals generally form basic oxides when combined with oxygen. Al_2O_3 and ZnO show the properties of both basic and acidic oxides, so these are known as amphoteric oxides.

08
- Metals such as potassium and sodium reacts violently with oxygen and catches fire if kept in open, so they are kept immersed in kerosene oil.
- Copper does not burn in air, but the hot metal gets coated with a black layer of copper (II) oxide.
- Silver and gold do not react with oxygen even at high temperatures.

09 **Anodising** is a process of forming a thick oxide layer of aluminium when exposed to air. This makes it resistant to further corrosion.

10 Metals react with water to form metal oxide and hydrogen gas. Metal oxides are soluble in water and forms metal hydroxides. All metals do not react with water.

11
- Metals like K, Na react violently with cold water and the reaction is so exothermic that the evolved hydrogen immediately catches fire.
- Ca reacts less violently with water. Ca starts floating as the bubbles of H_2 gas formed stick to the surface of metal.
- Mg does not react with cold water. It reacts with hot water and it also floats like Ca.
- Al, Fe and Zn do not react with either cold or hot water. They react with steam to form metal oxide and hydrogen gas.

12 Metals react with acids (dilute) to give a salt and hydrogen gas.

13 H_2 gas is not evolved when metal reacts with nitric acid, as HNO_3 is a strong oxidising agent. It oxides H_2 to H_2O and itself gets reduced to any of the nitrogen oxides (N_2O, NO, NO_2). Mn and Mg reacts with very dil.HNO_3 to evolve H_2 gas.

14 Aqua regia is a mixture of conc. HCl and conc. HNO_3 in a ratio of 3 : 1. It is a strong oxidising agent, which can dissolve gold and platinum.

15 Non-metals usually have properties contrary to metals. They usually form acidic oxides. They form negative ions and do not liberate hydrogen gas on reaction with dilute acids. Non-metals are either solids or gases, except bromine which is liquid.

16 Iodine is a non-metal, but it is lustrous.

17 Carbon is a non-metal that exists in different forms, called **allotropes.** Diamond, an allotrope of carbon is the hardest natural substance known and has a very high melting and boiling point. Graphite, another allotrope of carbon, is a good conductor of electricity.

18 **Metal Activity Series**

K > Na > Ca > Mg > Al > Zn > Fe > Pb > $\boxed{H}$ > Cu > Hg > Ag > Pt > Au

(i) Metals below hydrogen cannot displace hydrogen from acids.

(ii) Metals above hydrogen can displace it from dilute acids.

(iii) The higher the position, the more active is the metal.

(iv) More reactive metals can displace less reactive metals from their compunds in solution or molten form.

19 The compounds formed from the transfer of electrons from a metal to a non-metal are known as **ionic compounds.** *e.g.*, NaCl, $MgCl_2$, etc.

20 Ionic compounds are solids. They are hard and brittle. They are soluble in water and insoluble in solvents like petrol, kerosene, etc. Their melting and boiling points are very high. Their aqueous solution shows conductivity due to formation of ions. They conduct electricity in molten state, but not in solid state.

21 **Minerals** from which metals may be extracted economically are called ores and this process is called **metallurgy.**

22
- Metals at the bottom of the activity series (Au, Ag, Ca, Cu) are least reactive and are found in the free state. (Cu and Ag can be found in combined state as their sulphide or oxide ores).
- Metals at the top of the activity series (K, Na, Ca, Mg and Al) are very reactive and are never found in free state.
- Metals in the middle of the activity series (Zn, Fe, Pb, etc.) are moderately reactive and are found in the earth's crust as oxides, sulphides or carbonates.

23 Ores mined from the earth are usually contaminated with large amounts of impurities such as soil, sand, etc, called gangue.

24 Oxides of metals low in the activity series, can be reduced to metals by heating alone. *e.g.*, Cinnabar (HgS) on heating is first converted to HgO and then it is also reduced to Hg on further heating. Similarly, Cu can also be obtained from Cu_2S.

25 Metals in the middle of the activity series are usually present as sulphides or carbonates in nature.

26 Heating of sulphide ore in the presence of excess air is called **roasting.**

27 Heating of carbonate ore in the absence of air is called **calcination.**

28 The process of reducing the roasted ore is called **smelting.** The metal oxides can be reduced to metals by using suitable reducing agents like, carbon, highly reactive metals, etc.

29 The reaction of iron (III) oxide (Fe_2O_3) with aluminium is highly exothermic, so the metal is produced in molten state, which is used to join railway tracks or cracked machine parts. This is known as the **thermit reaction.**

$$Fe_2O_3(s) + 2Al\,(s) \longrightarrow 2Fe\,(l) + Al_2O_3(s) + \text{Heat}$$

30 Metals high up in the reactive series are obtained by **electrolytic reduction.**

31 **Refining of metals** can be carried by distillation, liquation, oxidation or by electrolytic methods.

32 • **Electrolytic refining** is done for metals like Cu, Zn, Sn, Ni, Au, Ag, etc. In this process, the impure metal is made anode, and a thin strip of pure metal is made the cathode. A metal salt solution is used as an electrolyte.

• The insoluble impurities which settle down at the bottom of the anode are called **anode mud.**

33 An **alloy** is a homogeneous mixture of one or more metals or non-metals.

34 The surface of some metals such as iron is corroded when they are exposed to moist air for a long period of time. This phenomenon is called **corrosion.**

35 The process of coating iron articles by zinc is known as **galvanisation.** This is an important method to prevent it from rusting.

36 **Alloying** is a good method for improving the properties of a metal.

37 The rusting of iron can also be prevented by painting, oiling, greasing, chrome plating or anodising.

38 Gold (Au), Silver (Ag) and Platinum (Pt) are least reactive metals. They are also known as **Noble metals.**

Intext Questions

On Page 40

Question 1 Give an example of a metal which

(i) is a liquid at room temperature.

(ii) can be easily cut with a knife.

(iii) is the best conductor of heat.

(iv) is a poor conductor of heat.

Sol. (i) Mercury (ii) Sodium

(iii) Silver (iv) Lead

Question 2 Explain the meanings of malleable and ductile.

Sol. **Malleable** Metals have a property that they can be beaten into thin sheets by hammering. Such metals are called malleable.

Ductile Metals which can be drawn into thin wires are called ductile metals.

On Page 46

Question 1 Why is sodium kept immersed in kerosene oil?

Sol. Sodium is a very reactive metal. It reacts with air and water vigorously at room temperature and catches fire. So, it is kept immersed in kerosene oil to prevent its exposure to air and water.

Question 2 Write equations for the reaction of

(i) iron with steam (ii) calcium with water

(iii) potassium with water

Sol. (i) $3Fe(s) + 4H_2O(g) \longrightarrow Fe_3O_4(s) + 4H_2(g)$

(ii) $Ca(s) + 2H_2O(l) \longrightarrow Ca(OH)_2(aq) + H_2(g)$

(iii) $2K(s) + 2H_2O(l) \longrightarrow 2KOH(aq) + H_2(g) + \text{Heat energy}$

Question 3 Samples of four metals *A*, *B*, *C* and *D* were taken and added to the following solution one by one. The results obtained have been tabulated as follows.

Metal	Iron (II) sulphate	Copper (II) sulphate	Zinc sulphate	Silver nitrate
A	No reaction	Displacement	—	—
B	Displacement	—	No reaction	—
C	No reaction	No reaction	No reaction	Displacement
D	No reaction	No reaction	No reaction	No reaction

Use the table above to answer the following questions about metals *A, B, C* and *D*.

(i) Which is the most reactive metal?

(ii) What would you observe if *B* is added to a solution of copper (II) sulphate?

(iii) Arrange the metals *A, B, C* and *D* in the order of decreasing reactivity.

Sol. Based on the activity series, the relative position, of metals present in the question is Zn > Fe > Cu > Ag. On the basis of results shown in the table we can conclude that

(i) *B* is the most reactive because it displaces Fe from iron (II) sulphate.

(ii) Cu will be displaced because *B* is more reactive than Fe, so it is also more reactive than Cu. So, blue colour of copper (II) sulphate fades away and a brown-red deposit of copper will be formed.

(iii) Metal *B* is most reactive as it displaces iron from its salt solution. Metal *A* is less reactive than *B* as it displaces less reactive copper from its salt solution. Metal *C* is even less reactive than *A* and *B* because it can displace only silver from its salt solution. Metals *D* is least reactive because it cannot displace any metal from its salt solution. Hence, the decreasing order of reactivity of the metals is

$$B > A > C > D.$$

Mistake Alert Only a more reactive metal can displace a lesser reactive metal from its salt solution.

Question 4 Which gas is produced when dilute hydrochloric acid is added to a reactive metal? Write the chemical reaction when iron reacts with dilute H_2SO_4.

Sol.

$$2Na + 2\ dil \cdot HCl \longrightarrow 2NaCl + H_2 \uparrow$$

Hydrogen gas is released when dil HCl reacts with a reactive metal.

$$Fe\ (s) + H_2SO_4(aq) \longrightarrow FeSO_4\ (aq) + H_2(g) \uparrow$$

Question 5 What would you observe when zinc is added to a solution of iron (II) sulphate? Write the chemical reaction that takes place.

Sol. When Zn reacts with $FeSO_4$, the pale green colour of the solution changes to colourless because Zn being more reactive than Fe, will displace it from its salt solution. Fine grey particles of Fe are also seen in the solution.

$$\underset{}{Zn} + \underset{\text{(Pale green)}}{FeSO_4} \longrightarrow \underset{\text{(Colourless)}}{ZnSO_4} + \underset{\text{(Grey solid)}}{Fe}$$

On Page 49

Question 1 (i) Write the electron-dot structures for sodium, oxygen and magnesium.

(ii) Show the formation of Na_2O and MgO by the transfer of electrons.

(iii) What are the ions present in these compounds?

◎ ***Thinking Process*** Electron-dot structures show the number of electrons present in the valence shell of an element valence skell is the outermost shell.

Sol. (i) **Sodium** (Na)

Atomic number = 11

Electronic configuration $\frac{2}{K}, \frac{8}{L}, \frac{1}{M}$; Valence shell e^- = 6

Electron dot structure $\dot{Na}$

(a) **Oxygen** (O)

Atomic number = 8

Electronic configuration $\frac{2}{K}, \frac{6}{L}$; Valence shell e^- = 6

Electron dot structure $:\ddot{O}:$

(b) **Magnesium** (Mg)

Atomic number = 12

Electronic configuration $\frac{2}{K}, \frac{8}{L}, \frac{2}{M}$; Valence shell e^- = 6

Electron dot structure $\ddot{Mg}$

(ii) **Formation of Na_2O**

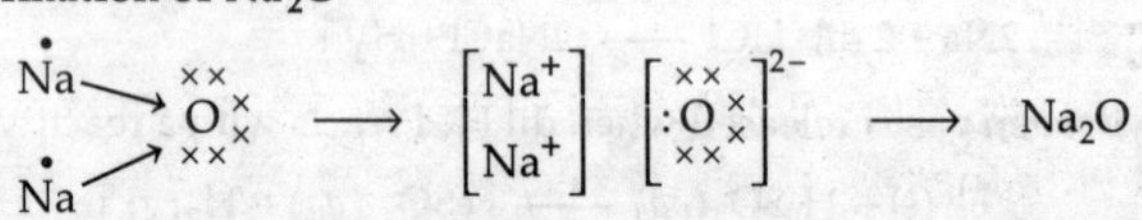

Sodium + Oxygen ⟶ Sodium ion Oxygen ion ⟶ Sodium oxide

Formation of MgO

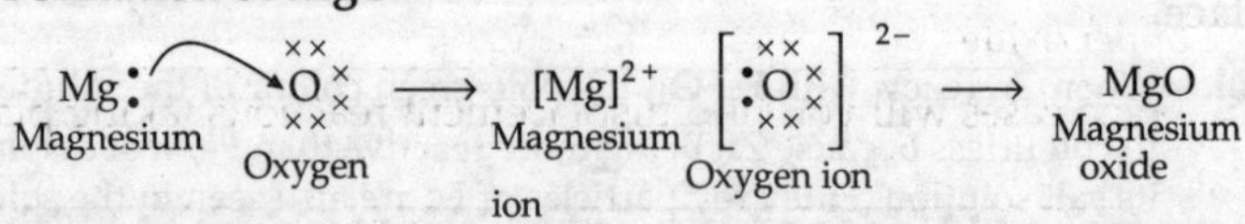

(iii) Na_2O contains Na^+ and O^{2-} ions.

MgO contains Mg^{2+} and O^{2-} ions.

Question 2 Why do ionic compounds have high melting points?

Thinking Process Ionic compounds are made up of two oppositely charged ions, *i.e.*, positive and negative ions. These ions are held by strong inter ionic force of attraction.

Sol. Ionic compounds have high melting points because a considerable amount of energy is required to break the strong inter ionic attraction existing in ionic compounds.

On Page 53

Question 1 Define the following terms.

(i) Mineral (ii) Ore (iii) Gangue

Sol. (i) **Minerals** The elements or compounds in the form of which metal occur naturally in the earth's crust are called **minerals.**

(ii) **Ores** Those minerals from which metals can be extracted easily and profitably are called **ores**.

(iii) **Gangue** The various impurities like sand, dust, rocky particles that are associated with the ore are called **gangue/matrix**.

Question 2 Name two metals which are found in nature in the free state.

Sol. Gold and silver are found in nature in free state because they are unreactive and inert.

Question 3 What chemical process is used for obtaining a metal from its oxide?

Sol. Reduction method is used to obtain a metal from its oxide, *e.g.*,

$$MO + C \longrightarrow CO + M \quad \text{(where } M = \text{metal)}$$

On Page 55

Question 1 Metallic oxides of zinc, magnesium and copper were heated with the following metals.

Metal	Zinc	Magnesium	Copper
Zinc oxide			
Magnesium oxide			
Copper oxide			

In which cases will you find displacement reactions taking place?

Sol.

Metal	Zn	Mg	Cu
ZnO	No displacement	Displacement	No displacement
MgO	No displacement	No displacement	No displacement
CuO	Displacement	Displacement	No displacement

[Because Mg > Zn > Cu is the reactivity order.]

Question 2 Which metals do not corrode easily?

Sol. Gold and platinum do not corrode easily as these are inert metals.

Question 3 What are alloys?

Sol. An alloy is a homogeneous mixture of two or more metals or a metal and a non-metal having a uniform composition.

Note Alloying is a very good method of improving the properties of a metal.

Exercises

Question 1 Which of the following pairs will give displacement reactions?

(a) NaCl solution and copper metal
(b) $MgCl_2$ solution and aluminium metal
(c) $FeSO_4$ solution and silver metal
(d) $AgNO_3$ solution and copper metal

Sol. (d) $AgNO_3$ solution will give displacement reaction with copper (Cu) because copper is placed above silver in the activity series. *i.e.*, copper is more reactive than silver. Thus, copper can displace silver from its salt solution.

$$2AgNO_3(aq) + Cu(s) \longrightarrow Cu(NO_3)_2(aq) + 2Ag(s)$$

Question 2 Which of the following methods is suitable for preventing an iron frying pan from rusting?

(a) Applying grease
(b) Applying paint
(c) Applying a coating of zinc
(d) All of the above

Thinking Process Iron undergoes rusting when it is exposed to moist air for a long time. This process can be prevented by coating the iron surface with various things or materials.

Sol. (d) All the given methods are helpful in preventing an iron frying pan from rusting.

Question 3 An element reacts with oxygen to give a compound with a high melting point. This compound is also soluble in water. The element is likely to be

(a) calcium (b) carbon (c) silicon (d) iron

Sol. (a) The compound is likely to be of calcium (Ca) because it combines with oxygen to give CaO (calcium oxide), which has a very high melting point. Calcium oxide dissolves in water to from calcium hydroxide.

$$2Ca + O_2 \longrightarrow 2CaO$$
$$CaO + H_2O \longrightarrow \underset{\text{Calcium hydroxide}}{2Ca(OH)_2}$$

Question 4 Food cans are coated with tin and not with zinc because

(a) zinc is costlier than tin.
(b) zinc has a higher melting point than tin.
(c) zinc is more reactive than tin.
(d) zinc is less reactive than tin

Sol. (c) Food cans are not coated with zinc because it is more reactive than tin, and it can react with organic acids present in the food.

Question 5 You are given a hammer, a battery, a bulb, wires and a switch.

(a) How could you use them to distinguish between samples of metals and non-metals?
(b) Assess the usefulness of these tests in distinguishing between metals and non-metals.

Thinking Process

- The ability of metals to be drawn into thin sheets by hitting them with a hammer is called malleability.
- Metals are also good conductors of heat and electricity.

Sol. (a)(i) Take the given samples, hammer them and observe. If the given sample breaks easily then it is a non-metal but if it doesn't break and can be drawn into sheets (malleable), then it is a metal.

(ii) Now create a circuit using a battery, a bulb, wires and a switch (as shown in the figure).

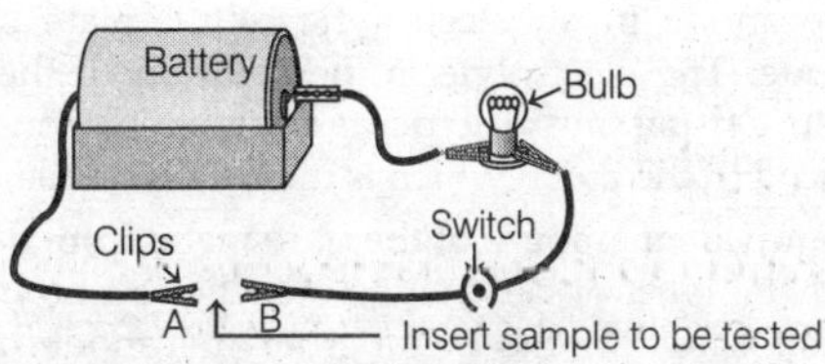

Insert any one sample between clips *A* and *B*. If the bulb glows it indicates that the sample is a good conductor of electricity and hence it is a metal. If the sample does not light the bulb then it is non-metal as it is a poor conductor of electricity.

(b) From the above tests it is clear that metals are malleable and good conductors of electricity whereas non-metals are non-malleable and poor conductors of electricity.

Question 6 What are amphoteric oxides? Give two examples of amphoteric oxides.

Sol. Some metal oxides, such as aluminium oxide, zinc oxide, etc., show the properties of acids as well as bases, *i.e.*, they react with acids and bases both to produce salts and water. These are called **amphoteric oxides**.

e.g., $Al_2O_3 + 6HCl \longrightarrow 2AlCl_3 + 3H_2O$

$$Al_2O_3 + 2NaOH \longrightarrow 2NaAlO_2 + H_2O$$

Question 7 Name two metals which will displace hydrogen from dilute acids, and two metals which will not.

Thinking Process The reactivity /activity series is a list of metals arranged in the order of their decreasing activities.

Sol. Metals which displace hydrogen from dilute acids are magnesium (Mg) and aluminium (Al), because these metals exist at higher position in activity series.

Metals which will not displace hydrogen from dilute acids are copper (Cu) and silver (Ag) because these metals exist at lower position in activity series.

Mistake Alert Only metals above hydrogen can displace it from dilute acids.

Question 8 In the electrolytic refining of a metal *M*, what would you take as the anode, the cathode and the electrolyte?

Sol. **Anode** Crude (Impure) metal *M*

Cathode Thin strip of pure metal *M*

Electrolyte Some salt solution of metal *M*

In electrolytic refining, the impure metal is converted into a block which is made anode in an electrolytic cell *A* plate of pure metal acts as the cathode. The electrolyte is the solution of the soluble salt of the same metal. On passing electric current, metal ions from the electrolyte are reduced to the metal which is deposited on the cathode.

An equivalent amount of the pure metal from the anode gets oxidised and the metal ions (or cations) go into the solution. This keeps on continuing till the whole of the metal from the anode dissolves and deposits on cathode, leaving behind impurities in the form of a mud below anode called the anode mud.

Question 9 Pratyush took sulphur powder on a spatula and heated it. He collected the gas evolved by inverting a test tube over it, as shown in figure below.

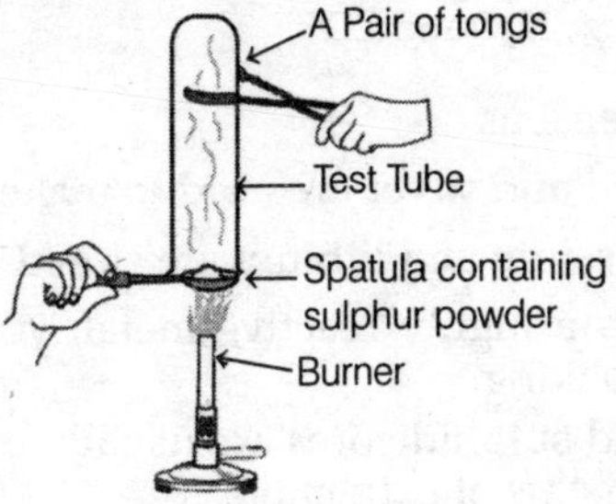

▲ Collection of gas

(a) What will be the action of gas on

(i) dry litmus paper? (ii) moist litmus paper?

(b) Write a balanced chemical equation for the reaction taking place.

Thinking Process

- Dry litmus paper only acts when it is dipped in a solution.
- Moist litmus paper can act on a gas.
- When a solution is acidic, blue litmus paper turns red. Whereas, when a solution is basic, red litmus paper turns blue.

Sol. (a) When sulphur powder is burnt in the air, sulphur dioxide is formed. It is an acidic oxide.

(i) SO_2 gas will have no action on dry litmus.

(ii) The gas will turn moist litmus paper from blue to red.

(b) Balanced equation is

$$S(s) + O_2(g) \longrightarrow SO_2(g)$$

$$SO_2(g) + H_2O(l) \rightleftharpoons H_2SO_3(aq) \rightleftharpoons 2H^+(aq) + SO_3^{2-}(aq)$$

Mistake Alert One can make a mistake in considering that dry litmus paper can act on a gas.

Question 10 State two ways to prevent the rusting of iron.

Sol. Ways to prevent rusting of iron

(i) By painting or greasing the surface of iron, it can be prevented from rusting because in this condition iron will not be in the direct contact with air/moisture.

(ii) By galvanising the iron surface. In galvanisation a layer of zinc is coated on the iron surface. Zinc is more reactive than iron, so it will be rusted in preference of iron.

Question 11 What type of oxides are formed when non-metals combine with oxygen?

Sol. Non-metals combine with O_2 to form **acidic oxide** (*e.g.*, CO_2 and SO_2) and **neutral oxides** *e.g.*, N_2O and CO

Question 12 Give reasons

(a) Platinum, gold and silver are used to make jewellery.
(b) Sodium, potassium and lithium are stored under oil.
(c) Aluminium is a highly reactive metal, yet it is used to make utensils for cooking.
(d) Carbonate and sulphide ores are usually converted into oxides during the process of extraction.

Sol. (a) Platinum, gold and silver are most ductile, malleable and lustrous metals. They are less reactive. These metals have little affinity for oxygen and thus are not attacked by moist air, hence they are suitable for making jewellery.

(b) Sodium, potassium and lithium are very reactive metals and react vigorously with air and water. They can even catch fire if kept in open air. So, they are stored under oil.

(c) Aluminium is a good conductor of heat and is resistant to corrosion. This is because it reacts with air to form a thin oxide layer Al_2O_3 which is very stable and prevents further corrosion of metal. It is also very light weight and malleable. Hence, it is used for making utensils.

(d) Carbonate and sulphide ores are usually converted into oxides during the process of extraction because it is easier to obtain a metal from its oxide as compared to its sulphides and carbonates.

Question 13 You must have seen tarnished copper vessels being cleaned with lemon or tamarind juice. Explain why these sour substances are effective in cleaning the vessels.

Sol. Carbon dioxide (CO_2) in air reacts with copper articles and tarnishes it. Copper slowly loses its shine and forms a green coating on its surface due to the formation of basic copper carbonate (green).

$$2Cu + \underbrace{H_2O + CO_2 + O_2}_{\text{Air}} \longrightarrow \underset{\substack{\text{Basic copper}\\\text{carbonate}}}{CuCO_3 \cdot Cu(OH)_2}$$

Basic copper carbonate is insoluble in water. So, copper vessels cannot be cleaned with water. Lemon juice contains citric acid, while tartaric acid exists in tamarind. These acids react with basic copper carbonate to form soluble salts. These salts are removed from the surface of copper metal and the metal shines again.

Question 14 Differentiate between metal and non-metal again on the basis of their chemical properties.

Thinking Process

- The ability of metals to lose electrons is known as electro positivity.
- The ability of non-metals to gain/attract electrons is known as electronic activity.

Sol.

Metal	Non-Metal
1. Metals are electropositive in nature. $M \longrightarrow M^+ + e^-$	Non-metals are electronegative in nature. $NM \xrightarrow{+e^-} NM^-$
2. Metals form basic oxides *e.g.,* $2Mg + O_2 \longrightarrow 2MgO$ (Basic oxide)	Non-metals form acidic/neutral oxides. *e.g.,* $C + O_2 \longrightarrow CO_2$ (Acidic oxide)
3. Metals replace hydrogen from dil. acids $M + \text{dil. HCl} \longrightarrow MCl + H_2 \uparrow$	Non-metals do not replace hydrogen from dil. acids.
4. Metals react with water to form metal oxide/metal hydroxide and hydrogen gas. $\text{Metal} + H_2O \rightarrow \text{Metal oxide} + H_2 \uparrow$ $\text{Metaloxide} + H_2O \rightarrow \text{Metal hydroxide}$	Non-metals do not react with water/steam to evolve H_2 as they can't give electrons to hydrogen ions of water.

Question 15 A man went door to door posing as a goldsmith. He promised to bring back the glitter of old and dull gold ornaments. An unsuspecting lady gave a set of gold bangles to him which he dipped in a particular solution. The bangles sparkled like new but their weight was reduced drastically. The lady was upset but after a futile argument the man beat a hasty retreat. Can you play the detective to find out the nature of the solution he had used?

Sol. The man used **'aqua-regia',** which is a mixture of conc. HCl and conc. HNO_3 in the ratio of 3 : 1 . This mixture can dissolve gold and platinum. Neither conc. HCl nor con. HNO_3 can do this alone. It is highly corrosive and since it can dissolve gold therefore the weight of bangles reduced drastically.

Mistake Alert One can make a mistake in considering the composition of aqua regia as a mixture of conc. HCl and conc. HNO_3 in the ratio of 1 : 3, instead of 3 : 1.

Question 16 Give reasons why copper is used to make hot water tanks and not steel (an alloy of iron).

Sol. The copper is used to make hot water tanks and not steel because

1. copper is one of the best conductors of heat, so it can heat water faster and evenly.
2. copper does not react with boiling water/steam, whereas steel (iron) reacts with steam.

DIKSHA APP Questions

☐ Multiple Choice Questions

Q.1 Graphite is an allotrope of

(a) lead (b) carbon (c) phosphorus (d) sulphur

◎ ***Thinking Process*** Allotropes are different physical forms in which an element can exist.

Sol. (b) Graphite is an allotrope of carbon. Graphite is used in nuclear reactors and lithium ion batteries, as it is a good conductor of electricity.

Q.2 The property of metals to be drawn into thin wires is called

(a) malleability (b) ductility (c) conductivity (d) sonority

Sol. (b) The property of metals to be drawn into thin wires is called ductility.

- Malleability is the property which allows the metals to be hammered into sheets.
- Sonority or sonorosity is that property of metals due to which metals make sound when hit with an object.

Q.3 The non-metal which exists as a liquid at room temperature is

(a) iodine (b) bromine (c) nitrogen (d) chlorine

Sol. (b) Bromine is the only non-metal that is exists as liquid at room temperature.

- It is a reddish brown liquid.
- It is used in the production of salts of bromine like AgBr, which is used in photography and KBr which is used in sleeping drugs.

Q.4 **Assertion** (A) The colour of copper sulphate solution changes when piece of zinc is dropped in it.
Reason (R) Copper is more reactive than zinc.

(a) Both A and R are true and R is the correct explanation of A.
(b) Both A and R are true but R is not the correct explanation of A.
(c) A is true but R is false.
(d) A is false but R is true.

Sol. (c) A is true but R is false.

The colour of copper sulphate solution changes when piece of zinc is dropped in it because zinc is more reactive than copper. In this reaction, zinc displaces copper from copper sulphate solution, leading to a colour change in the solution and appearance of a reddish brown solid (copper).

$$\underset{}{Zn(s)} + \underset{\text{(Blue colour)}}{CuSO_4(aq)} \longrightarrow \underset{\text{(Colourless)}}{ZnSO_4(aq)} + \underset{\text{(Reddish brown solid)}}{Cu(s)}$$

Q.5 The following questions consist of two statements Assertion (A) and Reason (R).

Answer the questions selecting the appropriate options given below.

Assertion (A) Metals like sodium and potassium are always found in combined state.

Reason (R) These metals are highly reactive.

(a) Both A and R are true and R is the correct explanation of A.
(b) Both A and R are true and R is not the correct explanation of A.
(c) A is true but R is false.
(d) A is false but R is true.

Sol. (a) Both A and R are true and R is the correct explanation of A.

Metals like sodium and potassium are always found in combined state, as these are highly reactive metals.

Q.6 Which of the following is used for dissolution of gold?

(a) Hydrochloric acid (b) Sulphuric acid
(c) Nitric acid (d) Aqua-regia

Sol. (d) Aqua-regia is used for dissolution of gold. Aqua-regia is a very powerful acid and latin meaning of its name is royal water. 3 parts conc. HCl + 1 part conc. HNO_3 is known as aqua-regia. It is used to dissolve gold (Au) and platinum (Pt).

Q.7 Which of the following represent the correct order of decreasing reactivity?

(a) Mg > Al > Zn > Fe (b) Mg > Zn > Al > Fe
(c) Al > Zn > Fe > Mg (d) Mg > Fe > Zn > Al

Sol. (a) The correct order of decreasing reactivity is Mg > Al > Zn > Fe. The activity series is a list that ranks metals based on their decreasing activities. Based on the activity series the order of reactivity for the mentioned metals is as follows:

- Mg ← Most reactive
- Al
- Zn
- Fe → Least reactive

Q.8 In the given reaction, $Al_2O_3 + NaOH \rightarrow X + H_2O$. What is element X ?

(a) $NaAlO_2$ (b) Na_3Al (c) Na_2O_3 (d) $NaAl_2O_3$

◎ **Thinking Process** Amphoteric oxides are metal oxides that react with acids and bases to produce water and salts.

Sol. (a) $X = NaAlO_2$ (sodium aluminate)

$Al_2O_3 + NaOH \longrightarrow 2NaAlO_2 + H_2O$

Al_2O_3 is an amphoteric oxides so, it reacts with base (NaOH) to give sodium aluminate ($NaAlO_2$) and water.

Q.9 Which metal from the following can displace Zn from $ZnSO_4$ solution?

(a) Lead (b) Copper (c) Magnesium (d) Silver

Sol. (c) Magnesium (Mg) can displace Zn from $ZnSO_4$ solution.

Magnesium (Mg) lies above Zn in the reactivity series and hence can displace Zn from zinc sulphate solution.

$$ZnSO_4(aq) + Mg(s) \longrightarrow MgSO_4(aq) + Zn(s)$$

Q.10 Sandhya took three beakers *A*, *B* and *C* containing zinc sulphate, silver sulphate and iron (II) sulphate solutions respectively. Copper pieces were added to each beaker. The solution will appear blue in the case of

(a) Beaker *A* (b) Beaker *B*
(c) Beaker *C* (d) Beaker *B* and *C*

Sol. (b) The solution will appear blue in the case of beaker *B* (containing silver sulphate solution).

(i) Copper (Cu) cannot displace zinc and iron from zinc sulphate and iron (II) sulphate solutions because zinc and iron are more reactive than copper.

(ii) Copper (Cu) can displace silver (Ag) from silver sulphate solution because copper is more reactive than silver. The reactive will be

$$Ag_2SO_4(aq) + Cu\,(s) \longrightarrow CuSO_4(aq) + 2Ag\,(s)$$

This reaction produces copper sulphate ($CuSO_4$) which is blue in colour.

Q.11 When brass, an alloy of Zn and Cu, is dissolved in dil. HCl, hydrogen gas is evolved. The evolution of gas is due to

(a) only copper reacts with dil. HCl.

(b) only zinc reacts with dil. HCl.

(c) both zinc and copper reacts with dil. HCl.

(d) zinc reacts with copper.

Sol. (b) When brass, an alloy of zinc (Zn) and copper (Cu) is dissolved in dil. HCl, hydrogen gas is evolved as only zinc reacts with dil. HCl.

Zinc is above hydrogen in the activity series, so it can displace it from dil. acid and result in the evolution of hydrogen gas. Whereas, copper is below hydrogen in the activity series, so it cannot react with dil. HCl to give H_2 gas.

☐ Very Short Answer Type

Q.1 Silver metal gets tarnished when left exposed for sometime. Explain.

Sol. Silver metal becomes black or gets tarnished after some time when exposed to air. This is because it reacts with sulphur in the air to form a coating of silver sulphide.

Q.2 An element '*A*' reacts with oxygen to form an oxide. This oxide dissolves in water to give an aqueous solution which turns red litmus blue.

(a) What is the chemical nature of the solution?

(b) Is element '*A*' a metal or a non-metal?

◎ ***Thinking Process*** Metals form basic oxides, whereas non-metals form acidic oxides.

Sol. (a) Element '*A*' reacts with oxygen to form an oxide which is basic in nature. This is because it is given that its aqueous solution turns red litmus blue, which is a characteristic property of a base.

(b) Element '*A*' is a metal as it forms basic oxide when reacted with oxygen.

$$\text{Metal} + \text{Oxygen} \rightarrow \underset{\text{(Basic in nature)}}{\text{Metal oxide}}$$

Q.3 Sodium and potassium are never found in free state in nature. Explain.

Sol. Sodium and potassium are the metals found at the top of the activity series. So, they are very reactive and are never found in nature as free elements.

Q.4 Name two metals that melt in hand.

Sol. Gallium and caesium are two metals that melt in hand because they have very low melting points.

Q.5 Name two metals which do not react with water at all.

Sol. Two metals which do not react with water at all are lead and copper.

☐ Short Answer Type

Q.1 How can we find whether a given element is a non-metal, if we know its electronic configuration?

◎ ***Thinking Process*** Electrons present in the outermost or valence shells are called valence electrons. On the basis of these valence electrons, we can classify elements into metals and non-metals.

Sol. Elements which have 1, 2 or 3 valence electrons are metals as they can lose electrons in a chemical reaction. Whereas, elements which have 4 or more valence electrons are non-metals as they have a tendency to gain electrons in a chemical reaction.

Q.2 How are ores different than minerals? .

Sol. The elements or compounds in the form of which metal occur naturally in the earth's crust are known as minerals.
Minerals from which metals can be extracted easily and profitably are called ores.

Mistake Alert Students should remember that all ores are minerals but all minerals are not ores.

Q.3 Aluminium is a reactive metal still it does not corrode. Comment.

Sol. Aluminium reacts with oxygen to form aluminium oxide, which is stable and forms a protective layer over the aluminium surface. This aluminium oxide coating makes the metal resistant to further corrosion.

Q.4 An oxide of metal '*X*' with valency 2 reacts with both acid (HCl) as well as base (NaOH) to produce salt and water.

(a) What is the name given to such an oxide?

(b) Identify the metal '*X*' and give the formula of its oxide.

Sol. (a) Amphoteric oxides are the oxides which reacts with both acids and bases to produce salt and water.

(b) The metal '*X*' which forms amphoteric oxide and has a valency of 2 is zinc. The formula of its amphoteric oxide is ZnO.

Q.5 How are metals high in the reactivity series obtained from their ores? Explain the process by taking an example.

Sol. The metals high up in the reactivity series (Na, Mg, Ca, Al, etc.) are very reactive. They cannot be obtained from their compounds by heating with carbon because these metals have more affinity for oxygen than carbon. These metals are obtained by **electrolytic reduction**.
For example, sodium, magnesium and calcium are obtained by the electrolysis of their molten chlorides. The metals are deposited at the cathode (the negatively charged electrode), whereas, chlorine is liberated at the anode (the positively charged electrode). The reactions are -

$$\text{At cathode}: Na^+ + e^- \rightarrow Na$$

$$\text{At anode}: 2Cl^- \rightarrow Cl_2 + 2e^-$$

Aluminium is also obtained by the electrolytic reduction of aluminium oxide.

□ Long Answer Type

Q.1 **How are ionic compounds different from covalent compounds in terms of their solubility, conductivity and physical state?**

Sol. (a) Ionic compounds are soluble in water, whereas covalent compounds are insoluble in water.

(b) Ionic compounds conduct electricity in molten state or in solution because ions in them move freely in these states and conduct electricity. While, covalent compounds are generally not good conductors of electricity.

(c) Ionic compounds are crystalline solids and are some what hard because of the strong force of attraction between the positive and negative ions. These compounds are generally brittle and break into pieces when pressure is applied on them. But, covalent compounds can be solids, liquids or gases.

Q.2 State three reasons:

(a) Sulphur is a non-metal. (b) Magnesium is a metal.

Sol. (a) Sulphur is a non-metal as :

(i) It is a poor conductor of electricity.
(ii) It is brittle.
(iii) It reacts with oxygen to form dioxide which is an acidic oxide.

(b) Magnesium is a metal because-

(i) It is a good conductor of electricity.
(ii) It is malleable and ductile.
(iii) It reacts with oxygen to form magnesium oxide which is basic in nature.

Q.3 What is thermit reaction? Give its one use.

Sol. The thermit reaction is a highly exothermic displacement reaction between aluminium powder (Al) and iron (III) oxide (Fe_2O_3). This reaction produces aluminium oxide (Al_2O_3) and iron (Fe) in a molten form. The reaction is as follows:

$$Fe_2O_3(s) + 2Al\,(s) \longrightarrow 2Fe(l) + Al_2O_3(s) + \text{Heat}$$

The reaction is highly exothermic, so it release a large amount of heat. This heat is sufficient to melt the iron, making the thermit reaction useful for welding and cutting metals. It is used to join railway tracks or cracked machine parts.

Carbon and Its Compounds

CHAPTER 04

Important Points

01 Carbon is a unique element that forms the basis for all living organisms and many of the things we use.

02 Carbon can form millions of compounds due to its **tetravalent** nature and the property of **catenation** (ability to form bonds with other elements). It forms **covalent bond** by sharing of valence electrons.

03 A separate branch of chemistry, known as **organic chemistry,** is known that includes the study of compounds of carbon, hydrogen and other elements including oxygen, sulphur, nitrogen, halogens, etc.

04 The element carbon occurs in different forms in nature, called **allotropes** of carbon. They have varying physical properties.

- In diamond, each carbon is bonded to four other carbon atoms forming a rigid three dimensional structure.
- In graphite, each carbon atom is bonded to three other carbon atoms in the same plane giving a hexagonal array. One of these bonds is a double-bond, and thus the valency of carbon is satisfied. These hexagonal arrays are placed in layers one above the other.
- Diamond is the hardest substance known, while graphite is smooth and slippery. Graphite is also a good conductor of electricity.
- Diamonds can be synthesized by subjecting pure carbon to very high pressure and temperature.
- Fullerenes is another class of carbon allotropes. C-60 is the first fullerene to be identified. It has 60 carbon atoms arranged in the shape of a football.

05 Carbon forms compounds containing a single covalent bond, called saturated compounds. It can also form compounds containing double and triple bonds between carbon atoms, called unsaturated compounds. Unsaturated compounds are more reactive than saturated compounds.

06 The carbon chains may be in the form of straight chains, branched chains or rings.

07 The ability of carbon to form chains give rise to a **homologous series** of compounds, in which the same functional group is attached to carbon chains of different lengths.

08 The compounds with identical molecular formula but different structures are called **structural isomers.**

09 Compounds containing only carbon and hydrogen are called **hydrocarbons.**

- Saturated hydrocarbons are called **alkanes.**
- Unsaturated hydrocarbons which contain double bonds are called **alkenes,** whereas those containing triple bonds are called **alkynes.**

10 The **functional group** is an atom or group of atoms that defines the structure and properties of organic compounds.

11 The important functional groups are alcohols, aldehydes, ketones and carboxylic acids.

12 As molecular mass of compounds increases, their melting and boiling points increases.

13 Nomenclature of organic compounds are modified by a prefix or suffix as shown below

Class of compounds	Prefix/suffix	Example
1. Haloalkane	Prefix-chloro, bromo, etc.	Chloropropane, Bromopropane, etc.
2. Alcohol	Suffix-ol	Propanol
3. Aldehyde	Suffix-al	Propanal
4. Ketone	Suffix-one	Propanone
5. Carboxylic acid	Suffix-oic acid	Propanoic acid
6. Alkenes	Suffix ene	Propene
7. Alkynes	Suffix-yne	Propyne

14 Carbon and its compounds are some of the major sources of fuels as it undergoes combustion to release heat and light.

$$C + O_2 \longrightarrow CO_2 + \text{heat and light}$$

15 Saturated hydrocarbons generally gives a clean blue flame, while unsaturated hydrocarbons gives a yellow flame with lots of black smoke. Incomplete combustion of even saturated hydrocarbons give a sooty flame.

16 Alcohols are converted into acids by using $KMnO_4$ (alkaline) or acidified $K_2Cr_2O_7$ by oxidation reaction.

17 Also, unsaturated hydrocarbons undergo addition reactions to form saturated hydrocarbons by addition of hydrogen in the presence of Ni or Pd catalyst. This reaction is commonly used in the hydrogenation of vegetable oils.

18 Saturated hydrocarbons also reacts with chlorine in the presence of sunlight. Cl replaces H atom of hydrocarbon one-by-one. This is called substitution reaction.

$$CH_4 + Cl_2 \xrightarrow{\text{Sunlight}} CH_3Cl + HCl$$

19 **Ethanol**, also commonly called as alcohol is used as solvent for preparing medicines, beverages, etc. It is soluble in water. It reacts with Na metal to form sodium ethoxide and hydrogen gas. It also gives unsaturated hydrocarbons when heated with conc. H_2SO_4 (at 443 K), by removal of water molecule from ethanol.

(a) $2Na + 2CH_3CH_2OH \longrightarrow \underset{\text{Sodium ethoxide}}{2CH_3CH_2O^-Na^+} + H_2 \uparrow$

(b) $CH_3 - CH_2OH \xrightarrow[443\,K]{\text{conc. } H_2SO_4} CH_2 = CH_2 + H_2O$

20 Alcohol's and carboxylic acids react together in presence of acid to form ester. Ester's have fruity or pleasent smell.

$$CH_3COOH + C_2H_5OH \xrightleftharpoons{\text{Acid}} CH_3COOC_2H_5 + H_2O$$

21 • Consumption of ethanol in large quantities, leads to slowing down of metabolic processes and depressing of the central nervous system. This causes lack of coordination, mental confusion and impaired judgement.

• Also, ingestion of even small amounts of methanol can be fatal, as it is oxidised to methanal in the liver, which coagulates cells and damages the optic nerve, leading to blindness.

22 To make industrial ethanol undrinkable, denatured alcohol is created by adding methanal and dyes to it, ensuring that it is easily identifiable and unsuitable for drinking.

23 Alcohol is used as an additive in petrol as it is a cleaner fuel because it burns to produce only CO_2 and H_2O, making it more environmental friendly. Alcohol is derived from sugarcane, which is a highly efficient plant in converting sunlight to chemical energy.

24 **Ethanoic acid**, also known as **acetic acid** is used in vinegar (5-8% solution of acetic acid) and as a preservative in pickles.

25 The melting point of pure ethanoic acid is 290 K, so it often freezes during winter and thus is called **glacial acetic acid.**

26 Acetic acid is a weak acid. It reacts with sodium, sodium hydroxide, sodium carbonate and sodium hydrogen carbonate to form sodium acetate.

- $CH_3COOH + NaOH \longrightarrow CH_3COONa + H_2O$
- $2CH_3COOH + Na_2CO_3 \longrightarrow 2CH_3COONa + CO_2 + H_2O$
- $CH_3COOH + NaHCO_3 \longrightarrow CH_3COONa + H_2O + CO_2$

27 On heating esters with sodium hydroxide (alkali), it gets converted back to alcohol and sodium salt of carboxylic acid. This is known as **saponification reaction** as it is used to prepare soaps.

28 Soaps are sodium or potassium salts of long chain carboxylic acids.

29 The ionic end of soap interacts with water, while the carbon chain interacts with oil (or dirt). The soap molecules thus form structures called **micelles,** where the hydrophobic end faces inwards towards the oil and hydrophilic end faces outside.

30 **Soap** helps to emulsify the oil (or dirt) and hence, causes its removal.

31 The micelles stay in solution as a colloid and will not come together to precipitate because of ion-ion repulsion. Thus, they scatter light and also appears cloudy.

32 **Soaps** form an insoluble substance, called **scum,** after washing with hard water because soap reacts with calcium and magnesium salts present in hard water.

33 **Detergents** are sodium salts of sulphonic acids or ammounium salts with chlorides or bromides ions, etc. They do not form scum and remain effective in hard water. Thus, they are usually used to make shampoos and products for cleaning clothes.

Intext Questions

On Page 61

Question 1 What would be the electron dot structure of carbon dioxide which has the formula CO_2?

Sol. Atomic number of C = 6

Atomic number of O = 8

Electronic configuration of C and O are

	K	L			K	L
C	2	4		O	2	6

Electron dot structure

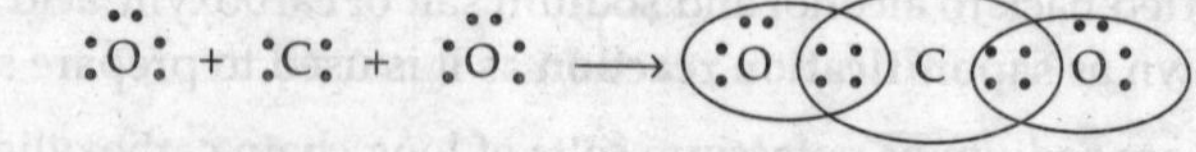

or O=C=O

Mistake Alert One can make a mistake of not writing the correct electron distribution in lewis dot structure.

Question 2 What would be the electron dot structure of a molecule of sulphur which is made up of eight atoms of sulphur?

(**Hint** The eight atoms of sulphur are joined together in the form of a ring.)

Sol Atomic number of S = 16

Electronic configuration = K L M
2 8 6

Electron dot structure of S_8

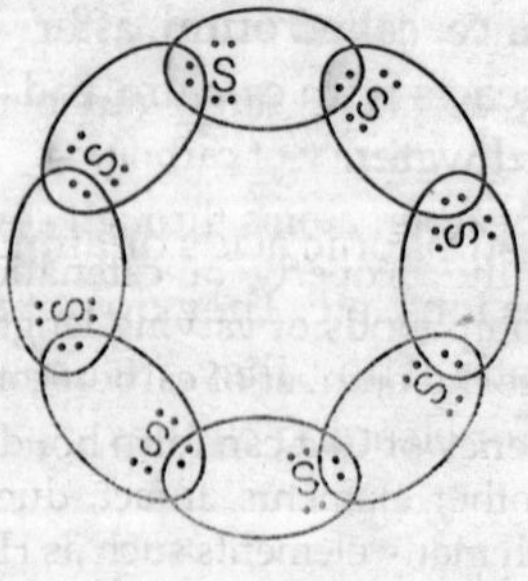

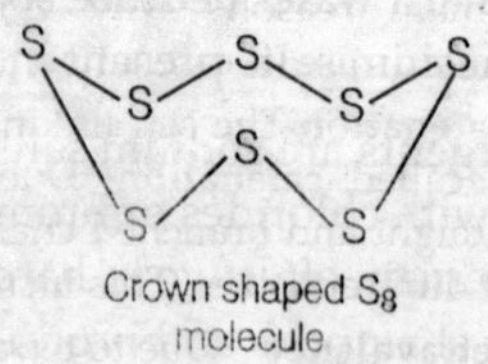

Crown shaped S_8 molecule

On Page 68

Question 1 How many structural isomers can you draw for pentane?

◎ *Thinking Process* Structural isomers have the same molecular formula but different structures.

Sol. Pentane (C_5H_{12}) has a skeleton of five carbon atoms. It can exist as straight chain as well as two branched chains. The possible structural isomers have been shown below.

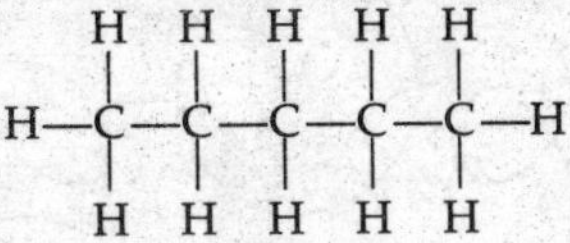

(*n*-pentane)

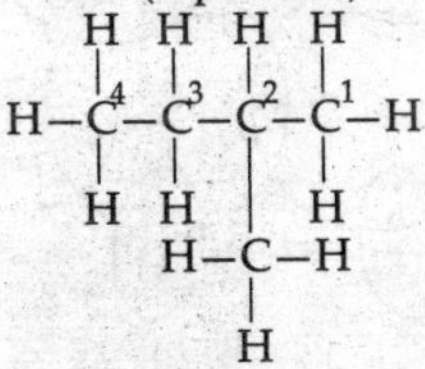

(2-Methylbutane) *iso*-pentane

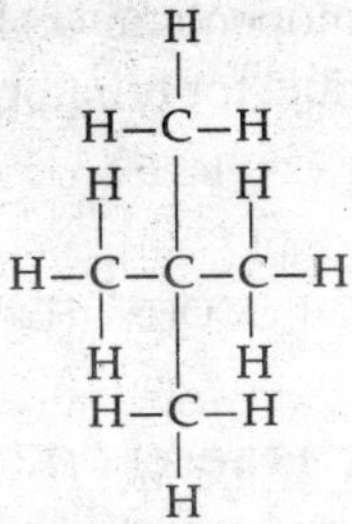

(2, 2-Dimethyl propane) (*neo*-pentane)

Question 2 What are the two properties of carbon which lead to the huge number of carbon compounds we see around us?

Sol. Two main reasons why carbon forms a huge number of carbon compounds are (i) catenation (ii) tetravalency of carbon.

(i) **Catenation** The self linking of carbon atoms through covalent bonds is called **catenation**. Due to the property of catenation, C forms straight and branched chain compounds of varying lengths and rings of different sizes. This increases the number of carbon compounds.

(ii) **Tetravalency** Due to tetravalency of C, it can form bonds either with other carbon atoms or some other elements. Infact, due to its small size, C forms strong bonds with many elements such as H, O, N, S and halogens, etc. In addition to this, C forms both double and triple bonds with itself or with other elements like O, N, etc. This further increases the number of carbon compounds.

Question 3 What will be the formula and electron dot structure of cyclopentane?

Sol. General formula of cycloalkane = C_nH_{2n}, In cyclopentane $n = 5$

$\therefore$ Formula of cyclopentane, $C_5H_{5\times 2} = C_5H_{10}$

Electron dot structure of cyclopentane

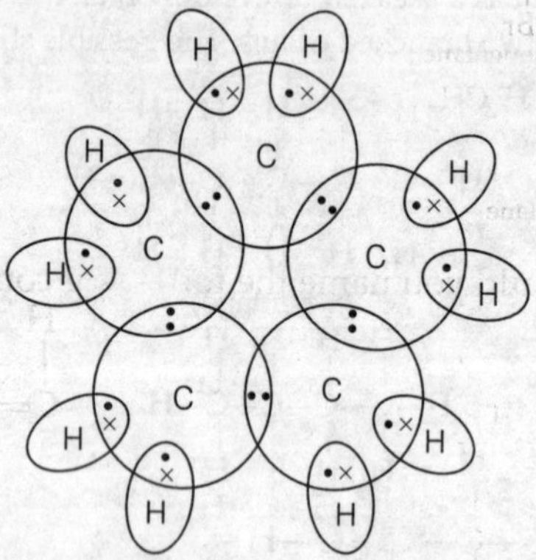

Question 4 Draw the structures for the following compounds.

(a) Ethanoic acid (b) Bromopentane (c) Butanone (d) Hexanal

Are structural isomers possible for bromopentane?

Sol.

(a) Ethanoic acid, CH_3COOH, 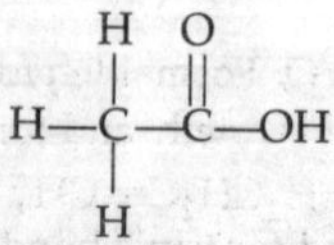

(b) Bromopentane, $CH_3CH_2CH_2CH_2CH_2Br$

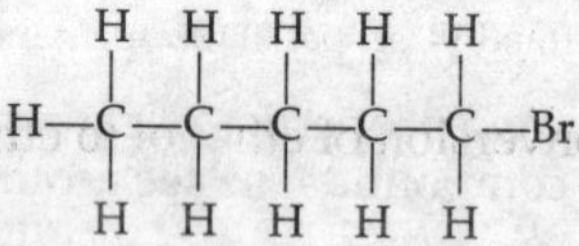

(c) Butanone, $CH_3CH_2\overset{\overset{O}{\|}}{C}—CH_3$ and 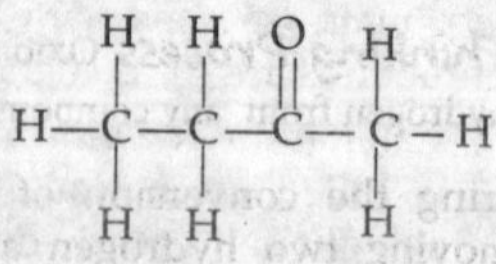

(d) Hexanal, $CH_3CH_2CH_2CH_2CH_2CHO$

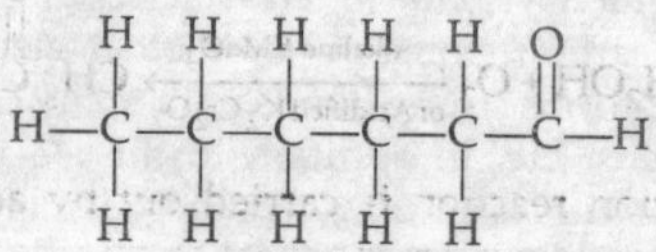

Yes, structural isomers of bromopentane are possible and they are

(i) $CH_3CH_2CH_2CH_2CH_2Br$
1-Bromopentane

(ii) $CH_3CH_2CH_2CHCH_3$ (with Br attached to the fourth carbon)
2-Bromopentane

(iii) $CH_3CH_2CHCH_2CH_3$ (with Br attached to the third carbon)
3-Bromopentane

Question 5 How would you name the following compounds?

(a) $CH_3—CH_2—Br$

(b) $H—\underset{}{\overset{H}{C}}=O$

(c) $H—\overset{H}{\underset{H}{C}}—\overset{H}{\underset{H}{C}}—\overset{H}{\underset{H}{C}}—\overset{H}{\underset{H}{C}}—C\equiv C—H$

Sol. (a) $CH_3—CH_2—Br$, Bromoethane (because for two carbons, root word is 'eth' and 'bromo' is the prefix for halogen atom).

(b) $H—\overset{H}{C}=O$, Formaldehyde or methanal (because for single carbon, root word is 'meth' and for aldehyde, suffix is 'al').

(c) $CH_3CH_2CH_2CH_2C\equiv CH$, 1-hexyne (because for 6 carbons, root word is 'hex' and for triple bond suffix is 'yne'.)

On Page 71

Question 1 Why is the conversion of ethanol to ethanoic acid an oxidation reaction?

◎ ***Thinking Process*** Oxidation is the addition of oxygen or removal of hydrogen from any compound.

Sol. During the conversion of ethanol to ethanoic acid we are actually removing two hydrogen and adding oxygen to ethanol, so it is an oxidation reaction.

$$CH_3CH_2OH + O_2 \xrightarrow[\text{or Acidified } K_2Cr_2O_7]{\text{Alkaline } KMnO_4} CH_3\overset{O}{\overset{||}{C}}—OH + H_2O$$

This oxidation reaction is carried out by adding oxidising agents like alkaline potassium permanganate or acidified potassium dichromate.

Question 2 A mixture of oxygen and ethyne is burnt for welding. Can you tell why a mixture of ethyne and air is not used?

Sol. We need a high temperature for welding, but when ethyne is burnt in air, it undergoes incomplete combustion and releases a lot of smoke and the temperature is also not very high.

In order to ensure complete combustion and to obtain the high temperature needed for welding, a mixture of ethyne and oxygen is used.

$$2CH\equiv CH + 5O_2 \longrightarrow 4CO_2 + 2H_2O + \text{heat} + \text{light}$$

On Page 74

Question 1 How would you distinguish experimentally between an alcohol and a carboxylic acid?

Sol. **Sodium bicarbonate test** ($NaHCO_3$ test)

$$\text{Alcohol} + NaHCO_3 \longrightarrow \text{No effervescence}$$

$$\text{Acid} + NaHCO_3 \longrightarrow \text{Brisk effervescence}$$

$$CH_3COOH + NaHCO_3 \longrightarrow CH_3COONa + H_2O + \underset{\text{Brisk effervescence}}{CO_2}$$

The sample which produces brisk effervescence when treated with $NaHCO_3$ due to release of CO_2 is a carboxylic acid. Whereas the sample which does not produce effervescence when treated with $NaHCO_3$, is an alcohol.

Question 2 What are oxidising agents?

◎ *Thinking Process* Oxidising agents itself gets reduced and oxidises the other substance.

Sol. Those substances which are capable of providing oxygen to other substances are called oxidising agents. *e.g.*, alk. $KMnO_4$ and acidified $K_2Cr_2O_7$ can both behave as oxidising agents.

$$CH_3CH_2OH \xrightarrow[\text{or alk. } KMnO_4 + \Delta]{\text{Acidified } K_2Cr_2O_7 + \Delta} CH_3COOH + H_2O$$

On Page 76

Question 1 Would you be able to check if water is hard by using a detergent?

◎ *Thinking Process* Detergents are sodium salts of sulphonic acids or ammonium salts with chlorides or bromides ions, etc. It remains effective in hard water. Hard water contains calcium and magnesium salts.

Sol. No, we cannot check if the water is hard by using a detergent, because detergent does not form insoluble calcium or magnesium salt (scum) with hard water.

Question 2 People use a variety of methods to wash clothes. Usually after adding the soap, they 'beat' the clothes on a stone, or beat it with a paddle, scrub with a brush or the mixture is agitated in a washing machine. Why is agitation necessary to get clean clothes?

Sol. When soap solution is made and dirty clothes are soaked in it then micelle formation occurs and oil or dirt is trapped in it. This results in the formation of an emulsion. To wash away the loosened dirt particles in the form of micelles from the surface of the cloth, it is either scrubbed mechanically or beaten or agitated in washing machine.

Exercises

Question 1 Ethane, with the molecular formula C_2H_6 has

(a) 6 covalent bonds (b) 7 covalent bonds
(c) 8 covalent bonds (d) 9 covalent bonds

◎ ***Thinking Process*** Covalent bonds are formed by sharing of electrons between two species.

Sol. (b) Structure of C_2H_6 is

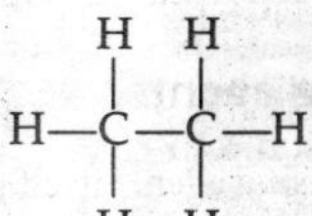

It is clear that it has 7 covalent bonds.

Question 2 Butanone is a four-carbon compound with the functional group

(a) carboxylic acid. (b) aldehyde.
(c) ketone. (d) alcohol.

◎ ***Thinking Process*** The suffix 'one' is used when the functional group present in the compound is ketone.

Sol. (c) In butanone, the function group is ketone (one) $>C{=}O$.

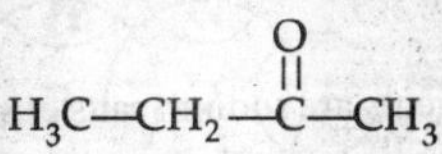

Butanone

Mistake Alert One can make a mistake in writing the 1 correct suffix corresponding to various functional groups in a compound.

Question 3 While cooking, if the bottom of the vessel is getting blackened on the outside, it means that

(a) the food is not cooked completely.
(b) the fuel is not burning completely.
(c) the fuel is wet.
(d) the fuel is burning completely.

◎ *Thinking Process* Incomplete combustion of fuel leads to a yellow sooty flame. Soot are unburnt carbon particles, which are black in colour.

Sol. (b) The unburnt particles of the fuel present in smoke blacken the vessel from outside. So, this indicates that the fuel is not burning completely.

Question 4 Explain the nature of the covalent bond using the bond formation in CH_3Cl.

Sol. The covalent bond is formed by sharing of electrons between the atoms. The shared pair of electrons belongs to the valence shell of both the combining atoms. For example CH_3Cl is a covalent compound. Atomic number of C = 6; H = 1; Cl = 17.

Electronic configuration

	K	*L*		*K*	*L*	*M*		*K*
C	2	4	Cl	2	8	7	H	1

C needs 4 electrons, H needs 1 and Cl also needs 1 electron to complete its octet.

∴ C shares its 4 electrons with each of the 3 H-atoms and 1 chlorine atom. It thus forms 4 covalent bonds as shown.

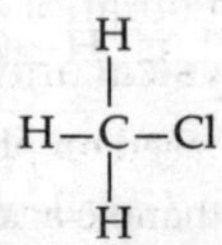

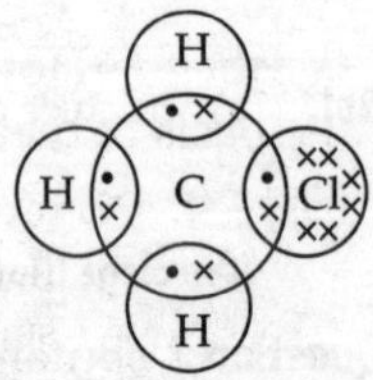

Question 5 Draw the electron dot structures for

(a) ethanoic acid (b) H_2S (c) propanone (d) F_2

Sol. (a) Ethanoic acid, CH_3COOH

(a) 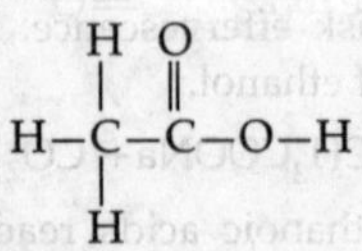

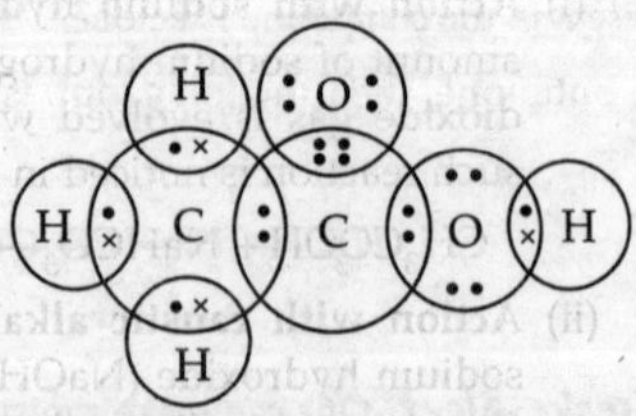

(b) H_2S, H–S–H

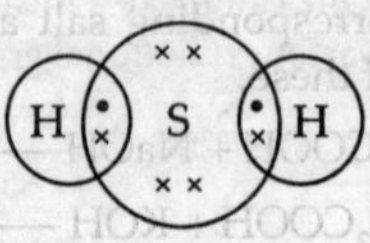

(c) Propanone, CH_3COCH_3

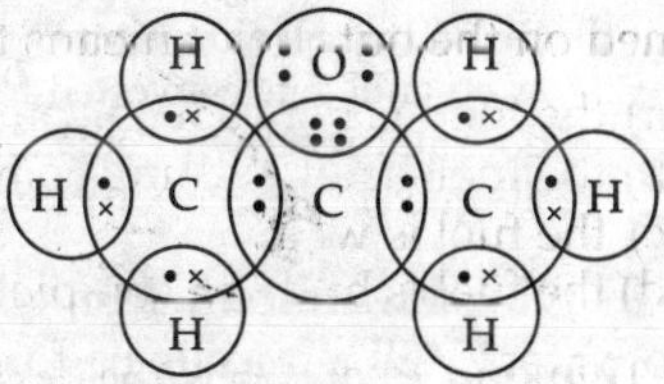

(d) F_2, F—F

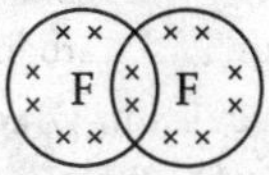

Question 6 What is a homologous series? Explain with an example.

Sol. **Homologous series** A series of similarly constituted compounds in which the members present have the same functional group and similar chemical properties, and any two succesive members in a particular series differ in their molecular formula by $-CH_2$ unit is called homologous series.

Example of homologous series

Alkane series C_nH_{2n+2}

CH_4 Methane, C_2H_6 Ethane

C_3H_8 Propane, C_4H_{10} Butane

C_5H_{12} Pentane

Question 7 How can ethanol and ethanoic acid be differentiated on the basis of their physical and chemical properties?

Sol. **I. Distinction based on physical properties**

(i) **Smell** Ethanoic acid has a pungent smell. Ethanol has a pleasant smell.

(ii) **Melting point** Ethanol has lower melting point (150 K) than ethanoic acid (290 K).

(iii) **Physical state** Pure ethanoic acid is solid (glacial acetic acid) in winters but ethanol is always a liquid.

II. Distinction based on chemical properties

(i) **Action with sodium hydrogen carbonate** On adding a small amount of sodium hydrogen carbonate to ethanoic acid, carbon dioxide gas is evolved with brisk effervescence. However, no such reaction is noticed in case of ethanol.

$$CH_3COOH + NaHCO_3 \longrightarrow CH_3COONa + CO_2\uparrow + H_2O$$

(ii) **Action with caustic alkalies** Ethanoic acids reacts with both sodium hydroxide (NaOH) and potassium hydroxide (KOH) to form corresponding salt and water. Ethanol fails to react with either of these.

$$CH_3COOH + NaOH \longrightarrow CH_3COONa + H_2O$$

$$CH_3COOH + KOH \longrightarrow CH_3COOK + H_2O$$

(iii) On adding alkaline $KMnO_4$ to ethanol, its pink colour disappears as ethanol gets converted to ethanoic acid. Whereas alk. $KMnO_4$ does not react with ethanoic acid and its pink colour does not disappear.

Question 8 Why does micelle formation take place when soap is added to water? Will a micelle be formed in other solvents such as ethanol also?

Sol. Soaps are the molecules in which the two ends have different properties, one is hydrophilic, (*i.e.,* water loving) while the other end is hydrophobic, (*i.e.,* water repelling or hydrocarbon loving). Inside water, these molecules have a unique orientation that keeps the hydrocarbon portion out of the water.

This is achieved by forming clusters of molecules in which the hydrophobic tails are in the interior of the cluster and the ionic ends are on the surface of the cluster. This formation is called a micelle. Soap in the form of a micelle is able to clean, since the oily dirt will be collected in the centre of the micelle. The micelles stay in solution as a colloid and will not come together to precipitate because of ion-ion repulsion. Thus, the dirt suspended in the micelles is also easily rinsed away.

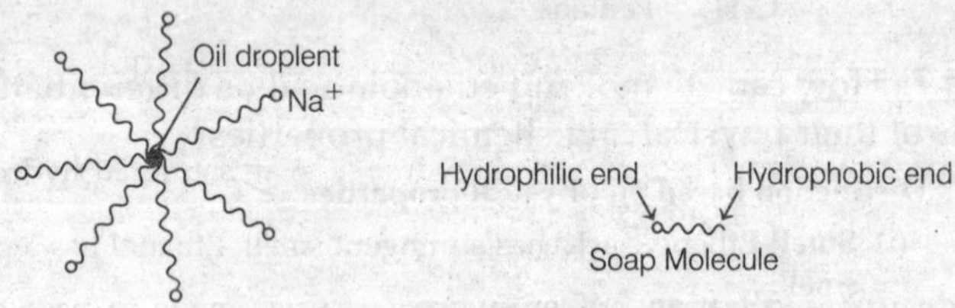

▲ Formation of Mecelles

No, micelle is not formed in other solvents like ethanol, because ethanol is less polar than water, so it is not as effective in stabilizing the hydrophilic heads of the soap molecule. Other such solvents also do not form micelle with soaps due to similar reason.

Question 9 Why are carbon and its compounds used as fuels for most applications?

Sol. Carbon burns in oxygen (air) to form carbon dioxide and water. During this reaction a large amount of heat and light are released. Hence, they are used as fuels.

$$C + O_2 \longrightarrow CO_2 + \text{heat} + \text{light}$$

Question 10 Explain the formation of scum when hard water is treated with soap.

Sol. Hard water contains calcium and magnesium salts. Soap is basically sodium or potassium salt of higher fatty acids. When soap is added to hard water, corresponding insoluble calcium and magnesium salts are formed. These are called **scum**.

Reaction taking place are shown below.

$$\underset{\text{(Hard water)}}{Ca^{2+}} + \underset{\text{(Soap)}}{2RCOONa} \longrightarrow \underset{\text{(Calcium salt ppt.)}}{(RCOO)_2Ca + 2Na^+}$$

$$\underset{\text{(Hard water)}}{Mg^{2+}} + \underset{\text{(Soap)}}{2RCOONa} \longrightarrow \underset{\text{(Magnesium salt ppt.)}}{(RCOO)_2Mg + 2Na^+}$$

Question 11 What change will you observe if you test soap with litmus paper (red or blue)?

◎ ***Thinking Process*** Soap is typically sodium or potassium salt of fatty acids. The preparation of soap involves reaction of esters with alkali and this is called saponification reaction. The alkali left in the solution is responsible for the alkaline nature of the soap.

Sol. Soap is alkaline in nature and hence its solution turns red litmus paper blue. It will have no effect on blue litmus paper.

Question 12 What is hydrogenation? What is its industrial application?

Sol. **Hydrogenation** The addition of hydrogen to unsaturated hydrocarbon in the presence of catalyst is known as hydrogenation.

nickel (Ni) or palladium (Pd)

Industrial application When hydrogen gas is made to pass through vegetable oil in the presence of nickel catalyst, it changes to solid fat (ghee).

$$\underset{\text{(Unsaturated)}}{\text{Vegetable oils} + H_2} \xrightarrow[\text{Heat}]{\text{Ni}} \underset{\text{(Saturated)}}{\text{Fats (ghee)}}$$

Question 13 Which of the following hydrocarbons undergo addition reactions?

$$C_2H_6, C_3H_8, C_3H_6, C_2H_2 \text{ and } CH_4$$

Sol. Unsaturated hydrocarbons containing double/ triple bond undergo addition reactions.

- C_2H_6, 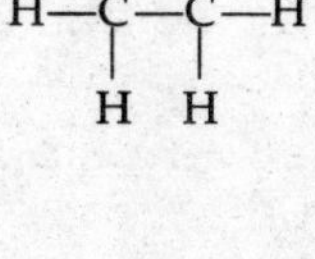

- C_3H_6, 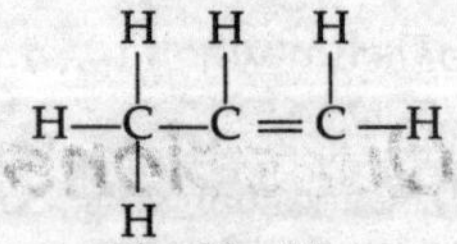
- C_3H_8, 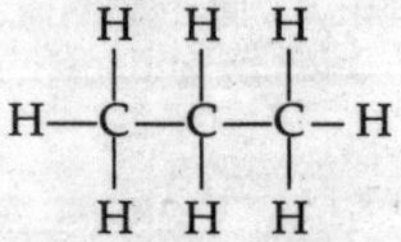
- C_2H_2, $H-C\equiv C-H$
- CH_4, 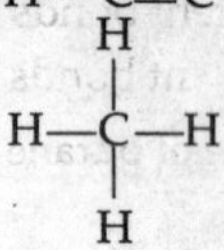

So, C_3H_6 and C_2H_2 will only undergo addition reactions.

Question 14 Give a test that can be used to differentiate between saturated and unsaturated hydrocarbons.

Sol. Unsaturated compounds are oxidised by alkaline $KMnO_4$ (oxidising agent which causes disappearance of its pink colour.

∴ When cooking oil is treated with a few drops of alkaline $KMnO_4$, pink colour of $KMnO_4$ disappears. With saturated hydrocarbons however, the pink colour $KMnO_4$ does not disappear.

Question 15 Explain the mechanism of the cleaning action of soaps.

Sol. Refer to 8 of exercises solution 8 of exercise.

DIKSHA APP Questions

☐ Multiple Choice Questions

Q.1 Butane has the molecule formula C_4H_{10}. It has

(a) 5 covalent bonds (b) 11 covalent bonds
(c) 13 covalent bonds (d) 15 covalent bonds

Sol. (c) The number of covalent bonds in the molecule of butane is thirteen. Butane has the formula C_4H_{10}.

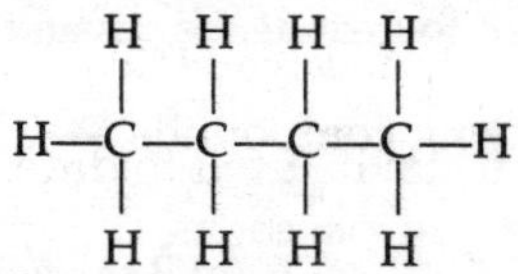

Butane is used as fuel for cigarette lighters, portable stoves, torches, etc. It is also found in LPG.

Q.2 The name of the compound CH_3CHO is

(a) propanal (b) propanone (c) ethanol (d) ethanal

Sol. (d) The name of the compound CH_3CHO is ethanal.

Ethanal (acetaldehyde) is usually used as an intermediate in the production of acetic acid. It is also used in the manufacturing of perfumes, drugs, flavouring agents, dyes, etc.

Q.3 Which of the following is an unsaturated compound?

(a) Chloromethane (b) Ethene (c) Ethane (d) Methane

◎ Thinking Process

- Saturated hydrocarbons have only single bonds.
- Unsaturated hydrocarbons have double or triple bonds present in them.

Sol. (b) Ethene is an unsaturated compound.

Ethene is prepared by heating ethyl alcohol with conc. H_2SO_4 at 443 K. It is used in making mustard gas, in ripening fruits artificially, in oxyethylene flame, in fruits preservation, etc. Ethene is first member of alkenes (also known olefins).

Q.4 When ethanol is heated with alkaline $KMnO_4$, it produces ethanoic acid. In the above reaction, alkaline $KMnO_4$ acts as

(a) dehydrating agent (b) reducing agent
(c) catalyst (d) oxidising agent

◎ *Thinking Process* An oxidising agent oxidises the other substance and itself gets reduced.

Sol. (d) When ethanol is heated with alkaline $KMnO_4$, it produces ethanoic acid. In this reaction alkaline $KMnO_4$ acts as oxidising agent.

$$C_2H_5OH \xrightarrow[\Delta]{\text{alkaline } KMnO_4} CH_3COOH$$

$KMnO_4$ is a strong oxidising agent that acts as a disinfect, deodrizer and astringent. It is used to treat dermatitis and cleanse wounds.

Q.5 In which of the following compounds, —CHO is the functional group.

(a) Propanone (b) Propanol
(c) Propanal (d) Propanoic acid

Sol. (c) Propanal compound has the —CHO functional group. Functional group is an atom or a group of atoms present in an organic compound. This group is responsible for the characteristic chemical properties of an organic compound. The given group in the question is —CHO, which represents an aldehyde.

Q.6 Alkynes may be represented by the general formula

(a) C_nH_{2n-1} (b) C_nH_{2n-2}
(c) C_nH_{2n} (d) C_nH_{2n+1}

Sol. (b) Alkynes may be represented by the general formula C_nH_{2n-2}. They contain atleast one carbon-carbon triple bond. Ethylene (C_2H_2) is the first member of alkyne homologous series.

Q.7 The bond between two identical non-metallic atom has a pair of electrons.

(a) unequally shared between two atoms.
(b) transferred completely from one atom to another.
(c) with identical spins.
(d) equally shared between them.

Sol. (d) The bond between two identical non-metallic atom has a pair of electrons equally shared between them. They form a covalent bond which is totally non-polar because of similar electronegativity.

Example C—C

(Non-polar covalent bond)

Q.8 Which one of the following green house gases is a contributor due to incomplete combustion of coal and petroleum?

(a) Oxide of nitrogen (b) Methane
(c) Carbon monoxide (d) Carbon dioxide

Sol. (c) Carbon monoxide gas is a contributor of green house gases and it is produced due to incomplete combustion of coal and petroleum. When the combustion of fuel takes place in insufficient supply of oxygen, it is called incomplete combustion.

e.g.
$$CH_4 + O_2 \xrightarrow{} CO + H_2O$$
(Insufficient supply of O_2)

Q.9 The functional group present in aldehydes is

(a) $-OH$ (b) $-CHO$ (c) $-COOH$ (d) $-COOR$

Sol. (b) The functional group present in aldehyde is $-CHO$.
General formula of aldehyde is $C_nH_{2n}O$. *e.g.*, formaldehyde (HCHO), acetaldehyde (CH_3CHO), etc.

Q.10 Which of the following does not belong to the same homologous series?

(a) C_2H_4 (b) C_2H_2 (c) C_4H_8 (d) C_3H_6

Sol. (b) C_2H_2 does not belong to the same homologous series. Homologous series is a series of compound, in which same functional group is attached to carbon chains of different lengths. Members of a homologous series are called homologous. *e.g.*, CH_4, C_2H_6, C_3H_8 belong to straight chain alkanes. All the members of a homologous series have similar chemical properties and they differ by a $-CH_2$ group.

Q.11 The reaction between CH_4 and chlorine in presence of sunlight is an example of

(a) substitution reaction. (b) combination reaction.
(c) addition reaction. (d) decomposition reaction.

Sol. (a) The reaction between CH_4 and chlorine in present of sunlight is an example of substitution reaction.

- Methane (CH_4) on reaction with Cl_2 in presence of diffused sunlight gives $CHCl_3$ as it replaces one H with Cl atom

$$CH_4(g) + Cl_2(g) \xrightarrow{h\nu} CH_3Cl(g) + HCl$$

Q.12 The tendency of carbon atoms to form long chains is called

(a) polymerisation (b) catenation (c) substitution (d) bonding

Sol. (b) The tendency of carbon atoms to form long chains is called catenation. Carbon atoms link with one another through covalent bonds to form chains and rings. This property of self linkage is called catenation. Due to property of catenation, carbon is able to exist in allotropic forms.

Q.13 Detergents are sodium or potassium salts of long chain of

(a) aldehydes (b) ketones

(c) carboxylic acid (d) sulphonic acid

Sol. (d) Detergents are sodium or potassium salts of long chain of sulphonic acid. Detergents are used as cleansing agent. They can be used both in soft and hard water because their calcium and magnesium salts are soluble in water, thus scum formation does not occur.

□ Very Short Answer Type

Q.1 Name the following

(i) an alcohol used in cough syrups.

(ii) a carboxylic acid used as a preservative .

Sol. (i) Ethanol is used in cough syrups.

(ii) Ethanoic acid is used as a preservative.

Q.2 A hydrocarbon 'X' does not react with H_2, but readily combines with chlorine in the presence of ultraviolet (UV) light. Predict the nature.

Sol. The hydrocarbon 'X' must be a saturated hydrocarbon as it reacts with chlorine in presence of UV light to give a substitution reaction. Also, it does not react with H_2 to give addition reaction, as it is a characteristic reaction of unsaturated hydrocarbons.

Q.3 An organic compound *A* with molecular formula $C_2H_4O_2$ turns blue litmus red and gives brisk effervescence with sodium hydrogen carbonate. Identify the compound.

Sol. The organic compound '*A*' is acetic acid, *i.e.*, CH_3COOH. It is acidic in nature so it turns blue litmus red. It also reacts with sodium hydrogencarbonate to give CO_2 gas, as brisk effervescence.

$$CH_3COOH + NaHCO_3 \rightarrow CH_3COONa + H_2O + CO_2$$

Q.4 Which is more reactive and why? C_2H_4 and C_2H_6.

◎ ***Thinking Process*** Unsaturated hydrocarbons are more reactive than saturated hydrocarbons.

Sol. Ethene (C_2H_4) is more reactive than ethane (C_2H_6) because ethene has a double bond between carbon atoms, which is more reactive and can readily participate in addition reactions, whereas ethane molecule has only single bonds and is less reactive.

Q.5 What is the difference in the molecular formula of any two consecutive members of a homologous series of organic compounds?

Sol. —CH_2 group (14u) is the difference in the molecular formula of any two consecutive members of a homologous series of organic compounds.

☐ Short Answer Type

Q.1 How will you convert ethanol to

(a) ethanoic acid

(b) ethene? Explain by giving suitable chemical equations.

Sol. (a) Ethanol is oxidised to ethanoic acid by using an oxidising agent like alkaline $KMnO_4$ or acidified potassium dichromate ($K_2Cr_2O_7$).

$$CH_3CH_2OH + [O] \xrightarrow[\text{Alkaline } KMnO_4 + \text{heat}]{\text{Acidified } K_2Cr_2O_7} CH_3COOH + H_2O$$

(b) To convert ethanol to ethene, a dehydration reaction is required, where ethanol is heated with a concentrated sulphuric acid at 443 K.

$$CH_3 - CH_2OH \xrightarrow[H_2SO_4]{\text{Hot Conc.}} CH_2 = CH_2 + H_2O$$

Q.2 What is a functional group? Give examples of two different functional groups.

Sol. A functional group is an atom or a group of atoms which replaces hydrogen from a hydrocarbon and provides specific properties to the compound, regardless of the length and nature of the carbon chain. Two different functional groups are: alcohol (-OH) and carboxylic acids (-COOH).

Q.3 Draw the structures for the following compounds.

(i) Ethanoic acid (ii) Bromopentane

(iii) Butanone (iv) Hexanal.

Sol. (i) $CH_3—COOH$

(ii) $CH_3—CH_2—CH_2—CH_2—Br$

(iii) $CH_3CH_2—COCH_3$

(iv) $CH_3CH_2CH_2CH_2CH_2CHO$

Q.4 Consumption of small quantities of dilute ethanol causes drunkenness. Even though this practice is condemned, it is a socially widespread practice. Describe its long-lasting harmful effects to spread awareness in society.

Sol. When large quantities of ethanol are consumed, it tends to slow metabolic processes and depresses the central nervous system. This results in lack of coordination, mental confusion, drowsiness, lowering of the normal inhibitions and finally stupour. The individual may feel relaxed but does not realise that his sense of judgement, sense of timing and muscular coordination have been seriously impaired.

Q.5 Explain why carbon generally forms compounds by covalent bonds.

Sol. Carbon cannot gain four electrons because it would be difficult for the nucleus with six protons to hold on to ten electrons. It also cannot lose four electrons because it would require a large amount of energy to remove four electrons leaving behind a carbon cation with six protons in its nucleus holding on to just two electrons. So, carbon can easily share its valence electrons to form covalent bonds.

☐ Long Answer Type

Q.1 Compare esterification and saponification reactions.

Sol. (a) Esterification is the reaction of formation of esters by reaction of carboxylic acid and alcohol in the presence of conc. sulphuric acid.

$$CH_3COOH + C_2H_5OH \xrightarrow{\text{Acid}} CH_3COOC_2H_5 + H_2O$$

In this reaction sweet smelling substance, esters are produced which are used in perfume and as flavouring agents.

(b) **Saponification reaction** is the alkaline hydrolysis of an ester to produce original alcohol and sodium salt of carboxylic acid.

$$CH_3COOC_2H_5 + NaOH \longrightarrow CH_3COONa + C_2H_5OH$$

The reaction is used for the preparation of soaps.

Q.2 Complete the following reactions.

(a) $CH_3COOC_2H_5 + H_2O \longrightarrow$

(b) $CH_3COOH + NaHCO_3 \longrightarrow$

(c) $CH_3COOH + C_2H_5OH \longrightarrow$

(d) $C_2H_2OH + Na \longrightarrow$

(e) $CH_3COOH + NaOH \longrightarrow$

Sol. (a) $CH_3COOC_2H_5 + H_2O \longrightarrow CH_3COOH + C_2H_5OH$

(b) $CH_3COOH + NaHCO_3 \longrightarrow CH_3COONa + CO_2 + H_2O$

(c) $CH_3COOH + C_2H_5OH \longrightarrow CH_3COOC_2H_5 + H_2O$

(d) $2C_2H_5OH + 2Na \longrightarrow 2C_2H_5ONa + H_2$

(e) $CH_3COOH + NaOH \longrightarrow CH_3COONa + H_2O$

Life Processes

CHAPTER 05

Important Points

01 Living organisms have the ability to perform basic life processes. This ability distinguishes them from the non-living organisms.

02 Life processes are the vital processes carried out by living organisms in order to maintain and sustain life.

03 There are special body parts which perform the various life processes in only multicellular organisms. No such organs are present in unicellular organisms.

04 All life processes require energy to carry out their functions and this is obtained from carbon-based food sources through the process called **nutrition**.

05 Nutrition is the process by which organisms obtain, absorb and utilise nutrients from external sources to support growth, maintain bodily function and provide energy.

Organisms can be classified based on their mode of nutrition into two categories, *i.e.,* autotrophs and heterotrophs.

06 **Autotrophs** (all green plants), make their own food using a green pigment known as chlorophyll. It plays a crucial role in converting the solar energy into chemical energy.

07 **Photosynthesis** is the process of synthesising of glucose using carbon dioxide and water in the presence of sunlight and chlorophyll. Glucose formed in this reaction is used by the plants to fulfill its various energy requirements. The excess amount of glucose is stored as starch in various parts of the plant. It can be expressed by following chemical reaction

$$6\,CO_2 + 12H_2O \xrightarrow[\text{Sunlight}]{\text{Chlorophyll}} C_6H_{12}O_2 + 6O_2 + 6H_2O$$

08 The following events occur during photosynthesis

(i) **Light Absorption** Chlorophyll in the chloroplasts absorbs light energy from the sun.

(ii) **Energy Conversion and Water Splitting** The absorbed light energy is converted into chemical energy and water molecules are split into hydrogen and oxygen. Oxygen is released as a by product.

(iii) **Carbon Dioxide Reduction** The chemical energy is used to convert carbon dioxide into carbohydrates.

09 Plants obtain carbon dioxide for photosynthesis through tiny pores called **stomata**, present on the surface of leaves. The stomata facilitate massive gaseous exchange during photosynthesis. This type of gaseous exchange also occurs across the surfaces of stems, roots and leaves.

10 The opening and closing of stomatal pores are regulated by guard cells, which control water loss and gaseous exchange. When guard cells absorb water, they swell, causing the stomatal pore to open and allowing carbon dioxide to enter. Conversely, when guard cells lose water, they shrink closing the pore to minimize water loss.

The following figure shows the stomata with guard cells

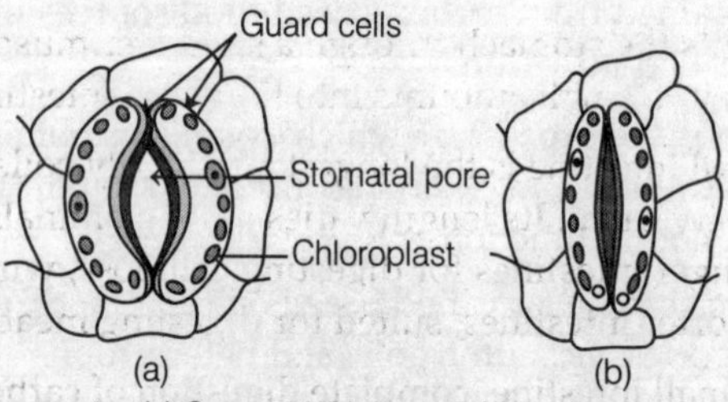

▲ (a) Open and (b) closed stomatal pore

11 **Heterotrophs** are organisms that depend on other organisms for their food. They can be classified into several types. Which are given below

Herbivores Organisms that eat plants, for *e.g.*, cow, goat, deer etc.

Carnivores Organisms that eat other animals, for *e.g.*, tiger, lion, sharks, etc.

Parasites Organisms that feed on other living organisms without killing them, for *e.g.*, *Cuscuta*, orchids, ticks, lice, leeches and tapeworms.

Saprophytes Organisms that feed on dead or decaying organic matter, for *e.g.*, fungi.

12 In *Amoeba*, digestion occurs in the food vacuole, formed by the engulfing of food particles using pseudopodia.

13 In *Paramecium*, the cell has a definite shape and food is taken in at a specific spot. Food is moved to this spot by the movement of cilia which cover the entire surface of the cell.

14 **Human alimentary canal** is a long tube extending from the mouth to the anus. The alimentary canal is made up of various organs and glands.

15 In mouth, food is crushed into small particles and mixed with saliva, which contains amylase for the digestion of starch.

16 Food is swallowed and moves to the stomach throught oesophagus. This movement is propelled by rhythmic muscle contractions known as peristalsis.

17 **Digestion** in the stomach is managed by gastric glands present in its wall. These glands secrete hydrochloric acid, the protein digesting enzyme (pepsin) and mucus. The hydrochloric acid creates an acidic environment that enhances the action of pepsin. Additionally, the acid also helps to kill bacteria present in the food. The mucus protects the inner lining of stomach from the corrosive effects of the acid.

18 Food exits the stomach through a sphincter muscle, which releases it in small amounts into the small intestine.

19 The small intestine is the longest and highly coiled part of the alimentary canal. Its length varies among animals, herbivores have longer intestines for digesting cellulose, while carnivores have shorter intestines, suited for digesting meat.

20 In the small intestine, complete digestion of carbohydrates, proteins and fats occur with the help of secretions from liver and pancreas.

21 The liver secretes bile, which neutralises the acidic food coming from the stomach and emulsifies fats into smaller droplets, making them easier to digest.

22 The pancreas produces pancreatic juice, containing enzymes such as trypsin (for proteins) and lipase (for fats). Additionally, the walls of small intestine secrete intestinal juice that finalises digestion, converting proteins to amino acids, carbohydrates to glucose and fats to fatty acids and glycerol.

23 The digestive food is absorbed by the walls of small intestine. The inner lining of the small intestine is covered with finger-like projections called villi, which increase the surface area for nutrient absorption. These villi are richly supplied with blood vessels that transport absorbed nutrients to cells, throughout the body, for obtaining energy, growth and repair of old tissues.

24 Undigested food then moves into the large intestine, where further water absorption occurs. The remaining waste is expelled from the body through the anus. The exist of waste is regulated by the anal sphincter.

25 **Respiration** is the breaking down of nutrients to release energy. During respiration, the digested food materials are broken down to release energy in the form of ATP.

26 Depending upon the requirement of oxygen, respiration occurs by the following two ways

(i) **Aerobic Respiration** It occurs in the presence of oxygen.

(ii) **Anaerobic Respiration** It occurs in the absence of oxygen.

27 In both kinds of respiration, the first step is breakdown of glucose into pyruvate. This process takes place in cytoplasm.

28 Depending on the presence or absence of oxygen different kind of products are formed in different cells, as given below.

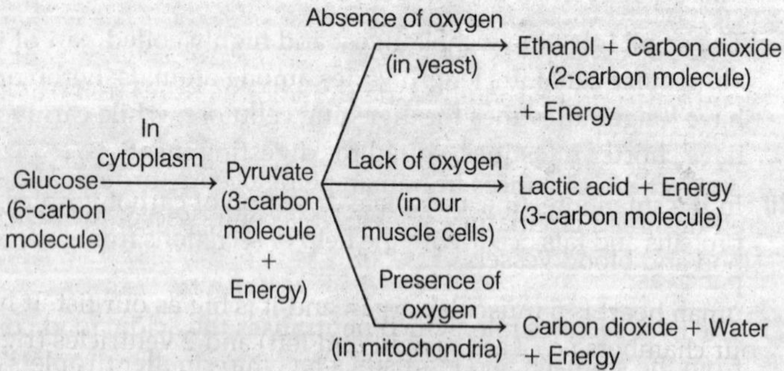

▲ **Breakdown of glucose by various pathways**

The energy released during cellular respiration is used to synthesis ATP, which is used to fuel all other activities.

29 Aerobic organisms rely on gaseous exchange to absorb oxygen for respiration and expel carbon dioxide.

Plants release CO_2 at night and oxygen during the day through stomata by the process of diffusion. The direction of diffusion depends upon the environmental conditions and the requirement of the plant.

30 The rate of breathing is faster in aquatic organisms, like fish, since, the amount of dissolved oxygen is very low in water compared to the amount present in air. Fishes, take in water through their mouth and force it to pass to the gills where the dissolved oxygen is taken up by the blood.

31 Terrestrial organisms use atmospheric oxygen for respiration. They have respiratory organs with structures that increases the surface area, enhancing contact with the oxygen-rich atmosphere.

32 In humans, when air enters through the nostrils, it follows the following path ways

Human → Nasal passage → Pharynx → Larynx → Trachea → Bronchi → Bronchioles → Alveoli

33 The alveoli of lungs are richly supplied with blood and are the sites, where the exchange of gases (O_2 and CO_2) occurs between blood and atmosphere. The respiratory pigment haemoglobin, carry oxygen from lungs to different tissues of the body. This pigment is present in red blood cells.

34 Blood transports carbon dioxide from body tissues to the alveoli for exhalation.

35 Transport of substances in human being occurs through a well-designed **circulatory system.** It is composed of the heart, blood and blood vessels.

36 Human heart is a muscular organ and it is big as our fist. It has four chambers *i.e.,* 2 atria (right and left) and 2 ventricles (right and left). Right half of the heart receives deoxygenated blood, whereas the left half receives oxygenated blood.

Ventricular walls are much thicker than atrial walls because the ventricles need to pump blood into various organs. Valves ensure that blood does not flow backwards when the atria or ventricles contract.

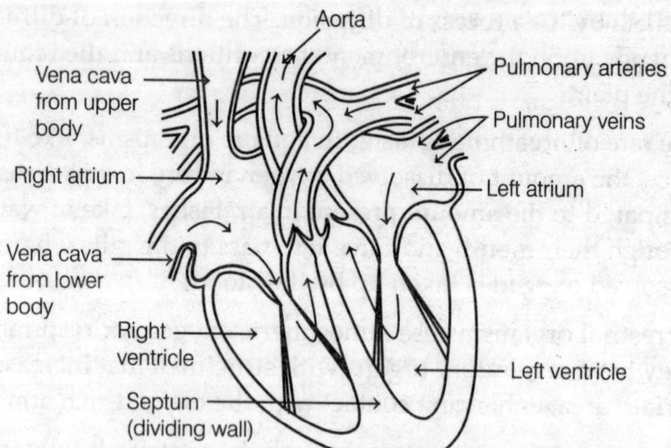

▲ Sectional view of the human heart

37 Blood is a fluid connective tissue which is made up of two parts. These are

(i) Plasma (ii) Blood corpuscles.

Plasma is the liquid part of the blood containing mostly water, dissolved salts and gases.

Blood corpuscles float in the plasma. They are of three kinds :

(i) **Red blood cells** contain haemoglobin which helps in transportation of oxygen.

(ii) **White blood cells** help in protection by killing the germs.

(iii) **Blood platelets** are essential for clotting of blood at the place of injury and thus, preventing blood loss.

38 **Arteries** carry blood from heart to different parts of the body, whereas **veins** deliver the blood back to the heart. Arteries are connected to veins by thin **capillaries**, wherein materials are exchanged between blood and cells.

39 Humans show **double circulation** and complete separation of oxygenated and deoxygenated blood. In double circulation, the blood passes through the heart twice during each cycle.

40 Such animals like amphibians or many reptiles, which have 3-chambered heart whreas fishes have only 2-chambered heart. In them, blood goes only once through the heart during one cycle and this is called **single circulation.**

41 **Lymphatic system** consists of lymph, lymph nodes, lymphatic capillaries and lymph vessels. Lymph is also important in the process of transportation.

42 Transportation in plants, occurs through the special tube-like structures called as **xylem** and **phloem tissues**.

43 Xylem is involved in transportation of water and nutrients obtained from the soil.

44 The xylem creates capillary effect and the water rises from ground to the top of the tree. In addition, evaporation of water through the leaves creates low pressure. This low pressure creates a pull effect. Both these factors combine resulting in transportation of water and minerals from roots to the top of the tree. This is called **ascent of sap**.

45 Root pressure and transpiration pull are the major forces involved in pulling water up the xylem.

46 The transportation of food is carried out through the phloem tissue from leaves and storage organs to other parts of the plant. This process is called **translocation** and requires energy from ATP.

47 Osmotic pressure in the phloem increase as substances, like sucrose, enters. This cause inward movement of water and create a pressure gradient that moves nutrients to areas with low pressure.

48 **Excretion** is the process of elimination of harmful metabolic nitrogenous wastes from the body.

49 In humans, a pair of kidneys, a pair of ureters, urinary bladder and urethra constitutes the excretory system.

50 **Nephrons** are the basic filtration units of kidneys. They carry out filtration, selective reabsorption and tubular secretion to form urine in kidney, which is then passed out through the urethra, *via* the ureters and urinary bladder.

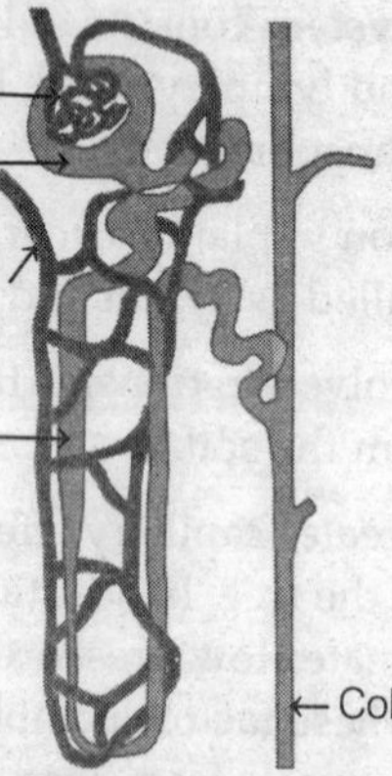

▲ Structure of a nephron

51 In case of kidney failure, an artificial kidney is used. This device remove nitrogenous waste products from the blood through the dialysis.

52 Plants do not have a well designed excretory system. They carry out excretion in various ways like transpiration, releasing wastes into surrounding soil, losing the leaves. They store some waste products in cell vacuoles and in old xylem in the form of resins, gums, latex, etc.

Intext Questions

On Page 81

Question 1 Why is diffusion insufficient to meet the oxygen requirements of multicellular organisms like humans?

Sol. In multicellular organisms, the demand for oxygen is high due to the need to perform various activities that require large amounts of energy. Diffusion is a slow process and cannot efficiently transport sufficient oxygen to meet the metabolic needs of all cells, especially those located far from the body surface. Therefore, specialised respiratory and circulatory systems are necessary to distribute oxygen quickly and effectively throughout the body.

Question 2 What criteria do we use to decide whether something is alive?

Sol. Living things exhibit certain characterstics, such as respiration, growth, reproduction, response to stimuli and the ability to adapt to their environment. These criteria help us determine if something is alive.

Question 3 What are outside raw materials used for by an organism?

Sol. Raw materials are substances which cannot be directly utilised by the organisms. They require further processing inside the body like digestion in animals and photosynthesis in plants. CO_2, water and minerals compounds are raw materials for plants, while water, carbohydrate, protein, fat and vitamins are raw material for the animals. These raw materials are to be taken from outside by plants and animals, respectively.

Question 4 What process would you consider essential for maintaining life?

Sol. Essential processes for maintaining life are nutrition, respiration, transportation, excretion, control and coordination. In absence of any one of these, the life become difficult. These processes ensure organism can obtain energy, eliminate waste and regulate its internal environment to survive.

On Page 87

Question 1 What are the differences between autotrophic nutrition and heterotrophic nutrition?

Sol. Difference between autotrophic and heterotrophic nutrition are as follows :

Autotrophic Nutrition	Heterotrophic Nutrition
Occurs in green plants, some bacteria, and some protists.	Occurs in animals and some plants.
Chlorophyll is necessary for trapping solar energy.	Chlorophyll is absent as they do not need to trap solar energy.
Food is manufactured using carbon dioxide (CO_2) and water as raw materials.	Food is obtained directly or indirectly from autotrophs.
Digestion of food does not occur.	Digestion is required to convert complex organic substances in food into simpler, soluble forms.
Autotrophs are at the bottom of the food chain as producers.	Heterotrophs are above autotrophs in the food chain as consumers.

Question 2 Where do plants get each of the raw materials required for photosynthesis?

Sol. Plants get each of the rawl material required for photosynthesis as follows.

(i) They absorb water by the roots from the soil.

(ii) CO_2 is obtained from air through stomata.

(iii) Light is obtained from Sun.

(iv) Other minerals like magnesium, phosphorus, iron, sulphur and nitrogen are taken up from the soil by the roots.

Question 3 What is the role of the acid in our stomach?

Sol. Role of HCl in the stomach are as follow :

(i) It provides acidic medium which is required for the activation of pepsin enzyme. Pepsin helps in digestion of protein into peptons and proteoses.

(ii) It kills various microbes present in food.

Question 4 What is the function of digestive enzymes?

Sol. Digestive enzymes in our body help in breaking down the food particles into smaller and simple absorbable form so that they can easily be absorbed by the cells and get used for the various important body functions.

Question 5 How is the small intestine designed to absorb digested food?

Sol. The inner wall of the small intestine is modified into tiny finger-like projections called villi, which increase the surface area for the absorption of digested food. These villi are highly vascularised, *i.e.*, richly provided with blood vessels. These vessels absorb the digested food and carry it to thc blood stream.

On Page 91

Question 1 What advantages over an aquatic organisms does a terrestrial organisms have with regard to obtaining oxygen for respiration?

Sol. Terrestrial organisms breathe in oxygen from the air, while aquatic organisms rely on the oxygen dissolved in water. Air contains about 21% oxygen, whereas water has less than 1% oxygen in a dissolved state. Oxygen also moves through air much faster than it does through water. Therefore, terrestrial organisms can get more oxygen quickly and with less effort. In contrast, aquatic organisms must work harder to obtain the same amount of oxygen from the water.

Question 2 What are the different ways in which glucose is oxidised to provide energy in various organisms?

Sol. The utilisation of glucose for the production of energy depends upon the availability of oxygen. In presence of oxygen, glucose is broken down aerobically in mitochondria, whereas in the absence of oxygen, glucose is broken down anaerobically in cytoplasm to produce comparatively lesser amount of energy.

Aerobic respiration It is a complete oxidation of food in the presence of oxygen to form CO_2, H_2O and large amount of energy is released.

$$\underset{(6C)}{\text{Glucose}} \xrightarrow[\substack{\text{(Cytoplasm)} \\ \text{No oxygen} \\ \text{required}}]{\text{Glycolysis}} \underset{(3C)}{\text{Pyruvic acid}} \xrightarrow[\text{Mitochondria}]{O_2 \text{ used}} CO_2 + H_2O + \text{Energy}$$

Anaerobic respiration It involves incomplete oxidation of food in the absence of oxygen. For example, skeletal muscles under hard work or vigorous exercise, respire in the absence of oxygen for some time to get extra energy.

$$\underset{\text{glucose}}{C_6H_{12}O_6} \xrightarrow{\text{in muscele cells}} \underset{\text{(Lactic acid)}}{2C_3H_6O_3} + \text{Energy}$$

$$\underset{\text{glucose}}{C_6H_{12}O_6} \xrightarrow[\text{in yeast}]{\text{Enzymes}} \underset{\text{(Ethanol)}}{2C_2H_5OH} + 2CO_2 + \text{Energy}$$

Question 3 How is oxygen and carbon dioxide transported in human beings?

Sol. In human beings, the transport of oxygen and carbon dioxide is primarily carried out by the blood.

Oxygen Transport Oxygen is transported by haemoglobin, a protein found in red blood cells. When we breathe in, oxygen enters the lungs and diffuses into the blood, where it binds to haemoglobin to form oxyhaemoglobin. This oxygenated blood is then pumped by the heart to all the cells in the body, where the oxygen is released for cellular respiration, a process that produces energy for the cells.

Carbon Dioxide Transport After the cells use oxygen, they produce carbon dioxide (CO_2) as a waste product. This CO_2 diffuses into the blood. Unlike oxygen, carbon dioxide is mainly transported in the blood in a dissolved form, as haemoglobin has a lower affinity for CO_2. The deoxygenated blood carries the carbon dioxide back to the lungs, where it is released into the alveoli and exhaled during breathing.

Question 4 How are the lungs designed in human beings to maximise the area for the exchange of gases?

Sol. The lungs in human beings are specially designed to maximise the area for the exchange of gases through millions of alveoli, which provide a large surface area. The exchange of gases occurs between the blood capillaries that surround the alveoli and the gases present in the alveoli. Alveoli are small, balloon-like structures and are the primary sites for the exchange of gases.

Each lung contains approximately 300-350 million alveoli, greatly increasing the surface area available for gas exchange. This large surface area, along with the rich supply of blood vessels surrounding the alveoli, ensures that the exchange of gases is efficient.

Note If the alveolar surface may spread out, it would cover about 80 m^2 area.

On Page 96

Question 1 What are the components of transport system in human beings? What are the functions of these components?

Sol. The transport system of human beings is composed of blood, heart, blood vessels and lymph.

(i) The blood transports O_2, CO_2, salts and nutrients in the body.

(ii) Heart collects deoxygenated blood from various body parts and pumps the oxygenated blood.

(iii) Blood vessels are arteries, veins and capillaries. The arteries carry blood away from heart, while veins collect blood from different organs. Exchange of material between blood and surrounding cells takes place through the thin wall of capillary.

(iv) Lymph is another type of fluid involved in transportation. It carries digested and absorbed fat from the intestine and drains excess fluid from extracellular space back into the blood.

Question 2 Why is it necessary to separate oxygenated and deoxygenated blood in mammals and birds?

Sol. In mammals and birds, separating oxygenated and deoxygenated blood is crucial because, they are warm-blooded and have high energy needs. They need a lot of energy to maintain a constant body temperature, which requires efficient oxygen delivery for ATP production.

The separation ensures that oxygen-rich blood efficiently reaches all body tissues, allowing these animals to meet their high metabolic demands and regulate their body temperature effectively.

Question 3 What are the components of transport system in highly organised plants?

Sol. Plant transport systems is highly organised consisting of two independent pathways for moving water and sugar. This system is composed of xylem and phloem.

(i) The transport water and minerals from root to leaves and other parts.

(ii) The phloem transport products of photosynthesis from leaves to other parts including roots.

Question 4 How are water and minerals transported in plants?

Sol. In plants, water and minerals are transported through xylem cells from soil to the leaves. Vessels and tracheids in xylem tissue of root, stem and leaves are interconnected to form the continuous water conducting channel reaching all parts of plant. The cells of root which are in contact of soil actively take up ions. To eliminate the concentration difference between root and soil, water moves into root from the soil.

Evaporation of water molecules from the cells of a leaf called transpiration creates a suction, which pulls water from the xylem cells of roots. Thus, the transportation helps in absorption and upward movement of water and minerals from root to the leaves.

Question 5 How is food transported in plants?

Sol. The transport of soluble products of photosynthesis is called translocation and it occurs through the phloem. Besides the products of photosynthesis, the phloem transports amino acids and other substances. The translocation of food and other substances takes place in the sieve tubes with the help of adjacent companions cells, both in upward and downward directions.

Material like sucrose is transferred into the phloem tissue using ATP. This increases the osmotic pressure of tissue causing water to move into it. This pressure moves the material in the phloem to tissue which have less pressure. This allows the phloem to move materials according to the need of plant.

On Page 98

Question 1 Describe the structure and functioning of nephrons.

Sol. Kidney is made up of large number of excretory units called **nephrons**. The nephron has a cup-shaped structure at its upper end which is called **Bowman's capsule**. The lower end of Bowman's capsule continues into U-shaped renal tube tubule. The Bowman's capsule and tubule together make the nephron. The one end of tubule is connected to Bowman's capsule and its other end is connected to a urine-collecting duct of the kidney.

The Bowman's capsule contains a bundle of blood capillaries known as **glomerulus**. One end of glomerulus is attached to renal artery which brings the blood containing urea waste into it while the other end of glomerulus comes out of Bowman's capsule, blood capillaries surround the tubule and finally joins a renal vein.

Functioning of Nephron

The function of glomerulus is to filter the blood passing through it. All small molecules like glucose, water, amino acids, minerals etc., (except the blood cells and proteins) pass through it. This is called **ultrafiltration**. As the filtrate move down the tubule, the useful substances like glucose, amino acids and most of the water are reabsorbed by the capillary around the tubule, but the waste material remains like urea remains in tubule. This liquid is called **urine**. The nephron carries urine into the collecting duct of kidney from where it is carried to the ureter.

Question 2 What are the methods used by plants to get rid of excretory products?

Sol. Plants use several methods to remove waste products some of them are given below.

1. **Gas Exchange** Oxygen and carbon dioxide, produced during photosynthesis and rospiration are expelled through tiny pores called stomata.
2. **Transpiration** Excess water is released from the plant through transpiration, mainly from the leaves.
3. **Storage** Some waste products are stored in leaves, bark or other parts of the plant that eventually fall off.
4. **Crystal Formation** Certain waste products are turned into crystals and stored in plant tissues.
5. **Useful Compounds** Some waste products are stored as resins and gums, especially in old xylem.

Question 3 How is the amount of urine produced is regulated?

Sol. The amount of urine produced is controlled by an Anti-Diuretic Hormone (ADH) produced by the anterior pituitary gland. If excess of water is present in the blood, then a more dilute urine is excreted, *i.e.*, less of water is reabsorbed and more of it is excreted out. In case of less water content in blood, concentrated urine is excreted. This process is called osmoregulation.

Exercises

Question 1 The kidneys in human beings are a part of the system for

(a) nutrition (b) respiration (c) excretion (d) transportation

Sol. (c) The excretory system of human beings includes a pair of kidneys, a pair of ureters, a urinary bladder and urethra. Excretion is the main function of excretory system.

Question 2 The xylem in plants are responsible for

(a) transport of water (b) transport of food
(c) transport in amino acids (d) transport of oxygen

Sol. (a) The xylem in plants are responsible for transport of water and minerals, while the food and amino acids are transported by phloem.

Question 3 The autotrophic mode of nutrition requires

(a) carbon dioxide and water (b) chlorophyll
(c) sunlight (d) All of these

Sol. (d) The autotrophic mode of nutrition requires carbon-dioxide, water, sunlight and chlorophyll for the process of photosynthesis.

Question 4 The breakdown of pyruvate to give carbon dioxide, water and energy takes place in

(a) cytoplasm (b) mitochondria (c) chloroplast (d) nucleus

Sol. (b) In the process of cellular respiration the glucose breaks into pyruvate in the cytoplasm, whereas the pyruvate breakdwn to carbon dioxide and water and gives energy by Krebs' cycle in mitochondria.

Question 5 How are fats digested in our bodies? where does this process take place?

Sol. In small intestine, the fat molecules are first of all emulsified by bile salts, to form tiny droplets of fat molecules. This emulsified fat is then digested by the enzyme lipase (pancreatic juice) and converted to fatty acids and glycerol. Digestion of fats starts in stomach and gets completed in small intestine.

(i) **Role of bile in fat digestion** Bile is secreted by liver. It emulsifies the fats, *i.e.,* breaks larger fat molecules to tiny droplets, thereby increasing the surface area of fats for the action of enzymes.

(ii) **Role of pancreatic and intestinal lipase**

$$\text{Emulsified fat} \xrightarrow[\text{Lipase}]{\text{Pancreatic}} \text{Fatty acids and glycerol.}$$

$$\text{Triglycerides} \xrightarrow[\text{Lipase}]{\text{Intestinal}} \text{Monoglycerides and fatty acids.}$$

Note Fats are not soluble in water. They form large globules which hinder the action of lipase on them. Bile helps to emulsify fats so as to increase the rate of digestion on fats by lipase.

Question 6 What is the role of saliva in the digestion of food?

Sol. Role of saliva in the digestion of food are given below.

(i) Saliva lubricates and moistens the food, making it easies to swallow and chew.

(ii) Enzyme salivary amylase (ptyalin) present in it helps in the digestion of starch present in food.

Question 7 What are the necessary conditions for autotrophic nutrition and what are its byproducts?

Sol. Autotrophic nutrition requires light, carbon dioxide, water and chlorophyll to produce glucose. Oxygen is produced as by products through photosynthesis.

Question 8 What are the differences between aerobic and anaerobic respiration? Name some organisms that use the anaerobic mode of respiraton.

Sol. Differences between aerobic and anaerobic respiration are as follows

S. No.	Aerobic Respiration	Anaerobic Respiration
1.	Takes place in the presence of O_2.	Takes place in the absence of O_2.
2.	Complete oxidation of food take place.	Incomplete oxidation of food take place.
3.	Large amount of energy is released (38 ATP).	Lesser amount of energy is released (2 ATP).
4.	End products are CO_2 and water.	End products are CO_2 and ethyl alcohol (in plants like yeast) or CO_2 and lactic acid (in animal tissue).

Anaerobic respiration takes place in yeast, *paramecium* etc.

Question 9 How are the alveoli designed to maximise the exchange of gases?

Sol. The bronchus, within the lungs, divides into smaller and smaller tubes (bronchioles) and finally terminate in balloon-like structures called 'alveoli'. The alveoli are made up of thin moist membranes which are richly supplied with blood and provide a very large surface area for the gaseous exchange.

Question 10 What would be the consequences of a deficiency of haemoglobin in our bodies?

Sol. Haemoglobin in the blood carries oxygen from the lungs to the body parts. In case of reduction in the amount of haemoglobin, the oxygen carrying capacity of the blood decreases. This leads to oxygen deficiency in the body. Which may lead to breathing problems, tiredness and lack of energy or even death or to heart failure (due to increased functioning of heart to pump more blood).

Question 11 Describe double circulation in human beings? Why is it necessary?

Sol. Double circulation means that blood passes through the heart twice during one cycle around the body. The human heart has two separate parts each with an upper chamber (auricle) and a lower chamber (ventricle).

1. **First Circulation** Blood moves from the heart to the lungs for oxygenation and then back to the heart.
2. **Second Circulation** Oxygen-rich blood is pumped from the heart to the rest of the body and then returns to the heart again.

This system is necessary because it keeps blood pressure maintained and ensures efficient delivery of oxygen to the body, which helps to meet the body's high energy needs.

Question 12 What are the differences between the transport of materials in xylem and phloem?

Sol. Differences between xylem and phloem are as follows

S. No.	Xylem	Phloem
1.	It helps in conduction of water and minerals from root to the leaves.	It helps in conduction of food prepared by the leaves to various parts of the plant.
2.	It consists of xylem vessels, tracheids xylem, parenchyma and xylem fibres.	It consists of sieve tubes, companion cells, phloem parenchyma and phloem fibres.

Question 13 Compare the functioning of alveoli in the lungs and nephrons in the kidneys with respect to their structure and functioning.

Sol. Comparison of alveoli and nephrons are as follows

Feature	Alveoli (Lungs)	Nephrons (Kidneys)
Function	Gaseous exchange	Blood filtration and waste removal, primarily urea.
Structure	Tiny, balloon-like sacs with a large surface area, surrounded by a network of capillaries.	Includes a glomerulus (capillary network) and a tubule for filtration and reabsorption.
Process	Oxygen diffuses from alveoli into the blood; carbon dioxide diffuses from blood into the alveoli.	Blood is filtered in the glomerulus; filtrate moves through the tubule where reabsorption and secretion occur to form urine.
Excretion	Primarily excretes carbon dioxide.	Primarily excretes urea and other waste products.

DIKSHA APP Questions

☐ Multiple Choice Questions

Q.1 Which enzyme is released in the stomach?

(a) Pepsin (b) Trypsin (c) Amylase (d) Bile juice

Sol. (a) Pepsin is the enzyme released in the stomach that helps break down proteins into smaller peptides.

Q.2 Which is the fundamental and structural unit of kidney?

(a) Alveoli (b) Ureter (c) Neuron (d) Nephron

Sol. (d) The nephron is the fundamental and structural unit of the kidney responsible for filtering blood and forming urine.

Q.3 Where does the digestion of food begin in the alimentary canal?

(a) Small intestine (b) Large intestine
(c) Mouth cavity (d) Stomach

Sol. (d) The digestion of food begins in the mouth cavity , where the enzyme **salivary amylase** starts breaking down carbohydrates.

Q.4 Which of the life processes convert chemical energy into heat energy?

(a) Nutrition (b) Excretion
(c) Transportation (d) Respiration

Sol. (d) Respiration is the life process that converts chemical energy from food into heat energy , which helps maintain body temperature.

Q.5 The food prepared in leaves in transported through this tissue

(a) xylem (b) meristematic (c) sap (d) phloem

Sol. (d) The food prepared in the leaves through photosynthesis is transported through the phloem tissue to other parts of the plant

Q.6 A glucose molecule is broken down into this molecule in cytoplasm during respiration.

(a) Haemoglobin (b)ATP
(c) Lactic acid (d) Pyruvate

Sol. (d) During respiration , a glucose molecule is broken down into **pyruvate** in the cytoplasm through a process called glycolysis.

Q.7 In which form is the food stored in leaves?

(a) Glucose (b) Glycogen
(c) Fructose (d) Starch

Sol. (d) In leaves , food is stored in the form of starch , which is a polysaccharide made up if glucose units.

☐ Very Short Answer Type

Q.1 Why does absorption of digested food occur mainly in the small intestine?

Sol. The absorption of digested food occur mainly in the small intestine because inner lining of small intestine is provided with villi which increases the surface area for absorption. As well as all of intestine is richly supplied with blood vessels which take the absorbed food to each and every cell of the body.

Q.2 Why is blood circulation in human heart called double circulation?

Sol. The blood circulation in human heart is called double circulation because the blood passes twice through the heart in one complete cardioe cycle *i.e* once through the right half in the form of deoxygenated blood and once through the left half in the form of oxygenated blood.

☐ Short Answer Type

Q.1 Draw and label the parts of the human excretory system.

Sol. Human excretory system given below.

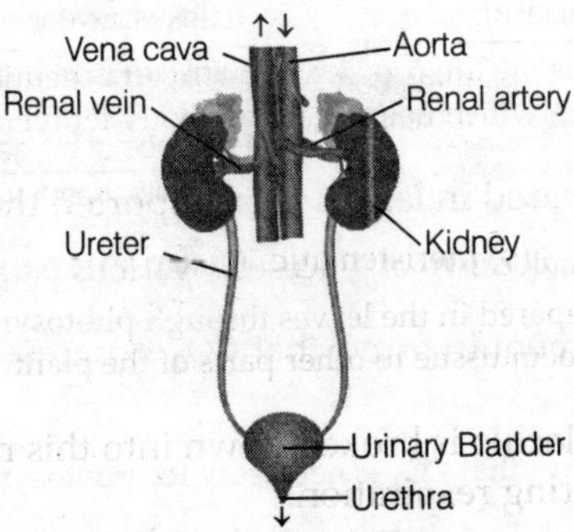

Q.2 (a) Draw a sectional view of the human heart and label on it, aorta, right ventricle, pulmonaryvein, pulmonary artery

(b) State the functions of

(i) blood (ii) lymph.

Sol. (a) Sectional view of the human heart with label given below.

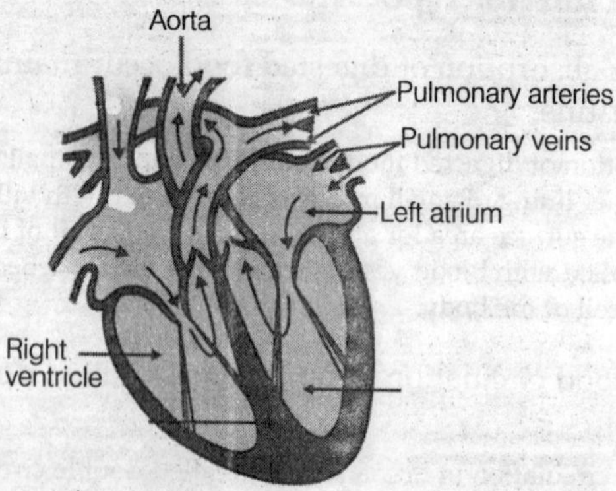

(b) (i) Blood transports nutrients, oxygen, CO_2, urea,hormones, etc

(ii) Lymph transport excess fluid from extra cellular space back into blood.

Q.3 Show break down of glucose by various pathways

Sol.

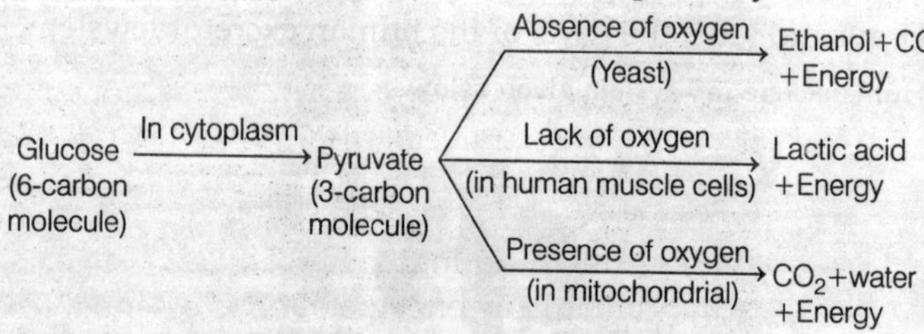

Break down of glucose by various pathways

Q.4 Give an experiment to prove that CO_2 is necessary for photosynthesis.

Sol. Experiment to prove that CO_2 is necessary for photosynthesis is as fallow.

Materials Required Two healthy potted plants, potassium hydroxide (KOH), two glass plates, two bell-jars, vaseline, iodine solution.

Procedure

1. Keep both plants in a dark room for 3 days.
2. Cover both plants with bell-jars.
3. Place a plate containing **KOH** in one jar (A).
4. Seal both the jars with vaseline and expose them to sunlight for 2 hours.
5. Pluck a leaf from each plant and test for starch using iodine solution.

Conclusion The plant with KOH will not show starch, proving that CO_2 is necessary for photosynthesis.

Q.5 What are the components of the gastric juice?Write their functions?

Sol. Gastric juice contains three components *i.e.*, hydrochloric acid, pepsin and mucus. Their functions are as follows. Hydrochloric acid in the stomach is used to make the medium acidic to facilitate the action of the enzyme pepsin and to kill germs if any.

Enzyme pepsin digests proteins and convert them in to peptones. The mucus helps to protect the stomach wall from its own secretions of hydrochloric acid.

Q.6 What are the end products formed during fermentation in yeast? Under what conditions a similar process takes place in our body that leads to muscle cramps?

Sol. The end products formed during anaerobic respiration or fermentation in yeast are carbon dioxide, ethanol and ATP. A similar process is seen in our body when there is lack of oxygen in muscles, leading to the muscle fatigue. It results due to the accumulation of lactic acid produced during anaerobic respiration of glucose. The energy or ATP produced during anaerobic respiration is much less as compared to aerobic respiration.

Q.7 Give reason

(i) Water enter continuously into the root xylem?

(ii) Bile does not contain any enzyme but it is essential for digestion.

Sol. (i) Water continously enter the root xylem due to the active uptake of ions by root cells, creating a concentration gradient that drives water movement from the soil into the root, forming a steady upward water column.

(ii) The bile salts breakdown the fat present in the food into smaller globules. This increases the efficiency of enzymes in the small intestine to digest the fat effectively.

Q.8 Give reason

(i) Separation of oxygenated and de-oxygenated blood is necessary in mammals.

(ii) The rate of breathing in a fish is faster than a pigeon.

(iii) We experience pain in our muscles after a strenuous physical exercise

Sol. (i) Mammals are warm blooded hence lot of energy is required to maintain a constant body temperature. The separation of oxygenated and deoxygenated blood in mammals is necessory to maintain high officiency in oxygen delivery to tissue supporting their high metabolic rate and constant body temperature.

(ii) A fish breathes in oxygen dissolved in water and the percentage of oxygen dissolved in water is less as compared to atmosphere.

(iii) Due to lack of oxygen during strenous exercise the anaerobic respiration occurs, resulting in formation of lactic acid. Accumulation of lactic acid causes pain in the muscles.

□ Long Answer Type

Q.1 (a) Draw a diagram of human alimentary canal and label on it: Oesophagus, buccal cavity,stomach,small intestine,large intestine(colon).

(b) Explain the statement, 'Bile does not contain any enzyme but it is essential for digestion'.

Sol. (a)

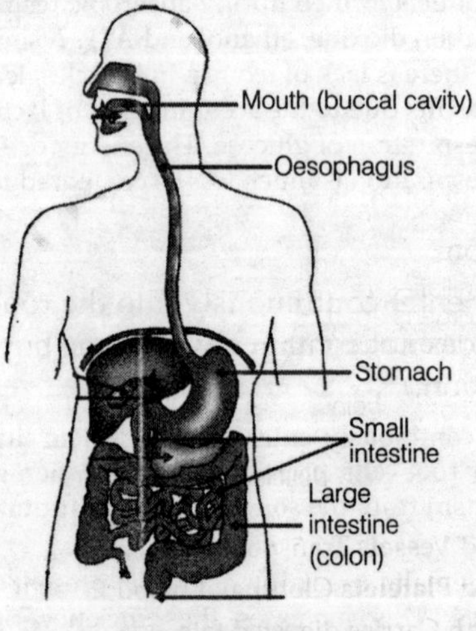

▲ Human alimentary cohal

(b) Bile does not contain any enzyme, but it plays an important role in digestion because:

(i) The bile salts emulsify fat by acting on large fat globules and breaking them into smaller globules. This increases the efficiency of pancreatic enzymes.

(ii) The food entering the small intestine is acidic. It is made alkaline by the action of bile juice so as to facilitate the action of pancreatic enzymes.

Q.2 (i) Elucidate the process of double circulatory system with the help of a diagram.

(ii) Write one function each of the following components of the transport system in human beings:

(a) Blood vessels (b) Blood platelets

(c) Lymph (d) Heart

Sol. (i) The deoxygenated blood from different parts of body is transported to heart from where it is carried to lungs for oxygenation. The oxygenated blood from the lungs returns to the heart, which is pumped again into different parts of the body by the heart. Thus, the blood passes twice through the heart making one complete round through the body. This is called double circulation.

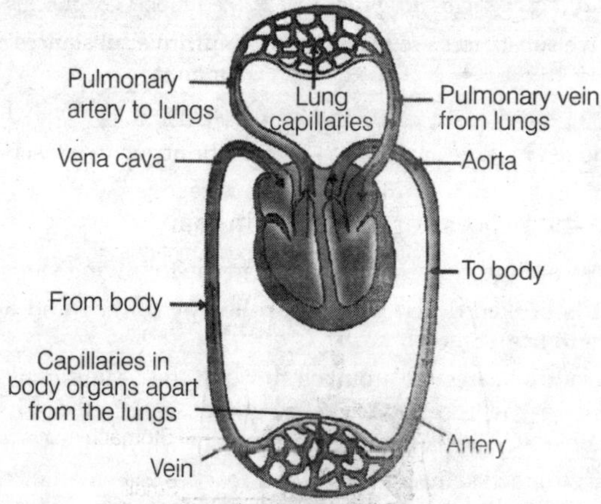

▲ Double circulatory system

(ii) (a) **Blood Vessels** Transport of blood.

(b) **Blood Platelets** Clotting of blood.

(c) **Lymph** Carries digested fats.

(d) **Heart** Helps to circulate blood in the whole body by acting as a pump.

Q.3 How does aerobic respiration differ from anaerobic respiration?

Sol. Aerobic respiration differ from anaerobic respiration in following ways.

Aerobic Respiration	Anaerobic Respiration
1. Aerobic respiration takes place in the presence of oxygen.	1. Anaerobic Respiration takes place in the absence of oxygen.
2. Complete breakdown of food occurs in it.	2. Incomplete breakdown of food occurs in it.
3. The end products are carbon dioxide (CO_2) and water (H_2O).	3. The end products are ethyl alcohol (C_2H_5OH) and carbon dioxide (CO_2) or lactic acid.
4. It produces a considerable amount of energy due to complete oxidation of food molecules.	4. Much less energy is produced due to incomplete oxidation of food.

Q.4 Differentiate between blood and lymph.

Sol. Difference between blood and lymph are as follows.

Blood	Lymph
1. Redin colour.	1. Colourless.
2. Red blood corpuscles are present.	2. Red blood corpuscles are absent.
3. Nutritive substances are more.	3. Nutritive substances are less in amount
4 Oxygen is more.	4. Oxygen is relatively less.
5 Fibrinogen in large amount.	5. Fibrinogen in less amount.

Q.5 Describe the process of digestion in man.

Sol. The process of digestion in man can be in the following steps.

1. Food is broken down by teeth, rolled by tongue and acted upon by saliva to from bolus.
2. This food reaches the stomach through the oesophagus by peristalsis where gastric juice from gastric glands is secreted. The gastric juice contains-HCI, pepsin and mucus.
3. From stomach semi digested food reaches the small intestine where it mixes with bile juice from liver and pancreatic juice from pancreas. These juices further helps in breaking down of food.
4. Finally digested food is absorbed by the walls of the small intestines, lined by villi.
5. The remaining undigested food moves into the large intestine. Here water is absorbed and the leftover material is prepared for elimination.
6. Finally the waste material is stored in the rectum until it is expelled from the body through anus.

Control and Coordination

CHAPTER 06

Important Points

01 A system of control and coordination is essential in living organisms to maintain homeostasis and respond to various stimuli.

02 Any change in the environment which forces a living organism to react is called a **stimulus** and the reaction due to this stimulus is called **response**.

03 In animals, control and coordination of the body are provided by the **nervous tissues** and the hormones circulating in the body.

04 **Neurons** are structural and functional unit of the nervous system. They use electrical and chemical signals to transfer information.

05 A neuron has three parts, *i.e.*, cell body, dendrites and axon. The axon conducts impulses from one neuron to another neuron through synapse.

06 Nerve impulses travel in the following manner from one neuron to the next neuron

Dendrites → Cell body → Axon → Nerve endings at the tip of axon → Synapse → Dendrite of next neuron.

07 Reflex action is an automatic, rapid and immediate reaction to a stimulus and is below the level of consciousness. No thinking is involved in reflex action.

08 Reflex arc is the neural pathway that mediates a reflex action. The pathway of reflex arc:

Receptor → Sensory neuron → Relay neuron → Motor neuron → Effector

09 The sensory neurons from various body parts synapse in the spinal cord which then activates the motor neurons without delay to execute a quick action, especially in case of emergencies. While these reflexes occur in the spinal cord the sensory information is still sent to the brain for processing.

10 Reflex actions, voluntary actions and involuntary actions are the various types of responses shown by the nervous system.

11 **Nervous system** consists of following three types:

(i) Central nervous system (CNS)

(ii) Peripheral nervous system (PNS)

12 **Central nervous system** includes brain and spinal cord.

13 Spinal cord controls the reflex actions and conducts messages between different parts of the body and brain.

14 The brain is divided into three main parts: fore brain, midbrain and hindbrain

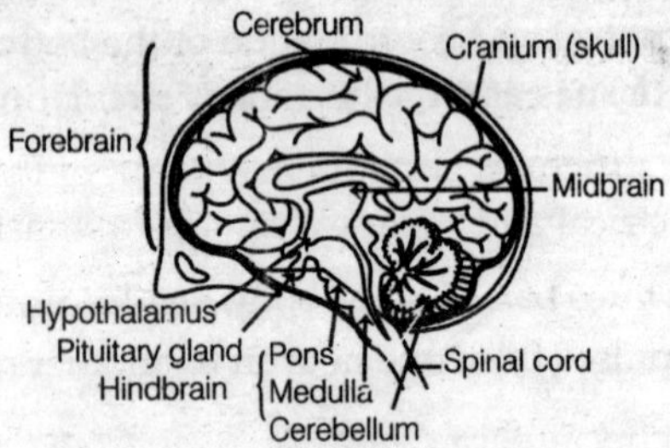

▲ Human brain

15 The forebrain is the brain's main thinking center, processing sensory inputs like sight, smell and hearing through specialised areas. It combines this sensory data with stored knowledge to make decisions, which are then sent to motor areas to control voluntary muscles. It also houses a separate center that manages sensations like hunger and satiety.

16 The **midbrain** also plays a role in auditory and visual reflexes, such as moving your head in response to a sudden sound or light.

17 The hindbrain controls involuntary actions such as blood pressure regulation salivation, and vomiting through the medulla. It also houses the cerebellum, which is responsible for precision in voluntary actions like walking, riding a bicycle, and picking up a pencil, while maintaining posture and balance without the need for conscious thought.

18 Brain is protected by a bony box called **cranium**, within which is fluid filled balloon present three layers of fluid-filled membranes for absorbing shock.

19 **Peripheral nervous system** connects body parts to the brain and spinal cord. It consists of spinal nerves and cranial nerves.

20 The sense organs detect changes in surroundings and pass this information to the central nervous system, which after processing the information, acts through the muscles.

21 The movements of muscle tissues are brought about by the contraction and relaxation of the contractile proteins in response to nerve impulses.

22 Plants lack nervous and muscular system. They respond to stimuli by showing two types of movements— **growth independent** and **growth dependent**.

23 Growth-independent movements also known as nastic movements:

(a) Growth-independent movements are usually quicker than growth-dependent ones and involves the use of electrochemical signals by the plant. To achieve this movement, plant cells change shape by altering their water content.

(b) These movements do not depend on the direction of the stimulus and happen in response to changes in the environment. For example, the **"Touch me not" plant** *(Mimosa pudica)* folds its leaves when touched. This is known as **thigmonasty** or **thigmotropism.**

24 Growth dependent movements, also known as tropic movements are slow, occurs either towards or away from the stimulus.

25 Tropic movements are shown in response to environmental factors such as light, gravity, water and chemicals.

26 These are movements where a plant grows in response to a specific stimulus. There are four main types:

1. **Phototropism** This is the growth of plants towards light.
2. **Geotropism** This is the movement of plant parts in response to gravity.
3. **Chemotropism** This is the movement of plants in response to chemicals.
4. **Hydrotropism** This is the movement of plant roots towards water.

27 In addition to electrochemical signals, plants and animals use hormones for control and coordination.

28 Hormones produced in one part of an organism move to another part to achieve the desired effect.

29 Some important plant hormones are auxin, gibberellin, cytokinin, abscisic acid and ethylene. Their important functions are given below

S.No.	Plant Hormone	Function
1.	Auxin	Helps in cell elongation.
2.	Cytokinin	Responsible for cell division.
3.	Gibberellin	Causes growth of stem.
4.	Abscisic acid	Inhibits growth.

30 Animal hormones promote controlled growth in various areas to maintain the body design.

31 The human body has several key endocrine glands that produce hormones, which control various processes in the body. Below is a table listing these glands, the hormones they secrete, and their functions

S.No.	Endocrine Gland	Hormone	Function
1.	Pituitary Gland	Growth Hormone	Controls the growth and development of the body.
2.	Hypothalamus	Releasing Hormones	Regulate pituitary gland to release hormones
3.	Thyroid Gland	Thyroxine	Regulates the metabolism of carbohydrates, proteins, and fats in the body
4.	Adrenal Glands	Adrenaline	Prepares the body to respond in emergency situations by increasing heart rate and energy supply.
5.	Pancreas	Insulin	Regulates blood sugar levels by helping cells absorb glucose.
6.	Testes (in males)	Testosterone	Causes the development of sex organs and secondary sexual characteristics in males, such as a deeper voice and facial hair.
7.	Ovaries (in females)	Oestrogen	Causes the development of sex organs and secondary sexual characteristics in females, such as breast development and menstrual cycle regulation.

32 Hormones must be secreted in precise amounts to ensure the body functions properly.

33 To control the timing and amount of hormone release, the body uses a system called **feedback mechanisms.**

34 Example of Feedback Mechanism is control of blood sugar by Insulin.

35 Feedback mechanisms ensure that hormone levels remain balanced, adjusting secretion based on the body's needs.

Intext Questions

On Page 105

Question 1 What is the differences between a reflex action and walking?

Sol. Differences between a reflex action and walking are as follows :

Reflex Action

- A reflex action is an automatic and quick response to a stimulus, like touching something hot and quickly pulling the hand away.
- Reflex actions happen without conscious thought or the need of willpower. They are controlled by the spinal cord is parts of the central nervous system.
- Examples include blinking when something approaches your eyes or jerking your leg when tapped on the knee.

Walking

- Walking is a voluntary action, meaning it requires conscious thought and control.
- It is controlled by the brain, specifically the cerebellum, which helps with balance and coordination.
- Walking involves the coordinated action of many muscles and requires the brain to send signals to the muscles to maintain balance and movement.

In summary, reflex actions are quick, automatic responses that don't involve thinking, while walking is a controlled, deliberate action that involves the brain's planning and coordination.

Question 2 What happens at the synapse between two neurons?

Sol. The nerve impulses are transmitted out by a small gap called synapse between a pair of neurons by means of a neurotransmitter. When the nerve impulse travelling through the first neuron reaches the axon endings. It releases tiny amount of a chemical substance into the synapse. This chemical substance crosses the gap and starts a similar electrical impulse in the dendrite of the next neuron. From dendrite, the nerve impulse is carried to the cell body and then to the end through axon. It can then be transferred to the third neuron in a similar way. This process continuous till the electrical impulse reaches the brain or spinal cord.

Question 3 Which part of the brain maintains posture and equilibrium of the body?

Sol. The cerebellum is the part of the brain that maintains posture and balance. It is located in the hindbrain and is responsible for coordinating voluntary movements and ensuring that the body stays balanced and upright.

Question 4 How do we detect the smell of an agarbatti (incense stick)?

Sol. To detect the smell of an agarbatti (incense stick), the following process occurs

1. **Olfactory Receptors** Special nerve cells called olfactory receptors, located in the nasal cavity, detect the scent molecules from the incense stick.
2. **Signal Transmission** When these receptors detect the smell, they send electrical signals through sensory neurons.
3. **Signal to Brain** These signals are then transmitted to the olfactory bulb in the brain, which is responsible for processing smells.
4. **Smell Perception** The brain interprets these signals as the specific smell of the agarbatti, allowing us to recognise and perceive the scent.

Question 5 What is the role of the brain in reflex action?

Sol. Reflex actions are simplest responses to an external stimulus which are not under consious control. They are controlled by the spinal cord. For example, when we touch a hot plate, we immediately remove our hand without thinking. Though, spinal reflexes are produced in the spinal cord, but the message of reflex action taken also goes to the brain. For any reflex action, various organs are involved, though the message to react is send by the spinal cord, but the activity of various organs to carryout the response is coordinated by brain.

On Page 108

Question 1 What are plant hormones?

Sol. Plant hormones, or phytohormones, are chemical substances in plants that help to control and coordinate various activities, such as growth, development, and responses to environmental stimuli.

Question 2 How is the movement of leaves of the sensitive plant different from the movement of a shoot towards light?

Sol. The main differences between the movement of leaves of a sensitive plant and movement of a shoot towards light are as follows:

S.No.	Movement of Leaves of a Sensitive Plant	Movement of Shoot Towards Light
1.	It is a nastic movement which does not depend on the direction of stimulus applied.	It is tropic movement which depends on the direction of stimulus applied.
2.	The stimulus is touch.	The stimulus is light.
3.	It is caused by the sudden loss of water from the swellings at the base of leaves.	It is caused by the unequal growth on the two sides of the shoot.
4.	It is not a growth movement.	It is a growth movement.
5.	It is very fast movement.	It is a slow movement.

Question 3 Give an example of a plant hormone that promotes growth.

Sol. Auxin is a plant hormone that promotes growth. Gibberellin also promotes growth but works effectively only in the presence of auxins.

Question 4 How do auxins promote the growth of a tendril around a support?

Sol. When the tip of tendrils touches a support, then the auxins present in its tip move to side which is away from the support. Auxins promote growth. So, due to more auxins in it, the side of tendril away from the support grows faster and becomes longer than the side which is in contact with the support causing the tendril curve and bend towards the support. This curving tendril can then encircle the support and ling around it.

Question 5 Design an experiment to demonstrate hydrotropism.

Sol. Experiment to Demonstrate Hydrotropism

Materials

- A tub filled with dry sand
- A porous pot filled with water
- A freshly germinated pea seedling

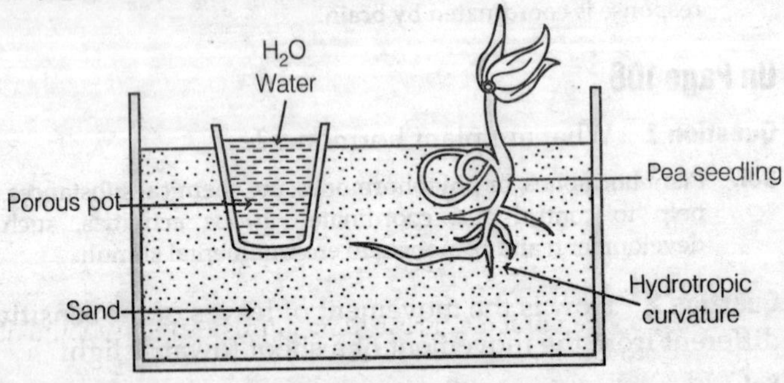

Hydrotrapism

Procedure

- Place the porous pot filled with water in the center of the tub filled with dry sand.
- Plant the pea seedling in the sand, positioning it so that the roots are near the porous pot.
- Observe the growth of the roots over time.

Observation

- The roots will grow towards the porous pot containing water.
- This demonstrates hydrotropism, where roots grow in response to the presence of water.

On Page 111

Question 1 How does chemical coordination take place in animals?

Sol. Chemical coordination in multicellular organisms take place through the special chemical substances called hormones, which are produced in endocrine glands.

These chemicals unlike nerve cells, reach all the cells of the body and bring about desirable changes For example, a hormone named adrenaline is directly secreted into the blood and carried to different parts of the body. It increase the heart beats and supply of oxygen to the muscles. The breathing rate also increases. All these responses enable the animal body to be ready to face the situation. Such hormones constitute a second way of control and coordination.

Question 2 Why is the use of iodised salt advisable?

Sol. Iodised salt is recommended because it contains iodine, which is essential for the production of thyroxine by the thyroid gland. Thyroxine regulates the metabolism of carbohydrates, fats, and proteins in the body. A deficiency of iodine can lead to a lack of thyroxine, resulting in a condition called goiter. Iodised salt helps prevent this deficiency by providing an adequate amount of iodine.

Question 3 How does our body respond when adrenaline is secreted into the blood?

Sol. When adrenaline is released into the blood, it triggers several immediate responses to prepare the body for a "fight or flight" situation:

1. **Increased Heart Rate** The heart beats faster to pump more oxygen-rich blood to the muscles.
2. **Redirection of Blood Flow** Blood flow to the digestive system and skin is reduced, and more blood is directed to the muscles.
3. **Increased Breathing Rate** Breathing rate rises to increase oxygen intake.
4. **Elevated Blood Glucose** More glucose is released into the blood to provide quick energy.

Question 4 Why are some patients with diabetes treated by giving injections of insulin?

Sol. In diabetic patient the pancreas does not produce enough insulin, a hormone that regulates blood sugar levels. Without sufficient insulin, blood sugar levels remain high. Insulin injections provide the necessary insulin to help lower the blood sugar levels and maintain proper glucose balance in the body.

Exercises

Question 1 Which of the following is a plant hormone?

(a) Insulin
(b) Thyroxin
(c) Oestrogen
(d) Cytokinin

Sol. (d) Auxin, gibberellin, and cytokinin are natural plant hormones.

Question 2 The gap between two neurons is called

(a) dendrite
(b) synapse
(c) axon
(d) impulse

Sol. (b) The synapse is the gap between the end knob of the axon of one neuron and the dendrite of another neuron.

Question 3 The brain is responsible for

(a) thinking
(b) regulating the heartbeat
(c) balancing the body
(d) All of the above

Sol. (d) The brain is involved in thinking (cerebrum), regulating the heartbeat and respiration (medulla oblongata), as well as balancing the body (cerebellum).

Question 4 What is the function of receptors in our body? Think of situations where receptors do not work properly. What problems are likely to arise?

Sol. **Function of Receptors** Receptors are specialised cells that detect and respond to specific stimuli (such as light, sound, touch, or chemicals) and send this information to the brain for processing.

Problems with Malfunctioning Receptors If receptors do not work properly, it can lead to various issues depending on the type of receptor affected:

- **Vision Problems** If eye receptors (photoreceptors) are damaged, it can result in vision impairment or blindness.
- **Hearing Loss** Damage to ear receptors (hair cells in the cochlea) can cause hearing loss or deafness.
- **Loss of Touch** If skin receptors are impaired, it can affect the sense of touch and cause difficulty in feeling rain, temperature or pressure.
- **Taste and Smell Issues** Problems with taste buds or olfactory receptors can impair the ability to taste or smell, affecting appetite and enjoyment of food.

Question 5 Draw the structure of a neuron and explain its function.

Sol. Structure of a Neuron and their function.

1. **Cell Body (Soma)** Contains the nucleus and other organelles; integrates information.
2. **Dendrites** Branch-like structures that receive signals from other neurons.
3. **Axon** Long, thin extension that transmits electrical signals away from the cell body.
4. **Axon Terminals** The endpoints of the axon where the neuron communicates with other neurons or muscles.
5. **Myelin Sheath** Fatty layer that covers the axon and speeds up signal transmission.
6. **Node of Ranvier** Gaps in the myelin sheath where the electrical signal is regenerated.
7. **Function** A neuron is the structural and functional unit of the nervous system. It carries electrical signals across long distances within the body. Sensory neurons transmit messages from sense organs to the brain and spinal cord. Motor neurons carry messages from the brain and spinal cord to muscles and glands, enabling movement and responses.

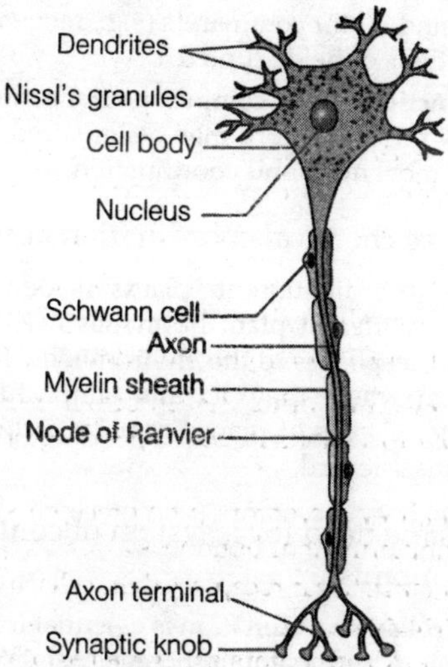

▲ Structure of a neuron

Question 6 How does phototropism occur in plants?

Sol. Phototropism is the growth response of a plant stem towards light. Here's how it occurs:

1. **Light Detection** When light falls on one side of the plant stem, auxin hormones accumulate on the shaded side.
2. **Auxin Distribution** The auxins promote faster growth on the side with less light (shaded side).
3. **Unequal Growth** Due to the higher concentration of auxins on the shaded side, that side grows faster than the side exposed to light.
4. **Bending Towards Light** This unequal growth causes the stem to bend towards the light source.

Question 7 Which signals will get disrupted in case of a spinal cord injury?

Sol. In case of a spinal cord injury, the following disruptions occur:

1. **Loss of Reflex Actions** Reflex actions below the level of the injury may not occur.
2. **Disrupted Communication** Nerves that carry signals between the brain and the rest of the body may be damaged, affecting both sensory and motor functions.
3. **Impaired Sensation and Movement** Sensory information (e.g., touch, pain) and motor commands (e.g., movement) might not reach their destinations or be disrupted.
4. **Complex Functions** More complex neural connections and processes controlled by the spinal cord may be impaired, leading to difficulties in voluntary movement and coordination.

Question 8 How does chemical coordination occur in plants?

Sol. The control and coordination in plants is done by plant hormones (phytohormones). Different plant hormones help to coordinate growth, development and responses to the environment. They are synthesised at places away from where they act and simply diffuse to the areas of actions. The major classes of plant hormone include auxins gibberellins cytokinins and abscisic acid.

Question 9 What is the need for a system of control and coordination in an organism?

Sol. A system of control and coordination is essential for organisms to respond effectively to stimuli and maintain homeostasis. When a stimulus affects the body, a coordinated reaction involving multiple organs is required to ensure an appropriate response. This system ensures that all organs work together harmoniously to produce the desired reaction and adapt to changes in the environment, thereby enhancing survival and functionality.

Question 10 How are involuntary actions and reflex actions different from each other?

Sol. **Reflex Actions**

- Controlled by the spinal cord.
- Rapid, automatic responses to external stimuli.
- Examples: Sneezing, coughing, quickly withdrawing a hand from a hot surface.

Involuntary Actions (Controlled by the Autonomic Nervous System):

- Controlled by the autonomic nervous system.
- Regulate internal processes and responses to internal stimuli.
- Examples: Heartbeat, digestion, sweating.

Question 11 Compare and contrasts nervous and hormonal mechanisms for control and coordination in animals.

Sol. Companson between nervous and hormonal mechanisms for control and co-ordination in animals are as follows :

S.No.	Nervous Mechanism	(Hormonal Mechanism)
1.	Made of neurons or nerve cells.	Made of secretory cells and glands.
2.	Messages transferred in the form of electrical impulses.	Messages transferred in the form of chemicals called hormones.
3.	Messages transmitted along the nerve fibres.	Messages transmitted through blood
4.	Messages travel very quickly.	Messages travel slowly.
5.	Effect of message usually last for a very short time.	Effect of message usually lasts longer.

Question 12 What is the difference between the manner in which movement takes place in a sensitive plant and the movement in our legs?

Sol. The movement of the leaves in a sensitive plant, takes place due to sudden loss of water in the pad-like swellings (called pulvinus) at the base of all leaves. The loss of water makes the pulvinus flaccid, leading to drooping and folding of leaves. On the other hand, the movement in our legs takes place due to the contraction of muscle on the leg bones, under the nervous control.

DIKSHA APP Questions

☐ Multiple Choice Questions

Q.1 Deficiency of iodine will cause this disease in the body.

(a) Beri Beri (b) Goitre (c) Marasmus (d) Night blindness

Sol. (b) Iodine is essential for the production of thyroxine hormone by the thyroid gland. A deficiency in iodine can lead to insufficient thyroxine production, causing the thyroid gland to enlarge, a condition known as goitre.

Q.2 The hormone which is responsible for the maintenance of sugar level in the blood

(a) growth Hormone (b) gibberellin (c) insulin (d) oestrogen

Sol. (c) Insulin, produced by the pancreas, regulates blood sugar levels by facilitating the uptake of glucose into cells, thus lowering the blood sugar level.

Q.3 Movement of root towards water is called

(a) phototropism (b) geotropism (c) hydrotropism (d) chemotropism

Sol. (c) Hydrotropism is the directional growth of plant roots towards water, allowing the plant to access this essential resource.

Q.4 Which is the receptor for taste?

(a) Olfactory receptor (b) Gustatory receptor
(c) Photo receptor (d) Thigmo receptor

Sol. (b) Gustatory receptors are specialised sensory receptors located on the tongue that detect taste stimuli.

Q.5 Which is the main thinking part of the brain?

(a) Fore brain (b) Mid brain (c) Hind brain (d) Hypothalamus

Sol. (a) The fore brain, particularly the cerebrum, is responsible for complex cognitive functions such as thinking, reasoning, and memory.

Q.6 Which one of the following is not a tropic movement?

(a) Movement of shoot towards light
(b) Movement of roots toward water
(c) Movement of roots towards gravity
(d) Drooping of leaves of *Mimosa pudica*, on touching

Sol. (d) Tropic movements are directional growth movements in response to stimuli like light or gravity. The drooping of *Mimosa pudica* leaves is a nastic movement, which is a non-directional response to stimuli.

Q.7 Pancreas release following hormone

(a) insulin (b) glucagon
(c) Both 'a' and 'b' (d) None of the above

Sol. (c) The pancreas produces both insulin, which lowers blood sugar levels, and glucagon, which raises blood sugar levels.

Q.8 Precision in voluntary action is due to

(a) pons (b) medulla oblongata
(c) cerebrum (d) cerebellum

Sol. (d) The cerebellum coordinates voluntary movements, ensuring they are smooth and precise, such as maintaining balance and posture.

Q.9 Which of the following hormone is not found in human beings?

(a) Thyroxine (b) Insulin
(c) Oestrogen (d) Cytokinin

Sol. (d) Cytokinin is a plant hormone involved in cell division and growth. The other hormones listed (thyroxine, insulin, and oestrogen) are found in humans.

Q.10 Which is the largest part of the brain?

(a) Medulla Oblongata (b) Pons
(c) Cerebellum (d) Cerebrum

Sol. (d) The cerebrum is the largest part of the human brain and is involved in various functions such as thought, memory, and voluntary movement.

□ Very Short Answer Type

Q.1 Name the largest cell present in the human body.

Sol. The largest cell in the human body is the neuron or nerve cell.

Q.2 Enlist the alternative name for "Hormones".

Sol. Hormones are also known as chemical coordinators or messengers.

Q.3 The sensation of feeling full is because of the center associated with hunger is present in which part of the brain?

Sol. The sensation of feeling full is due to the hunger center located in the forebrain.

Q.4 What will happen if the intake of iodine in our diet is low?

Sol. If iodine intake is low, the release of thyroxine from the thyroid gland will be reduced, affecting the metabolism of proteins, carbohydrates, and fats. A person might develop goiter due to iodine deficiency.

Q.5 Why are roots called positively geotropic?

Sol. Roots are called positively geotropic because they grow towards the direction of gravity.

☐ Short Answer Type

Q.1 Pancreas is an example of a heterocrine gland. Justify.

Sol. Heterocrine glands release their secretions both into the blood (hormones) and into ducts (digestive juices). The pancreas is a heterocrine gland because it releases hormones like insulin and glucagon into the bloodstream and secretes pancreatic juice into the pancreatic duct.

Q.2 Define neurons and identify the parts of a neuron where information is transmitted to another neuron.

Sol. Neurons are the structural and functional units of the nervous system. They are specialised cells that transmit impulses between the brain and other parts of the body. The synapses, junction between two neuron, are the sites where information is transmitted from one neuron to another.

Q.3 Read the functions of the following plant hormones and name them:

(a) Promote cell enlargement, cell differentiation, and fruit growth. ....

(b) Promote cell enlargement, and cell differentiation in the presence of auxins, and help in breaking the dormancy in seeds and buds. ....

(c) Promote cell division, promote the opening of stomata and fruit growth, help in breaking the dormancy of seeds and buds, and delay the aging of leaves. ....

(d) Promote dormancy in seeds and buds, promote the closing of stomata, and cause leaf fall. ....

Sol. (a) Auxins

(b) Gibberellins

(c) Cytokinin

(d) Abscisic acid

Q.4 (a) The stimulus in the blooming of flowers and a sunflower aligning itself in the direction of sunlight is light. How are these movements different from each other?

(b) What type of movement do roots exhibit?

Sol. (a) The differences between movement during blooming of Flowers and Sunflower alignment are as fallows

Blooming of Flowers	Sunflower Alignment
1. It shows nastic Movement (Non-directional)	1. It shows tropic Movement (Directional)
2. Growth-independent movement	2. Growth-dependent movement

(b) Roots exhibit negative phototropism (grow away from light) and positive geotropism (grow towards gravity).

Q.5 Match the following

1. Olfactory receptors	a. Tongue
2. Thermo receptors	b. Eye
3. Gustato receptors	c. Nose
4. Photo receptors	d. Skin

Sol. 1-(c), 2-(d), 3-(a), d-(b)

☐ Long Answer Type

Q.1 Why is it important that hormones are secreted in precise quantities? How is this achieved in the animal body?

Sol. Hormones must be secreted in precise quantities to maintain proper physiological balance and ensure that bodily functions are regulated accurately. Hormone levels are regulated by feedback mechanisms. For example, if blood sugar levels rise, the pancreas detects this change and secretes more insulin to lower the sugar levels. As blood sugar levels decrease, insulin secretion is reduced. This feedback loop helps to maintain homeostasis by adjusting hormone levels as needed.

Q.2 What are plant hormones? Name them and give their functions.

Sol. Plant hormones, or phytohormones are chemical messengers that coordinate growth, development, and responses to environmental stimuli. They are produced in one part of the plant and act in another part. The main plant hormones include:

- **Auxins** Promote stem elongation and growth, and are involved in plant tropisms.
- **Gibberellins** Promote stem elongation, seed germination, and flowering.

- **Cytokinins** Stimulate cell division and are found in higher concentrations in areas of rapid growth such as fruits and seeds.
- **Abscisic Acid (ABA)** Inhibits growth, helps close stomata, and promotes leaf senescence.

Q.3 How are the brain and spinal cord protected in the human body?

Sol. The brain and spinal cord are protected by several structures:

- **Cranium** The brain is encased in the cranium (skull), which shields it from physical injury.
- **Vertebral Column** The spinal cord is protected by the vertebral column (backbone), which surrounds and supports it.
- **Meninges** Both the brain and spinal cord are covered by three protective membranes called meninges (dura mater, arachnoid mater, and pia mater).
- **Cerebrospinal Fluid (CSF)** The space between the meninges is filled with cerebrospinal fluid, which acts as a cushion to protect the brain and spinal cord from mechanical shocks.

Q.4 What happens at the synapse between two neurons?

Sol. At the synapse between two neurons, the following process occurs:

1. An electrical impulse traveling along the axon reaches the end of the axon (axon terminal).
2. This impulse triggers the release of neurotransmitters (chemical messengers) into the synaptic cleft (the gap between neurons).
3. The neurotransmitters cross the synaptic cleft and bind to receptors on the dendrite of the next neuron.
4. This binding initiates a new electrical impulse in the second neuron, continuing the transmission of the signal.
5. This process ensures that the nerve impulse is transmitted from one neuron to another, allowing communication throughout the nervous system.

How do Organisms Reproduce?

CHAPTER 07

Important Points

01 Reproduction is a biological process of producing new individuals of the same species by existing organisms or parents.

02 Reproducing organisms create the offsprings resemble their parents due to the inheritance of genetic material.

03 The basic event in reproduction is the creation of a DNA copy. Cells uses chemical reactions to build copies of their DNA.

04 The copying of DNA is proceded by cellular division. This process makes sure that each new cell (called a daughter cell) gets all the important parts it needed, including a full set of DNA, so it can function properly.

05 The process of DNA copying is not always accurate, resulting in variations arising during reproduction, that is the basis for evolution.

06 These variations may or may not be beneficial for the individual, but helps in the survival of the species during adverse conditions.

07 The modes of reproduction may be different depending on the body design of the living organisms. It can be broadly divided into two types

(i) Asexual reproduction (ii) Sexual reproduction

08 **Asexual reproduction** can occur in several ways, depending on the organism. The main modes of asexual reproduction are given below.

09 **Fission** occurs in unicellular organisms like bacteria and protozoa through simple cell division. Depending on the number of daughter cells formed, fission may be binary fission or multiple fission.

10 **Fragmentation** occurs in some multicellular organisms with simple body organisation *e.g., Spirogyra*. Their body, on maturation simply breaks up into smaller fragments, each of which developing into new individual.

11 **Regeneration** is the ability of organisms like *Hydra* and *Planaria* to regrow a complete body from their body parts after being cut. The process of regeneration involves specialised totipotent cells which proliferate and differentiate to form the complete body.

12 **Budding** is a process in which organisms like *Hydra* develop an outgrowth (bud) due to repeated cell division at a specific site. The bud grows, matures into new individuals and separate from the parent body then detached.

13 **Spore formation** is found in some simple multicellular organisms like *Rhizopus*. It include formation of thick walled spores have the capacity to develop into new individuals on the availability of suitable conditions.

14 **Vegetative propagation** occurs in plants through the roots, stems or leaves of parent plant under appropriate conditions. For example, the buds produced in the notches along the leaf margin of *Bryophyllum* fall on the soil and develop into new plants.

15 **Sexual reproduction** requires both male and female individuals to produce the new offspring.

16 The offspring is produced by the union of the male and female germ cells, which contain only half of the chromosome number.

17 In simpler organisms, such as some algae and fungi, the male and female germ cells (gametes) are often very similar in size and shape, or even identical. These gametes fuses to create a new individual.

18 But, in complex organisms, the germ cells are also specialised. In such cases, the male gamete is smaller and motile, whereas the female gamete is larger not-motile and stores food.

19 In plants like angiosperms, flower is the site of sexual reproduction. Stamen, the male productive part consist of anther and filament. Carpel, the female reproductive part is composed of stigma, style and ovary.

20 **Unisexual flowers** contain either stamens or carpels as reproductive organs, *e.g.*, papaya and watermelon. **Bisexual flowers** contain both stamens and carpels, *e.g.*, mustard and *Hibiscus*.

21 **Pollination** is the transfer of pollen grains from anther to the stigma. It may be either self-pollination or cross-pollination. The transfer of pollen grain from one flower to another is carried out by agents like wind, water or animals.

22 Pollen tube carries the male gamete from stigma to the female gamete in ovary.

23 **Fertilisation** occurs when both gametes unite to form a zygote, which then develops into an embryo. After fertilisation, the ovule becomes a seed, and the ovary ripens to form a fruit. The seed contains the embryo, which will grow into a seeding under optimum conditions, process called **germination.**

24 Human uses sexual mode of reproduction.

25 Puberty is the period when a child's body begins to develop and mature sexually. Before puberty, the body focuses on growth and development. Puberty marks the transition to physical maturity, preparing the body for reproduction.

26 During puberty changes such as appearance of pimples on face, development of body odor, growth of thick hair in armpits and genital areas occur in both boys and girls.

27 In girls, increase in breast size, darkening of nipples and occurrence of menstruation are puberty related changes. In boys, facial hair growth, cracking of voice and occasional enlargement of penis occur during puberty.

28 **Male reproductive system** in humans is composed of a pair of testes, vas deferens, seminal vesicles, prostate gland, urethra and a penis.

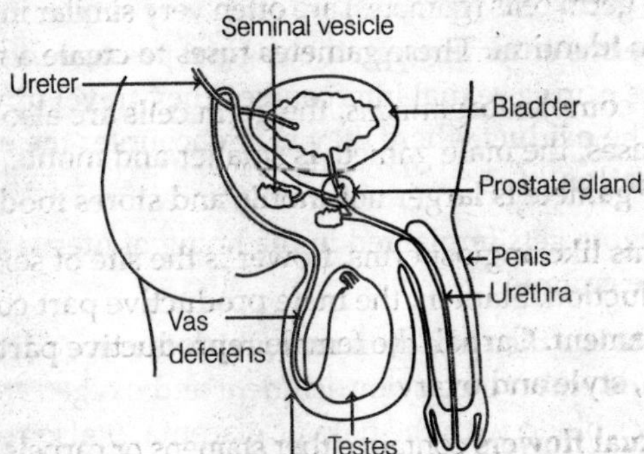

▲ Male reproductive system

29 Testes are situated outside the abdominal cavity in scrotum and are responsible for the formation of sperms.

30 Vas deferens and urethra are the thin tubes through which sperms are transported from testes to outside.

31 Sperms are male germ cell consisting of a small head and a long tail.

32 **Female reproductive system** is made up of ovaries, Fallopian tubes, uterus, cervix and vagina.

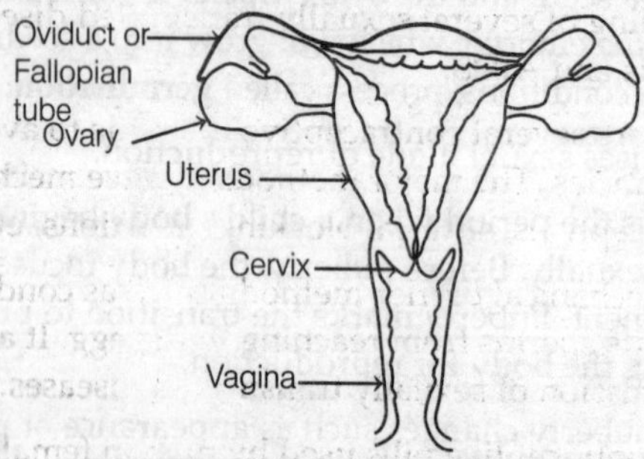

▲ Female reproductive system

33 The ovaries are responsible for producing ova (eggs) and for secreting the hormones **oestrogen** and **progesterone.**

34 The ovaries of a girl already contain thousands of immature eggs before puberty.

35 On reaching puberty, one of the ovaries releases a mature egg every month. This is called **ovulation**. This mature egg is carried by the Fallopian tube.

36 The sperms enter through the vaginal passage into the vagina of females during sexual intercourse. They travel upwards and reach the oviduct where they may encounter the egg, resulting in **fertilisation.**

37 The zygote gets implanted in the lining of uterus and develops into the embryo.

38 Placenta is a disc-like structure which is embedded in the uterine wall. The embryo gets nourishment and oxygen from the mother's blood with the help of placenta. It also removes the waste generated by the developing embryo.

39 The development of child inside the mother's body takes about nine months in humans After this, the child is born due to rhythmic contraction of uterine muscular.

40 In case fertilisation does not occur, the released egg along with the thickened lining of the uterus is shed out through the vagina. This cycle occurs every month in human females and is called menstruation or menstrual cycle and it lasts for about 2 to 8 days.

41 The unprotected sexual act can cause pregnancy as well as spreading of several sexually transmitted diseases like gonorrhea, syphilis and AIDS.

42 There are several contraceptive methods to avoid unwanted pregnancies. The major methods involve mechanical barriers, oral contraceptives, surgical blocking, abortions, etc.

43 The mechanical barrier methods, such as condom diaphragm prevents sperms from reaching to the egg. It also prevents transmission of sexually transmitted diseases.

44 Oral contraceptive pills used by human females, alter the hormonal balance, thereby preventing the egg from being released.

45 Surgical methods, such as blocking the vas deferens in males or the oviducts (Fallopian tubes) in females, effectively prevent pregnancy.

46 Abortions can be done to remove unwanted pregnancies. But, this method is being misused in our country to carryout female foeticide. This is leading to imbalance in female-male sex ratio. Due to this, child sex ratio is declining in alarming rate, although there is ban in prenatal sex determination in India.

47 Contraceptive methods play important role in maintaining the size of a human population.

Intext Questions

On Page 114

Question 1 What is the importance of DNA copying in reproduction?

Sol. DNA copying is crucial in reproduction for the following reasons:

1. **Transmission of characteristics** It ensures that parental traits are passed to offspring, maintaining the genetic continuity of the species.
2. **Genetic variation** It brings variations, which can be beneficial for evolution and adaptation, leading to the diversity within a species.

Question 2 Why is variation beneficial to the species but not necessarily for the individual?

Sol. An individual with variation can survive a lifetime without getting any benefits of variation, but during adverse conditions variation can help a species to survive and not become extinct, For example if there would be a population of bacteria living in temperate water and temperature rises due to global warming, most of the bacteria will die but only the variants resistant to heat will be able to survive,

On Page 119

Question 1 How does binary fission differ from multiple fission?

Sol. The difference between binary fission and multiple fission are as follows :

S.No.	Binary fission	Multiple fission
1.	In binary fission, the parent cell splits to form two new daughter cells.	In multiple fission, the parents cell splits into many new daughter cells.
2.	It takes place during favourable environmental conditions.	It takes place during unfavourable environmental conditions.
3.	It takes place in organisms like *Amoeba, Paramecium, etc.*	It takes place in organisms like *Plasmodium.*

Question 2 How will an organism be benefited if it reproduces through spores?

Sol. Spores are tiny, spherical, asexual reproductive bodies that benefit the organisms by enabling them to survive in unfavourable conditions and colonisation of new. As they have a tough protective wall and can germinate under favourable conditions.

Question 3 Can you think of reasons why more complex orgainsms cannot give rise to new individuals through regeneration?

Sol. Complex organisms cannot reproduce through regeneration because of following reasons

Complexity of Structure In complex organisms, the body has specialised cells, tissues, and organs that work together. Regenerating an entire organism from a single part requires a high level of organisation and control over these specialised structures, which is not feasible in more complex systems.

Energy and Resources Regenerating a whole organisms requires significant amounts of energy and resources, which complex organisms may not have. For larger, more complex animals, the process of regenerating a whole body would be extremely taxing on the organism.

Question 4 Why is vegetative propagation practised for growing some types of plants?

Sol. Vegetative propagation is practiced for the following reasons.

1. It helps in growing plants that do not produce viable seeds.
2. It allows the propagation of plants with superior traits, ensuring offspring are genetically identical to the parent.
3. It is useful for plants that take longer to mature. It is a cheaper, easier and more rapid method.
4. It is beneficial for plants that require extensive care during early development stages.

Question 5 Why is DNA copying an essential part of the process of reproduction?

Sol. DNA copying is essential in reproduction because

Genetic Continuity During reproduction, the genetic material in the parent organism needs to be replicated and passed on to the offspring to maintain consistency across generations.

Inheritance of Traits DNA contains the instructions for the development and functioning of an organism. By copying DNA, offspring inherit traits from their parents, ensuring they develop similar characteristics.

Cell Division In both sexual and asexual reproduction, cell division (such as mitosis or meiosis) requires DNA replication so that each new cell has a complete set of genetic material, allowing the organism to grow, develop, and reproduce.

On Page 126

Question 1 How is the process of pollination different from fertilisation?

Sol. The process of pollination different from fertilisation are as follows :

S.No.	Fertilisation	Pollination
1.	The fusion of male and female gamete to form zygote is called fertilisation.	The transfer of pollen grains from anther to the stigma of a flower is called pollination.
2.	It involves both male and female gametes.	It involves only the male gamete (pollen grain).

Question 2 What is the role of the seminal vesicles and the prostate gland?

Sol. Secretions from seminal vesicles and prostate gland provide nutrition to the sperms and make their transport easier by providing them a fluid medium.

Question 3 What are the changes seen in girls at the time of puberty?

Sol. Changes seen in girls at the time of puberty are as follows

(i) Growth of hair in armpits and pubic region.

(ii) Mammary glands (breast) develop and hips broaden.

(iii) Begining of menstruation.

Question 4 How does the embryo get nourishment inside the mother's body?

Sol. The embryo gets nutrition from the mother's blood with the help of special tissue called placenta. This is a disc-like tissue which develops between the uterine wall and embryo. It has villi on embryo side of the tissue. On the mothers side are blood spaces, which surrounds the villi. This gives a large surface area for oxygen and glucose to pass from the mother to the embryo.

Question 5 If a women is using a copper-T, will it help in protecting her from sexually transmitted diseases?

Sol. No, copper-T does not prevent the transmission of sexually transmitted diseases. Copper-T only prevents implantation. Condoms are the one of the safest method, which is used to prevent the transmission of sexually transmitted diseases.

Exercises

Question 1 Asexual reproduction takes place throught budding in

(a) *Amoeba*

(b) Yast

(c) *Plasmodium*

(d) *Leichmania*

Sol. (b) Yeast. Asexual reproduction through budding occurs in yeast, while *Hydra* also reproduces this way. *Amoeba* reproduces by binary fission, *Plasmodium* by multiple fission, and *Leishmania* also by binary fission.

Question 2 Which of the following is not a part of the female reproductive system in human beings?

(a) Ovary

(b)Uterus

(c) Vas deferens

(d) Fallopian tubes

Sol. (c) Vas deferens. The vas deferens is part of the male reproductive system. The ovary, uterus and Fallopian tube are all parts of the female reproductive system.

Question 3 The anther contains

(a) sepals (b) ovules

(c) pistil (d) pollen grains

Sol. (d) Pollen grains. The anther, which is part of the stamen in plants, contains pollen grains, which are the male gametes. Sepals are part of the flower's outer structure, ovules are found in the ovary and the pistil is the female reproductive part.

Question 4 What are the advantages of sexual reproduction over asexual reproduction?

Sol. There are a number of advantages of sexual reproduction over asexual reproduction. These include

(i) Sexual reproduction created variations which are useful for ensuring survival of a species.

(ii) Two different individuals in a population would have quite diffferent patterns of accumulated variations.

(iii) The desired phenotype can be promoted by sexual reproduction.

These advantages are not available with asexual reproduction.

Question 5 What are the functions performed by the testes in human beings?

Sol. Functions of testes

(i) Produce male sex cells-sperms.

(ii) Produce male sex hormone testosterone.

Question 6 Why does menstruation occur?

Sol. Menstruation occurs when the egg released during ovulation is not fertilised. Every month uterus prepares itself to receive a fertilised egg, thus its lining becomes thick and spongy. In case, the egg is not fertilised this lining breaks and discharged out of the body through the vagina in the form of blood and mucous.

Question 7 Draw a labelled diagram of the longitudinal section of a flower.

Sol.

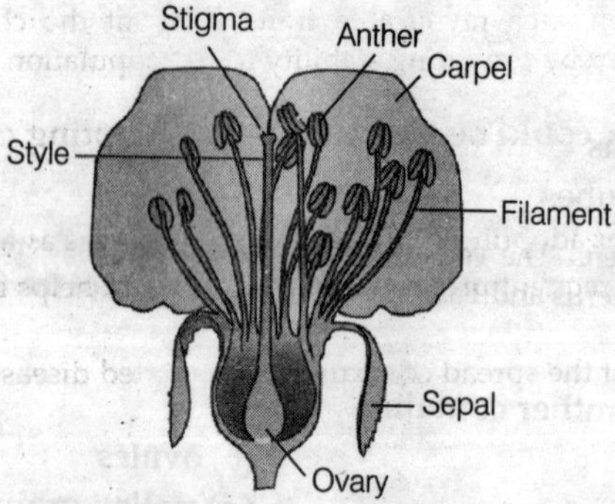

▲ Longitudinal section of a flower

Question 8 What are the different methods of contraception?

Sol. The different methods of contraception are as follows

1. **Barrier methods** In barrier methods, the physical devices such as condoms and diaphragm are used. They prevent sperms from meeting the eggs.
2. **Chemical methods** In the chemical methods, the females use pills-oral pills that contain hormones which stop ovaries from releasing ovum.
3. **Surgical methods** In males, a small portion of sperm duct is cut by surgical methods and the cut end is tied properly **(vasectomy)**. This prevents the sp... ns from coming out.

In females, a ... part of the ovi...t is cut and tied **(tubectomy)**. This prevents the ... om entering the ov...t.

Question 9 How are the modes for reproduction different in unicellular and multicellular organisms?

Sol. Unicellular organisms are made up of only single cell, in which all the functions are performed by the single cell. So, reproduction is done by simple, asexual methods but in multicellular organisms various cells perform different functions. So, production of specialised cells *i.e.,* germ cells is required and simple methods for reproduction are insignificant.

Question 10 How does reproduction help in providing stability to populations of species?

Sol. Reproduction leads to certain variations in the characteristics of the offspring. This may allow organism to exist in diverse habitats and niches. Certain variations present in the individuals of certain population may enable the individuals to survive under unfavourable conditions. Organism with such favourable traits transmit the characters to their offsprings, thereby providing stability to the population of a species.

Question 11 What could be the reasons for adopting contraceptive methods?

Sol. The reasons for adopting contraceptive methods are as follows

(i) To avoid frequent pregnancies, which in turn helps in population control.

(ii) To prevent the spread of sexually transmitted diseases.

DIKSHA APP Questions

Multiple Choice Questions

Q.1 The method of contraception in humans which is permanent is

(a) physical barrier method

(b) chemical method

(c) intra uterine contraceptive device

(d) surgical method

Sol. (d) The **surgical method** is a permanent contraception method involving procedures like vasectomy or tubal ligation to prevent reproduction.

Q.2 The part of the flower that produces female germ cell is

(a) filament (b) anther

(c) stigma (d) ovary

Sol. (d) The ovary is the part of the flower that produces the female germ cell, called the ovum or egg cell, located inside the ovule

Q.3 In human males organ that produces the male germ cell is

(a) penis (b) vas deferens

(c) testis (d) seminal vesicles

Sol. (c) Testis produces sperm (male germ cell) and the hormone testosterone in males.

Q.4 An example of an organism that reproduces by multiple fission is

(a) yeast (b) *Plasmodium*

(c) *Amoeba* (d) *Spirogyra*

Sol. (b) *Plasmodium* reproduces by multiple fission, where the nucleus divides multiple times before the cell splits into several daughter cells.

Q.5 The cell organelle which plays an important role in cell division is

(a) nucleus (b) endoplasmic reticulum

(c) lysosome (d) vacuole

Sol. (a) The nucleus controls and regulates cell division through its genetic material (DNA), ensuring the proper replication and distribution of chromosomes.

Q.6 Reproduction is essential for living organisms to order

(a) keep the individual organism alive

(b) maintain growth

(c) fulfill their energy requirements

(d) continue the species generation after generation

Sol. (d) Reproduction ensures the survival and continuity of a species by producing offspring. It is not essential for the survival of an individual organism.

Q.7 The reproductive part of plant is called

(a) sepal (b) petal (c) seed (d) flower

Sol. (d) The flower is the reproductive part of a plant, containing structures for sexual reproduction such as stamens (male) and carpels (female).

Q.8 In a flower, the parts that produce male and female gametes are

(a) stamen and style (b) filament and stigma

(c) stamen and stigma (d) anther and ovary

Sol. (d) The **anther** produces male gametes (pollen grains), and the **ovary** produces female gametes (ovules).

Q.9 Which contraceptive is not an example of mechanical/Barrier method?

(a) Condom (b) Cervical caps

(c) Diaphragm (d) Mala D Tablets

Sol. (d) **Mala D tablets** are a type of oral contraceptive that works through hormonal regulation not as a mechanical barrier.

□ Very Short Answer Type

Q.1 How is reproduction in *Leishmania* different from that in *Plasmodium* though both are unicellular?

Sol. *Leishmania* shows binary fission. *Plasmodium* shows multiple fission.

Q.2 Which part of the flower changes into seed after fertilisation?

Sol. Ovule

Q.3 Cell division is a type of reproduction in unicellular organisms. Justify with an example.

Sol. In *Amoeba,* cell division results in 2 daughter cells (binary fission), each of which develop into a new individual. Hence cell division is a type of reproduction in unicellular organisms.

Q.4 Name a surgical contraceptive method in case of females.

Sol. Tubectomy

Q.5 The fertilised egg always has one……… chromosome.

Sol. X

Q.6 Animals produce gametes which fuse to form a ………

Sol. Zygote

Q.7 Name any two sexually transmitted diseases.

Sol. HIV AIDS and Syphillis.

Q.8 What is the ratio of number of chromosomes between a germ cell and a zygote?

Sol. The ratio of number of chromosomes between germ cell and a zygote is 1:2 as the former is a haploid cell while the latter is a diploid cell.

Q.9 Why do we see the growth of bread mould on slices of bread more frequently during rainy season?

Sol. The growth of bread mould on slices of bread is seen more frequently during rainy season due to the increase amount of moisture in the air.

Q.10 Why do offsprings from sexual reproduction exhibit more variation?

Sol. They exhibit more variation because their genetic composition is a combination of genetic material from two parents of the same species.

Q.11 List two changes that occur in human females during adolescence.

Sol. Two changes that occur in human females during adolescence period include change in hair growth pattern and enlargement of mammary glands.

Q.12 Draw the diagram of binary fission in *Amoeba*.

Sol.

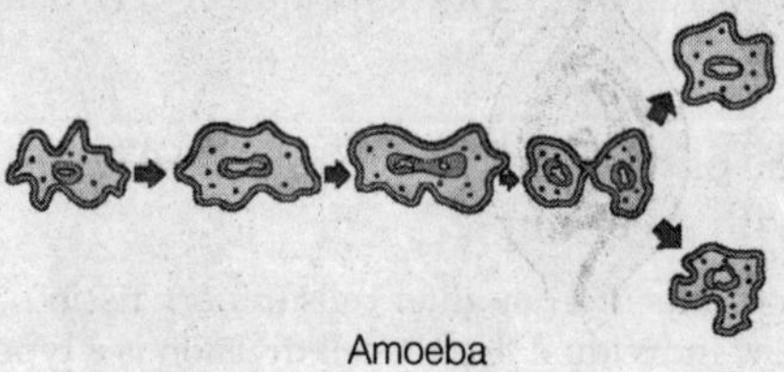

Amoeba

Q.13 What is the difference between asexual and sexual reproduction?

Sol. Difference between sexual and sexual reproduction are as follows

Asexual reproduction:
1. Only one parent is required. 2 The offsprings are clone of their parents. 3. sexual activity is involved.

Sexual reproduction:
1. Two parents are required for sexual reproduction. 2. It produces variations in offsprings. 3. Sexual activity is involved.

Q.14 Name two types of fission in organisms.

Sol. Binary fission and multiple fission.

Q.15 Why there is a need to understand the importance of birth control?

Sol. Birth control methods are adopted to check increase in population and to satisfy the requirements of upcoming generations in a sustainable way.

☐ Short Answer Type

Q.1 (a) Explain the terms:

(i) Implantation (ii) Placenta

(b) What is the average duration of human pregnancy?

Sol. (a) (i) Implantation is the event during which a fertilised egg or zygote adheres to the wall of the uterus, inside the female body.

(ii) Placenta is a disc like vascular structure embedded in the uterine wall. The placenta supplies nutrients like glucose and oxygen to the developing embryo. It also removes waste substances generated by the embryo,

(b) The average duration of human pregnancy is nine months.

Q.2 (i) Label the following diagram.

(ii) Which process is being shown in the diagram?

Sol. (i)

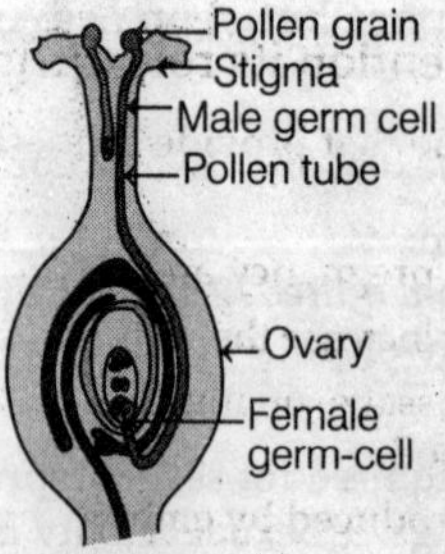

(ii) The diagram show the process of germination of pollen on stigma, which is necessary for passage of male gametes to ovary. In this process the pollen grains travel through pollen tube which then enters the ovary and releases the 2 male gametes. One of which participate in syngamy and the other in triple fusion.

Q.3 Discuss spore formation in fungi.

Sol. The spores in fungi vary in shape. Spores are usually unicellular, thick walled, spherical structures. The thick wall provide protection till they come in contact with other surface and begin to grow. Sometimes the spores may be multi cellular also.

Sometimes the spores are produced endogenously in Special saclike asexual reproductive bodies called sporangia. Spores in such cases are called sporangiospores. Spores on falling on ground or substratum grow new hypha, *e.g., Rhizopus*.

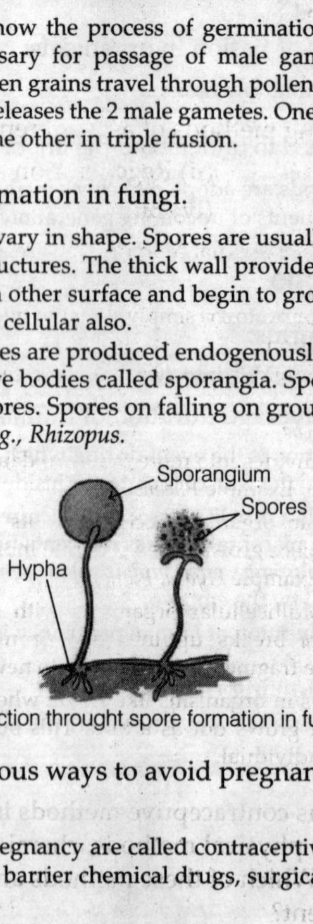

Reproduction throught spore formation in fungus

Q.4 What are the various ways to avoid pregnancy?Elaborate any one method?

Sol. Methods to avoid pregnancy are called contraceptive methods. They includes mechanical barrier chemical drugs, surgical methods and Intra-uterine drugs.

Surgical methods Vasectomy refers to surgical method in which vas deferentia in human males are cut and sealed to prevent pregnancy by making semen devoid of sperms .Tubectomy refers to surgical process in which oviducts in human females are cut and sealed to prevent pregnancy by inhibiting the release of egg

Q.5 What is placenta ? Mention its role during pregnancy

Sol. Placenta is a special tissue that provide connection between embryo and uterine wall.

Role of placenta during pregnancy are as follows

1. It possesses villi that increase the surface area for absorption of nutrients.
2. It facilitates the passage of nutrition and oxygen to embryo from mother through blood.
3. Waste substances produced by embryo are removed through placenta into mother's blood.

☐ Long Answer Type

Q.1 Explain the following methods of asexual reproduction.

(i) Fission (ii) Regeneration

(iii) Fragmentation (iv) Budding

Sol. The following methods of asexual reproduction are as follows

(i) **Fission**

- Many bacteria or protozoa simply split into two or more equal halves during cell division.
- When the cell divides into two daughter cells, it is called binary fission.
  Example : *Amoeba*
- When the cell divides into more than two daughter cells, it is called multiple fission. Example *Plasmodium*

(ii) **Regeneration** If an organism accidently cuts or breaks into many pieces and each piece grows into a separate individual; this is known as regeneration. Example *Hydra, Planaria*

(iii) **Fragmentation** Multicellular organisms with simple body designs such as *Spirogyra* breaks up into two or more fragments upon maturation. These fragments then grow into new individual.

(iv) **Budding** It occurs in organisms like *Hydra* where a small part of the body of a parent grows out as a bud. This bud then detaches and becomes a new individual.

Q.2 Mention the various contraceptive methods in human beings. Categorise them as physical methods, chemical methods and surgical methods. Which of these methods are temporary and which are permanent?

Sol. Contraceptive methods are used to prevent pregnancy and can be classified into different categories based on their function. The various contraceptive methods in humans are as follows

1. **Physical Methods** These methods create a barrier to prevent sperm from reaching the egg. Example include **condoms, diaphragm** and **cervical cap.**
2. **Chemical Methods** These methods involve chemicals or hormones to prevent pregnancy. Examples include **oral contraceptives, injection** and **spermicides.**
3. **Surgical Methods** These are permanent methods that surgically prevent pregnancy. Examples include vasectomy for men and **tubal ligation** for women.

Among various contraceptive methods, physical methods (such as condoms, diaphragm, cervical cap) and chemical methods (such as oral contraceptives, injections, spermicides) are temporary, while surgical methods (such as vasectomy and tubal ligation) are permanent.

Q.3 Trace the events that could take place in a flower from the time the pollen grains of the same species fall on the sigma up to completion of fertilisation.

Sol. Events taking place in a flower from time of pollen grains of same species Fall the stigma upto completion of fertilisation are as follow

After th pollen grain falls on the stigma, formation of pollen tube occurs.

↓

The male germ cell in the pollen grain moves through the pollen tube towards the ovary

↓

On reaching the ovary, the male germ cell fuses with the female germ cell to form a unicellular zygote(fertilisation)

↓

The zygote divides several times to form multicellular embryo within the ovule

↓

Maturation of ovule into seeds and ovary into fruit occurs

Q.4 What is the process 'implantation'? Where does implantation does takes place? Mention its structure and function.

Sol. The embedding of the embryo in the inner uterine walls is known as implantation. It takes place in the inner lining of the uterus. Uterus is the muscular bag like organ. The growth and development of the growing fetus takes place here. The foetus stays in the uterus for approximately 9 months. Here it receives nutrition from the mother's body to grows and matures. The connective tissue called placenta is responsible for exchange of glucose and oxygen.The developing embryo also generates waste substances into mothers blood via placenta only.

Heredity

CHAPTER 08

Important Points

01 Reproduction produces offspring of identical designs of the parents. However, they are not exactly identical, but show a great deal of variation from the parents.

02 Variations arising during the process of reproduction can be inherited. In asexual reproduction, a few variations can occur, whereas much more variations occur in sexual reproduction.

03 During asexual reproduction, the minor variations occur due to slight inaccuracies in DNA copying.

04 In sexual reproduction, variations are mainly caused by crossing over during the process of cell division.

05 Different individuals have different kinds of advantages. Beneficial variations help the species to survive better in the environment.

06 The beneficial variations forms the basis of evolution on natural basis.

07 Heredity rules determine the process by which traits and characteristics are inherited of from parents to offsprings.

08 In humans, both the father and mother contribute equal amount of genetic material to the child. It means that each trait can be influenced by both paternal and maternal DNA. Thus, for each trait, humans have two versions of genes, called alleles.

09 **Gregor Johann Mendel** conducted a large number of experiments on pea plants. He carried out large number of monohybrid and dihybrid crosses using many contrasting characteristics and put forward several important conclusions.

10 In a monohybrid cross, with pure vareties of plants, taking only one character, the phenotypic ratio obtained in F_2 generation is 3:1 and genotypic ratio will be 1 : 2 : 1.

11 In case of a dihybrid cross with two pairs of contrasting characters, the phenotypic ratio obtained in F_2-generation is 9:3:3:1. From his experiments, Mendel concluded that any pair of contrasting characters, one is dominant and the other one is recessive. The homozygous dominant trait is denoted by two capital letters, whereas the homozygous recessive trait is denoted by two small letters.

12 During gamete formation, the genes controlling a particular trait separate from each other. Therefore, each gamete contains pure character with respect to contrasting characters are considered.

13 When two or more traits are involved in gametes formation, their genes assort independently, irrespective of the combinations present in the parents.

14 Mendel's experiment interpret that both parents contribute equally to the DNA of the progeny during sexual reproduction. For this mechanism, each germ cell contains only one gene set.

15 Each gene set is present as separate independent pieces, each called as a **chromosome.**

Thus, each cell will have two copies of each chromosome, one each from the male and female parents. Every germ cell will take one chromosome from each pair and these may be of either from mother or from father.

16 Genes carry information for proteins synthesis which in turn control the various body characteristics.

17 The male and female germ cells combine during fertilisation and produce a diploid zygote. Thus, the normal diploid number of chromosomes in the offspring is restored.

18 Sex determination in different individuals occurs by different mechanisms. Some rely on environmental cues. For example in few reptiles, the temperature at which fertilised eggs are kept determines the sex.

In other animals such as snails individuals can change sex as their sex is not genetically determined. The sex of human offspring is genetically determined.

(i) Humans have 22 pairs of autosomes and one pair of sex chromosomes.

(ii) Males have an heterogametic pair of sex chromosomes, *i.e.*, XY, while females always have similar perfect pair, *i.e.*, XX.

(iii) In a woman, all eggs carry only X-chromosome. Whereas in male two types of sperms are produced, one carrying X-chromosonal and other carrying Y-chromosonl.

(iv) Sex of a child depends on which type of sperm fuses with the egg.

(v) If the sperm carrying X-chromosome fuses with the egg, a girl child will be produce and if the sperm carrying Y-chromosome fuses with the egg, it will result in to birth of a baby boy.

Intext Questions

On Page 124

Question 1 If a trait 'A' exists in 10% of the population of an asexually reproducing species and a trait 'B' exists in 60% of the same population, which trait is likely to have arisen earlier?

Sol. In asexual reproduction, when cells copy their DNA, small mistakes can happen, leading to variations in the offspring. These variations can create new traits in the population.

Now, if a trait is found in only 10% of the population, it means this trait probably appeared more recently. On the other hand, if a trait is found in 60% of the population, it's more likely that this trait has been around for a longer time. So, trait B, which is in 60% of the population, most likely appeared before trait A, which is in only 10% of the population.

Question 2 How does the creation of variations in a species promote survival?

Sol. Sometimes, the environment changes in ways that make it hard for a species to survive. For example, if the water temperature suddenly increases most bacteria living in that water might die. However, if some bacteria have a variation that makes them resistant to heat, they will survive. These variations can help the species continue to exist, even in tough conditions.

But remember, not all variations are helpful. Some may not be useful at all. So, while variations can help the species survive, they don't always benefit every individual organism.

On Page 133

Question 1 How do Mendel's experiments show that traits may be dominant or recessive?

Sol. Mendel crossed a pure tall pea plant (TT) with pure dwarf pea plant (tt) and observed that all the progeny were hybrid tall (Tt), in the F_1 generation.

TT	×	tt	P
(Tall parent)	↓	(Dwarf)	
	(Tt)		
	(All hybrid tall)		F_1

However, when he self crossed plants of F_1 generation, he observed that one fourth of the plants were dwarf and three fourth were tall.

Tt × Tt F_1

↓

TT Tt Tt (Tall) tt (Dwarf)

Thus, he concluded that although the F_1 progeny had both tall and short traits, only tall plants were observed in the F_1 generation, which means tallness is a dominant trait. Thus, it was concluded that the gene causing tallness is dominant while the gene causing dwarfness is recessive. The trait expressing itself in the hybrid is the dominant one.

Question 2 How do Mendel's experiments show that traits are inherited independently?

Sol. Mendel used a dihybrid cross between pure pea plants to show that traits are inherited independently.

He selected pea plants with round yellow seeds (RRYY) with wrinkled green seeds (rryy).

Round, Yellow seeds Wrinkled, Green seeds

P RRYY x rryy

↓

F_1 RrYy

(All round yellow seeds) hybrid

In F_1 generation, 4 types of gametes are formed

RY, Ry,rY, ry

F_1

Gametes	RY	Ry	rY	ry
RY	RRYY	RRYy	RrYY	RrYy
Ry	RRYy	RRyy	RrYy	Rryy
rY	RrYY	RrYy	rrYY	rrYy
ry	RrYy	Rryy	rrYy	rryy

Yellow round 9

Yellow wrinkled 3

Green round 3

Green Wrinkled 1

The variety of combination in the offspring shows that inheritance of seed colour does not affect the inheritance of seed shape.

Thus it can be concluded that green yellow traits and round wrinkled traits can be inherited independently.

Question 3 A man with blood group 'A' married a woman with blood group O and their daughter has blood group 'O'. Is this information enough to tell you which of the traits blood group A or O is dominant? Why or why not?

Sol. The given information is not enough to determines which of the traits - blood group A or O- to be dominant. As in blood heredity, blood type O is always recessive where as blood type A is always dominant. In this case father's blood group can be (heterozygous) AO or homozygous (AA) and mother's blood group will be OO.

For daughter to be have blood group O. She must recessive O gene each from both. For this father must have AO blood group and mother must have OO blood group.

Question 4 How is the sex of the child determined in human beings?

Sol. Genetics is involved in determination the sex of a child. A male cell has one X-chromosome and one Y-chromosome, so it produces two types of sperms with genotype A + X and A + Y. Female sex is homogametic. A female cell has both X-chromosomes, so it produces similar type of eggs with genotype 'A + X'.

Sex of the child depends upon what happened during fertilisation.

(i) If a sperm carrying X-chromosome fertilises the egg, the child born will be female.

(ii) If a sperm carrying Y-chromosome fertilises the egg, the child born will be male.

Thus, the sperm (or the male cell) determines the sex of the child.

44 + XX (Female) → 22 + X (Gamete) (22 + X)

44 + XY (Male) → 22 + X, 22 + Y (Gametes) (22 + X), (22 + Y)

44 + XX (Female) 44 + XY (Male)

Exercises

Question 1 A Mendelian experiment consisted of breeding tall pea plants bearing violet flowers with short pea plants bearing white flowers. The progeny all bore violet flowers, but almost half of them were short. This suggests that the genetic make-up of the tall parent can be depicted as

(a) TTWW (b) TTww (c) TtWW (d) TtWw

Sol. (c) In a pea plant, the tall height and violet colour represent the dominant phenotype while short height and white colour represent the recessive phenotype.

- Since the recessive trait (short pea plant) appears in the progeny, there is the presence of the recessive allele in the parent. But as it is given that the parent is tall, therefore there should be an allele for the tall trait as well. Hence, the genotype for height is heterozygous dominant (Tt)
- Also, all plant bear violet flower (dominant trait), allele from the recessive trait is absent.
- Therefore, the genotype for flower colour is homozygous dominant.

Question 2 A study found that the children with light-coloured eyes are likely to have parents with light-coloured eyes. On this basis, can we say anything about whether the light eye colour trait is dominant or recessive? Why or why not?

Sol. From this study, we cannot make any inference whether light eye colour trait is recessive or dominant, because as both the parents have light colour eye, all the children will definitely have light colour eye (though certain variations may occur.)

Question 3 Outline a project which aims to find the dominant coat colour in dogs.

Sol. In order to find a dominant coat colour in dogs, homozygous black (BB) male dog and a homozygous white (bb) female dog are allowed to cross-breed in order to produce offspring (F_1-generation).

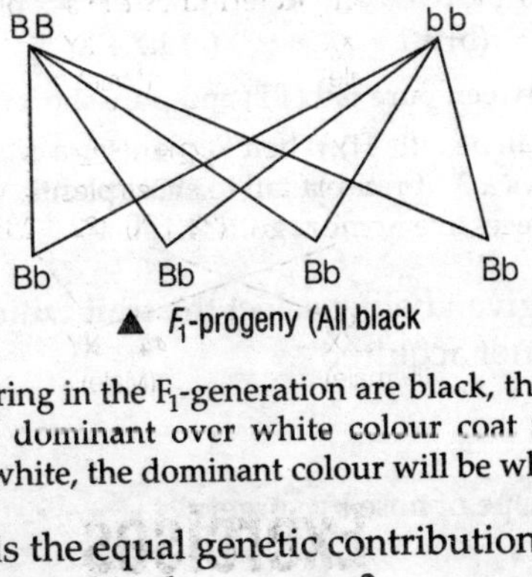

▲ F_1-progeny (All black

If all the offspring in the F_1-generation are black, this concludes that black colour coat is dominant over white colour coat in dogs and if all the offspring are white, the dominant colour will be white.

Question 4 How is the equal genetic contribution of male and female parents ensured in the progeny?

Sol. The male and female reproductive cells divide by meiosis to form haploid gametes. These gametes have equal genetic material. The zygote is formed by the fusion of male and female gamete, *i.e.*, it has equal genetic contribution from male and female parents. The individual is then developed from the zygote.

DIKSHA APP Questions

☐ Multiple Choice Questions

Q.1 Which of the following is not a direct conclusion that can be drawn from Mendels Experiment?

(a) Only one parental trait is expressed

(b) Two copies of each trait is inherited in sexually reproducing organism

(c) For recessive trait to be expressed, both copies should be identical

(d) Natural selection can alter frequency of an inherited trait.

Sol. (d) Mendel's experiments did not address natural selection, which was later explained by Darwin.

Q.2 What is the probability that the male progeny will be a boy?

(a) 50% (b) 56% (c) 47.43% (d) It varies

Sol. (a) The probability of male progeny being a boy is 50%, as it depends on whether the sperm carries an X or Y chromosome, with each having an equal chance.

Q.3 In peas, a pure tall plant (TT) is crossed with a short plant (tt). The ratio of short plants to pure tall plants in F_2 is

(a) 1:3 (b) 3:1 (c) 1:2:1 (d) 2:2

Sol. (a) In a cross between pure tall (TT) and pure short (tt) plants, the F_1 generation will all be tall (Tt).When F_1 plants are crossed, the F_2 generation shows a 3 : 1 ratio of tall to short plants, with the short plants appearing in a recessive homozygous (tt) state.

Q.4 From the list given below select the trait which can be inherited but not acquired

(a) colour of eye

(b) weight loss

(c) change in shape of nose by surgery

(d) swimming

Sol. (a) Eye colour is an inherited trait controlled by genetics, while weight loss is an acquired trait influenced by lifestyle or environmental factors.

Q.5 Name the scientist who worked out on the rules of inheritance

(a) G.J Mendel (b) J.G Mendel (d) Mendeleev (d) Batson

Sol. (a) Mendel is known for his work on the principles of inheritance, formulating the laws of inheritance based on his experiments with pea plants.

Q.6 A white flowered plant is denoted as pp and a purple flowered plant is denoted as PP. If the two plants are cross bred with each other, then: What will be the likely flower colour of the plants of F_1 generation?

(a) White (b) Purple
(c) Both purple and white (d) Light purple

Sol. (b) The flower colour of the F1 generation will be purple (Pp) as purple is dominant over white.

Q.7 What will be the genotypic and phenotypic ratio of the cross between Rr and rr respectively (R is dominant allele, and r is recessive allele)?

(a) 1:2:1 and 3:1 (b) 1:2:1 and 1:1
(c) 1:1 and 3:1 (d) 1:1 and 1:1

Sol. (d) The genotypic ratio is 1 Rr: 1 rr, and the phenotypic ratio is 1 dominant : 1 recssive.

Q.8 Offspring formed by sexual reproduction exhibit more variation than those produced by asexual reproduction

(a) sexual reproduction is a lengthy process
(b) more DNA is involved in sexual reproduction
(c) genetic material comes from two different species
(d) gametes of parents involved have qualitatively different composition

Sol. (d) Sexual reproduction involves the fusion of gametes from two parents, resulting in offspring with genetic variation, while asexual reproduction produces genetically identical offspring.

Q.9 Which part of DNA codes for a single functional product (protein/RNA) which causes differences or resemblances between organisms?

(a) Chromosome (b) Promoter
(c) Trait (d) Gene

Sol. (d) A gene is a segment of DNA that codes for a single functional product, such as a protein or RNA.

☐ Very Short Answer Type

1. Why did Mendel choose pea plant for his experiment?

Sol. Mendel chose pea plant for his experiment because they are

- Easy to grow
- Short lifespan.
- Easy distinguishable characters.
- Produce large number of offsprings.
- Self pollinated.

Q.2 What will be the sex of the offspring if a sperm carrying X Chromosome fertilises the egg?

Sol. Female

Q.3 Mention any two strategies that are used by different species for determining sex of their new borns.

Sol. Environmental cues and genetic determination.

Q.4 Differentiate between genotype and phenotype

Sol. Genotype is the genetic constitution of an organism and phenotype is the external appearance

Q.5 Which is a better mode of reproduction sexual or asexual? Why?

Sol. Sexual reproduction is considered to be a better mode of reproduction because it leads to variations that enable organisms to adapt to the changing environment and adds survival value to particular species.

Q.6 Why some phenotypes are closely associated in a given population?

Sol. Some phenotypes are closely associated in a given population because their genes might be linked so there are higher chances of them being transferred together in each generation.

Q.7 Name the Father of Genetics.

Sol. Gregor Johann Mendel

Q.8 What is gene?Where are genes located?

Sol. Gene is a segment of DNA or chromosomes occupying specific position. Genes are located on chromosomes.

Q.10 What is the function of a gene?

Sol. Gene is the carrier of the genetic information from one generation to the next.

Q.11 Newly formed DNA copies may not be identical at times. Give reason.

Sol. Newly formed DNA copies may not be identical at times if there is error or inaccuracies in DNA copying.

Q.12 What is the phenotypic ratio obtained in Mendels dihybrid cross?

Sol. 9:3:3:1

Q.13 Mention any two forms of wild cabbage.

Sol. Broccoli/cauliflower/kale/cabbage.(any two)

Q.14 What are inherited traits?

Sol. Those which are passed on from parents to offsprings.

Q.15 Mendel performed his experiments on ......

Sol. Garden pea.

☐ Short Answer Type

Q.1 A woman has only sons. Analyse the situation and give suitable explanation.

Sol. The females are homogametic i.e. they have XX chromosome. They can only give X chromosome. The sex of a child is determined by the chromosomes which they inherit from their father. In this situation also, the child is getting only Y chromosome from the father.

Q.2 A woman has only daughters. Analyse the situation genetically and provide a suitable explanation.

Sol. The woman produces ova with 'X' chromosome The man produces sperms with X and Y chromosome which actually determines the sex of the baby. If a Y-bearing sperm fertilises the egg, the zygote has the 44 + XY composition, and the resulting embryo grows to be a boy. When an X-bearing sperm fertilises the egg, the resulting zygote has the 44 + XX composition. This embryo develops into a girl. Fusion of ova with X chromosome with sperm having X chromosome has lead to daughters only.

Q.3 Do the sex chromosomes of the mother play a significant role in determining the sex of a new born?

Sol. No, because mothers have a pair of X-chromosomes. All children will inherit an 'X' chromosome from their mother regardless of whether they are boys or girls.

Q.4 (a) Will geographical isolation be a major factor in the speciation of a self-pollinating plant species? Why or why not?

(b) Will geographical isolation be a major factor in the speciation of an organism that reproduces asexually? Why or why not?

Sol. (a) Geographical isolation will not be a major factor in the speciation of a self-pollinating plant species because it does not have to look for other plants to carry out its process of reproduction.

(b) Geographical isolation will not be a major factor in the speciation of an organism that reproduces asexually because it does not require any other organism to carry out reproduction.

Q.5 How is the sex of the child determined in human beings?

Sol. In human beings, sex of the child depends upon the kind of male gamete that fertilises the female gamete. If sperm carrying X chromosomes fertilises the ovum carrying X chromosome, then the child born will be a girl. If a sperm carrying Y chromosome fertilises the ovum which carries X chromosome, then the child born will be a boy.

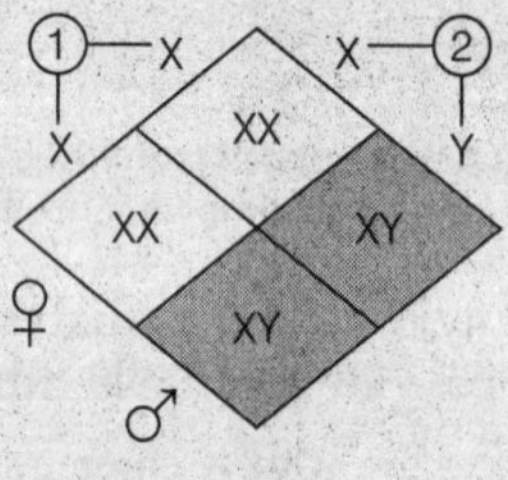

Q.6 Mention the total number of chromosomes along with the sex chromosomes that are present in a human female and a human male. Explain how in sexually producing organisms the number of chromosomes in the progeny remains the same as that of the parents.

Sol. Human male has 22 pairs of chromosomes along with XY sex chromosome. Human female has 22 pairs of chromosomes along with XX sex chromosome and males, have 22 pairs of chromosomes along with XY sex chromosomes. The original number of chromosomes (the amount of DNA) becomes half during gamete formation. When the gamete fuse to form a zygote the original number of chromosomes (the amount of DNA) is restored in the progeny.

Light : Reflection and Refraction

CHAPTER 09

Important Points

01 Reflection of Light The phenomenon of bouncing back of light rays on striking a smooth surface, is called reflection of light.

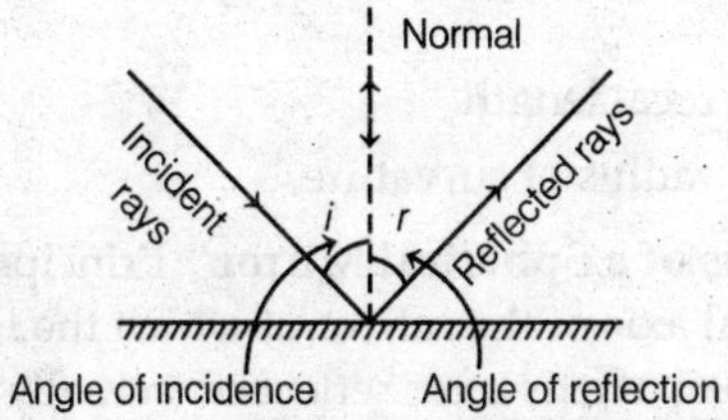

02 Laws of Reflection There are two laws of reflection

(i) The incident ray, the reflected ray and normal at the point of incidence, all lie in the same plane.

(ii) Angle of incidence is always equal to angle of reflection

$$\angle i = \angle r$$

03 Spherical Mirror If the reflecting surface of the mirror is spherical, then the mirror is called a spherical mirror. Spherical mirrors are of two types

(i) The spherical mirror with outward curved reflecting surface is called **convex mirror.** A beam of light generally diverges after reflection from its surface, hence it is also called **divergent mirror.**

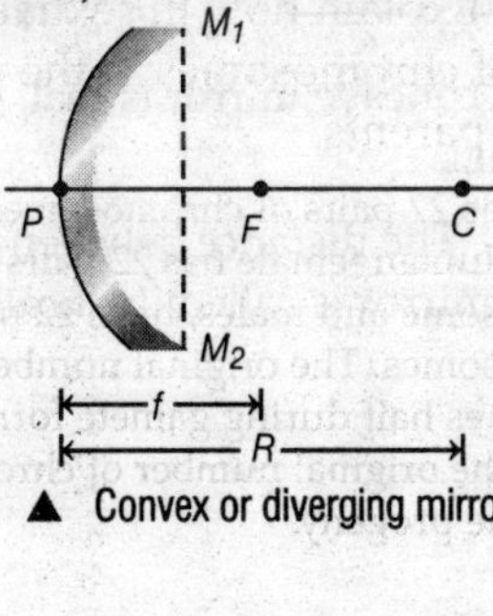

▲ Convex or diverging mirror

(ii) The spherical mirror with inward curved reflecting surface is called **concave mirror**. A beam of light generally converges after reflection from its surface, hence it is also called **convergent mirror**.

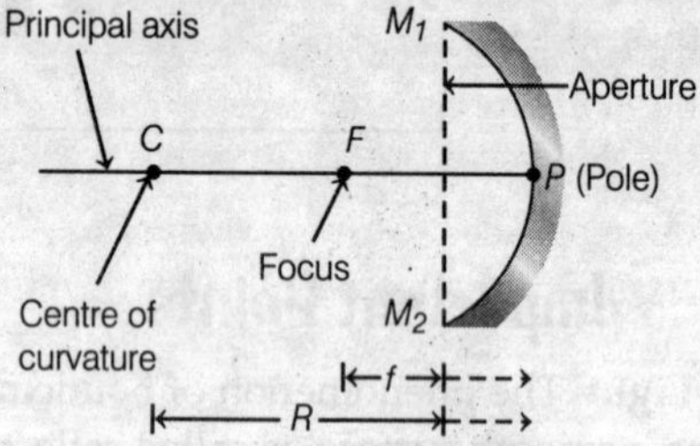

▲ Concave or converging mirror

Here, f = focal length

R = radius of curvature.

04 Principal Focus of a Spherical Mirror Principal focus is a point on the principal axis of the mirror at which the light rays coming parallel to principal axis after reflection actually meet or appear to be coming from.

For a concave mirror, the focus is in front of the mirror, while for a convex mirror, the focus is behind the mirror.

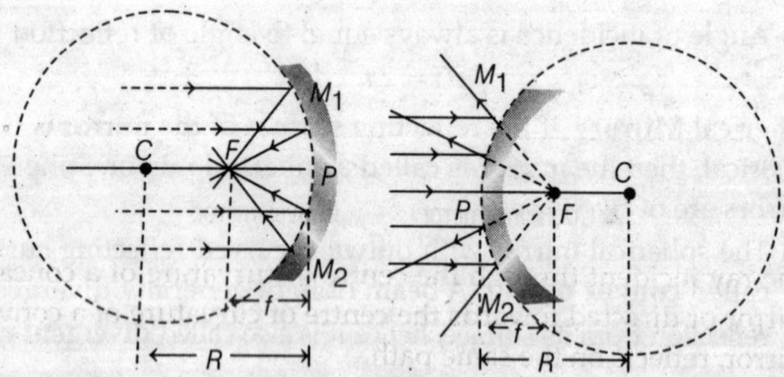

The focus of a concave mirror is real, while the focus of a convex mirror is virtual.

05 Focal Length The distance between pole and principal focus of a spherical mirror is called its focal length. It is represented by f.

06 Relation between Focal Length and Radius of Curvature of a Spherical Mirror If the aperture of the mirror is small, then

$$f = \frac{R}{2}$$

07 Reflection by Spherical Mirrors The reflection follows the same two rules everywhere. However, due to spherical nature of the surface, some interesting cases are observed

(i) The rays incident parallel to the principal axis, pass through the focus after reflection in case of concave mirror or appear to come from focus in convex mirror.

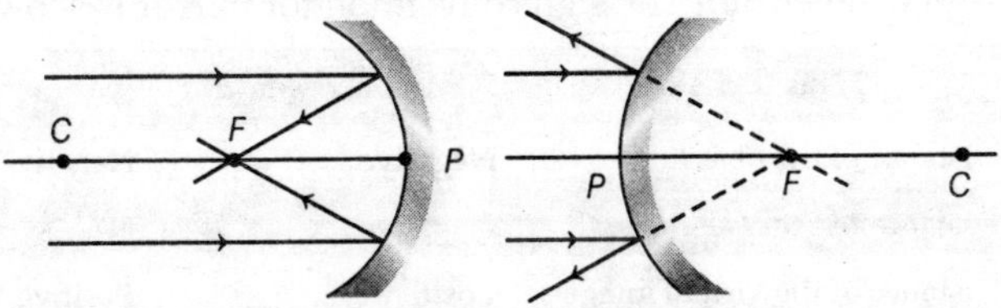

▲ Concave mirror Convex mirror

(ii) The rays incident through the focus of a concave mirror or directed towards focus of a convex mirror, become parallel to principal axis after reflection from the mirror.

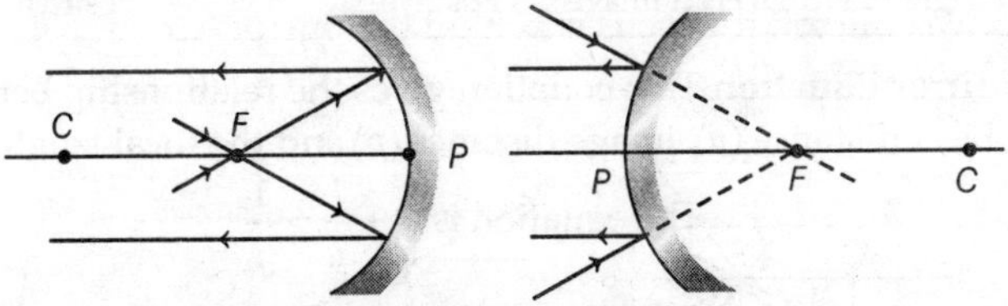

▲ Concave mirror Convex mirror

(iii) The ray incident through the centre of curvature of a concave mirror or directed towards the centre of curvature of a convex mirror, reflects on the same path.

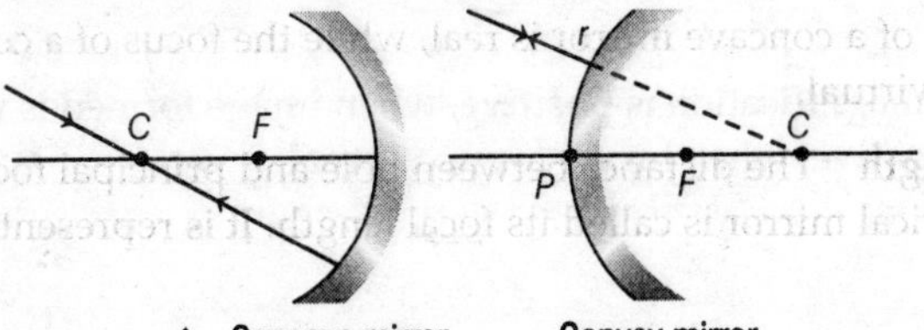

▲ Concave mirror Convex mirror

(iv) A ray incident obliquely to the principal axis, towards a pole P on the concave or convex mirror is reflected obliquely, following the laws of reflection,

i.e., $\angle i = \angle r$

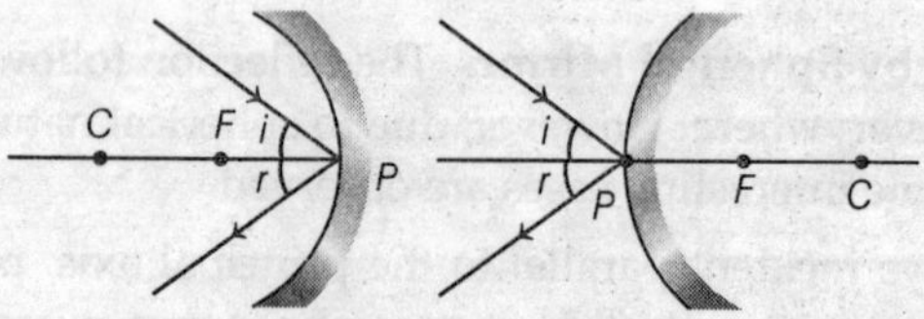

▲ Concave mirror Convex mirror

08 Sign Convention The sign convention for mirror is shown below.

Measurements	For concave mirror	For convex mirror
Distance of the object	Negative	Negative
Distance of the real image	Negative	NA
Distance of the virtual image	Positive	Positive
Focal length	Negative	Positive
Height of the object	Positive	Positive
Height of inverted real image	Negative	NA
Height of virtual erect image	Positive	Positive

09 Mirror Equation This equation gives the relationship between object distance (u), image distance (v) and the focal length (f).

The equation is $\frac{1}{v} + \frac{1}{u} = \frac{1}{f}$

10 Linear Magnification This equation is the ratio of the height of image to the height of object.

$$m = \frac{h_i}{h_o}$$
$$= -\frac{v}{u}$$

Linear magnification is **positive**, when image formed is **virtual** and **negative**, when image formed is **real**.

11 Refraction Change in path of a light ray as it passes from one medium to another is called **refraction**. When light travels from a rarer medium to a denser one, it bends towards the normal $(i > r)$ and when travels from a denser medium to a rarer one, it bends away from the normal $(i < r)$.

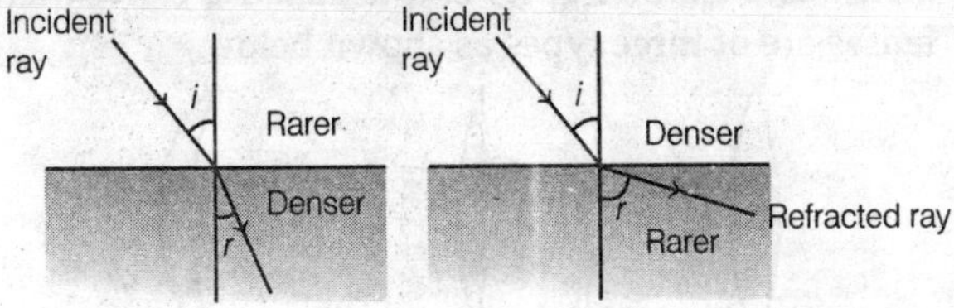

▲ Refracted ray

12 Laws of Refraction

(i) Incident ray, normal and the refracted ray, all lie in the same plane.

(ii) Ratio of sine of angle of incidence to sine of angle of refraction for light of single wavelength is constant for a given pair of media (Snell's law)

i.e., $$\frac{\sin i}{\sin r} = \mu, \text{ constant } (\mu \text{ or } \eta)$$

This constant is known as refractive index μ.

13 Refractive Index $_1\mu_2$ represents refractive index of medium 2 with respect to medium 1, when light is going from medium 1 to medium 2.

$$_1\mu_2 = \frac{\mu_2}{\mu_1} = \frac{\sin i}{\sin r}$$

where, μ_2 is called the absolute refractive index of medium 2. It is the refractive index of the medium with respect to air/vacuum.

For glass-water interface.

$$_w\mu_g = \frac{_a\mu_g}{_a\mu_w}$$

Note Refractive index of air (1.0003) is minimum and refractive index of diamond (2.42) is maximum.

14 Lens Lens is a transparent medium bounded by two surfaces, atleast one of which is curved.

Lenses are of two types

(i) **Convex or convergent lens** A lens which is thicker at the centre and thinner at its end is called a convex lens. Convex lenses are of three types as shown below.

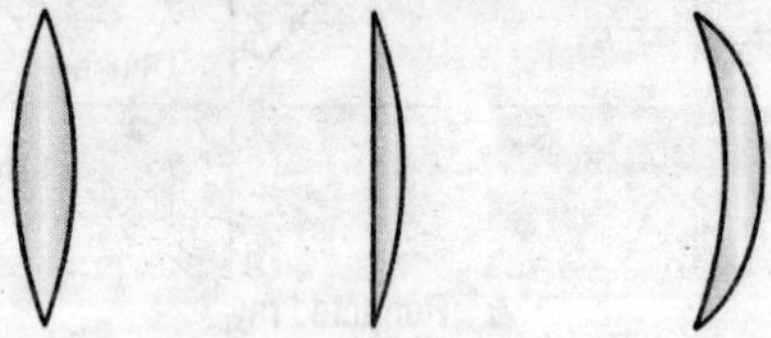

(a) Double convex lens (b) Plano-convex lens (c) Concavo-convex lens

A convex lens is also known as a converging lens because it converges a parallel beam of light rays passing through it.

(ii) **Concave or diverging lens** A lens which is thinner at the centre and thicker at its end is called a concave lens. Concave lenses are of three types as shown below.

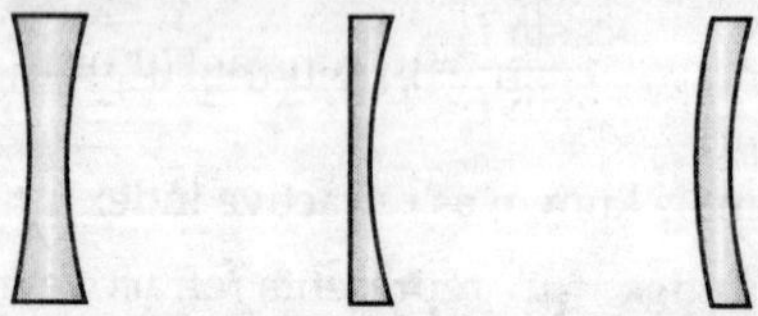

(a) Double concave lens (b) Plano-concave lens (c) Convexo-concave lens

A concave lens is also known as a diverging lens because it diverges a parallel beam of light rays passing through it.

15 Refraction Through a Lens

(i) Rays incident parallel to the principal axis, after refraction will pass through principal focus in case of convex lens and will appear to be coming from principal focus in case of concave lens.

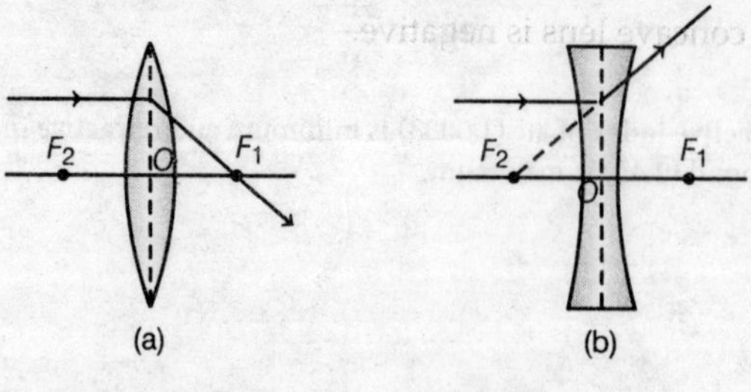

(a) (b)

(ii) Ray incident through or directed towards focus will emerge parallel to the principal axis after the refraction.

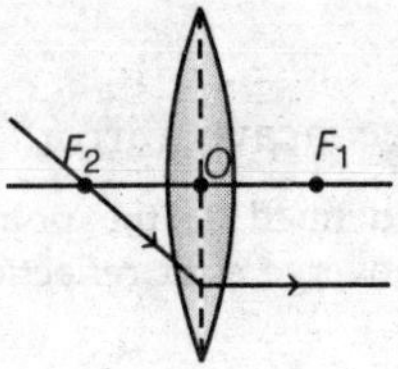

(c)

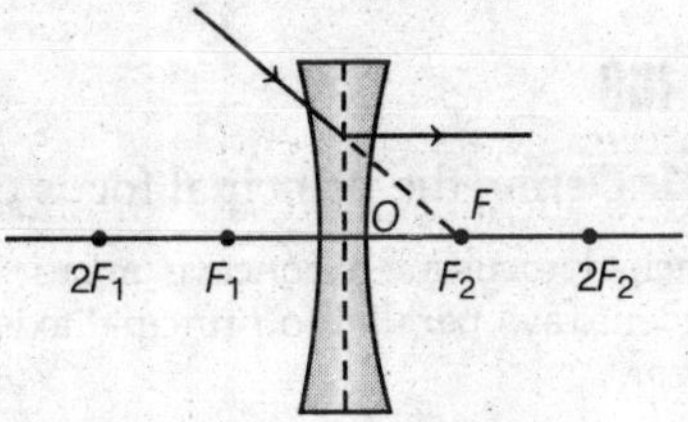

(d)

(iii) Ray directed towards optical centre will emerges out undeviated.

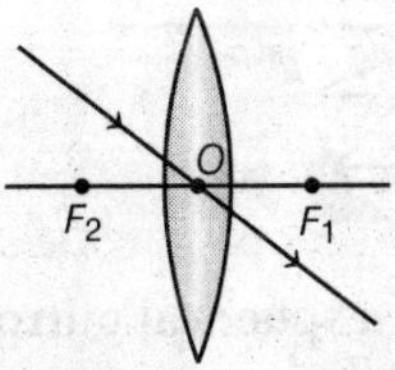

(e)

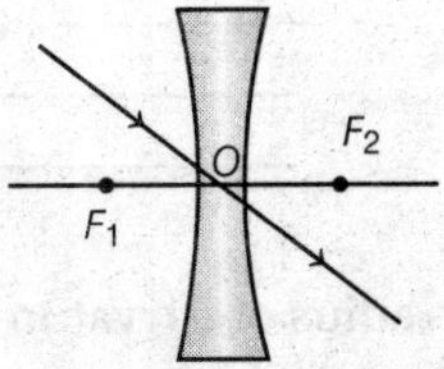

(f)

16 Lens Formula This formula gives the relationship between object distance (u), image distance (v) and the focal length (f). The lens formula is expressed as

$$\frac{1}{v} - \frac{1}{u} = \frac{1}{f}$$

17 Power of a Lens Power of a lens is defined as the reciprocal of its focal length.

$$P = \frac{1}{f}$$

SI unit of power is dioptre (D).

1 dioptre is the power of a lens whose focal length is 1 metre.

- Power of convex lens is positive.
- Power of concave lens is negative.

Intext Questions

On Page 168

Question 1 Define the principal focus of a concave mirror.

Sol. Principal focus of a concave mirror is defined as the point at which incident rays parallel to principal axis converge after reflection from the mirror.

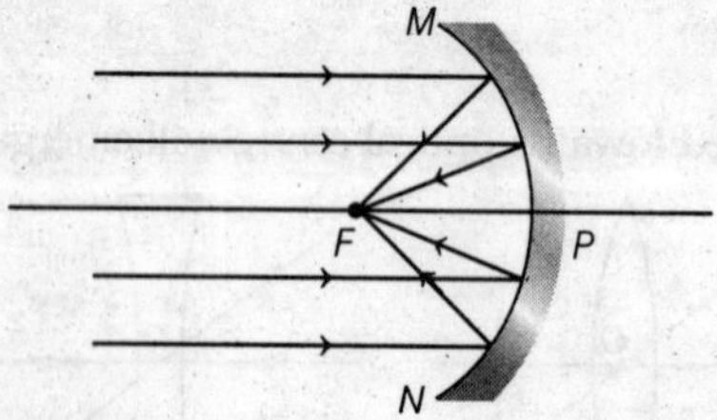

Question 2 The radius of curvature of a spherical mirror is 20 cm. What is its focal length?

Sol. Focal length $= \frac{1}{2} \times$ Radius of curvature $= \frac{1}{2} \times 20$ cm $= 10$ cm

Question 3 Name a mirror that can give an erect and enlarged image of an object.

Sol. Concave mirror.

Question 4 Why do we prefer convex mirror as a rear view mirror in vehicles?

Sol. Convex mirror has a larger aperture. So, it has a bigger field of view. So, this enables the driver of the vehicle to view larger area behind his vehicle.

On Page 171

Question 1 Find the focal length of a convex mirror whose radius of curvature is 32 cm.

Sol. Focal length $= \frac{1}{2} \times$ Radius of curvature $= \frac{1}{2} \times 32 = 16$ cm

Question 2 A concave mirror produces three times magnified (enlarged) real image of an object placed at 10 cm in front of it. Where is the image located?

Sol. Real image is inverted. So, magnification is negative.

Thus, $$m = -3 = \frac{\text{Image size}(h_i)}{\text{Object size}(h_0)}$$

$$= -\frac{\text{Image distance}}{\text{Object distance}} = -\frac{v}{u}$$

$$\Rightarrow \quad -3 = \frac{-(v)}{(-10)} \quad (\because \text{Object is placed in front of mirror})$$

$$\Rightarrow \quad -3 = \frac{v}{10}$$

Image distance $= -30$ cm

Negative sign shows that image is real, so it will be formed in front of the mirror.

On Page 176

Question 1 A ray of light travelling in air enters obliquely into water. Does the light ray bend towards the normal or away from the normal? Why?

Sol. Light bends towards the normal on entering water. This happens because water is an optically denser medium than air. When light travels from a rarer medium to denser medium, it bends towards the normal.

Question 2 Light enters from air to glass having refractive index 1.50. What is the speed of light in the glass? The speed of light in vacuum is 3×10^8 ms^{-1}.

Sol. Given, refractive index of glass ${}_a\mu_g = 1.50$

and speed of light in vacuum $c = 3 \times 10^8$ ms^{-1}

$${}_a\mu_g = \frac{\text{Speed of light in air}}{\text{Speed of light in glass}}$$

$$\text{Speed of light in glass} = \frac{c}{{}_a\mu_g}$$

$$= \frac{3 \times 10^8}{1.5} = 2 \times 10^8 \text{ m s}^{-1}$$

Mistake Alert The speed of light in any medium other than vaccum/air will be less than the speed of light in air. Sometimes, after calculation if the speed comes out to be greater than 3×10^8 ms^{-1}, recheck your calculations.

Question 3 Find out, from table 10.3, the medium having highest optical density. Also find the medium with the lowest optical density.

Sol. Absolute refractive index of some material media.

Material medium	Refractive index	Material medium	Refractive index
Air	1.0003	Canada Balsam	1.53
Ice	1.31	Rock salt	1.54
Water	1.33	Carbon disulphide	1.63
Kerosene	1.44	Ruby	1.71
Fused quartz	1.46	Sapphire	1.77
Turpentine oil	1.47	Diamond	2.42
Benzene	1.50		
Crown glass	1.52		

The medium with highest refractive index will have highest optical density. So, diamond has highest optical density.

The medium with lowest refractive index will have lowest optical density. So, air has lowest optical density.

Question 4 You are given kerosene, turpentine and water. In which of these does light travel the fastest? Use the information given in table 10.3.

Given $\mu_{kerosene} = 1.44$

$\mu_{turpentine} = 1.47$

$\mu_{water} = 1.33$

Sol. Light travels the fastest in a medium having minimum optical density or lowest refractive index.

Since, $\mu_{water} = 1.33$ is the lowest, speed of light is maximum in water.

Question 5 The refractive index of diamond is 2.42. What is the meaning of this statement?

Sol. Refractive index of any medium w.r.t. another medium indicates the extent to which bending of light takes place when it enters from first medium to the given medium.

The given value of refractive index also indicates that speed of light in diamond is $\frac{1}{2.42}$ times the speed of light in vacuum.

On Page 184

Question 1 Define 1 dioptre of power of a lens.

Sol. The power of lens is 1 dioptre when focal length of the same lens is 1 metre.

Question 2 A convex lens forms a real and inverted image of a needle at a distance of 50 cm from it. Where is the needle placed in front of convex lens if the image is equal to the size of object? Also, find the power of the lens.

Sol. Given image distance, $v = +50$ cm

Magnification, $m = -1$ (image is inverted)

$$m = \frac{v}{u}$$

$$u = \frac{v}{m} = \frac{50}{-1} = -50 \text{ cm}$$

So, needle is placed at 50 cm in front of the lens.

By lens formula,
$$\frac{1}{f} = \frac{1}{v} - \frac{1}{u}$$

$$\frac{1}{f} = \frac{1}{50} - \frac{1}{-50} = \frac{1}{25}$$

$$f = 25 \text{ cm} = 0.25 \text{ m} \qquad [\because 1 \text{ m} = 100 \text{ cm}]$$

Power,
$$P = \frac{1}{f} = \frac{1}{0.25} = 4 \text{ D}$$

Question 3 Find the power of a concave lens of focal length 2 m.

Sol.
$$\text{Power} = \frac{1}{\text{Focal length}} = -\frac{1}{2} = -0.50 \text{ D}$$

Negative sign arises due to the divergent nature of concave lens.

Exercises

Question 1 Which one of the following material cannot be used to make a lens?

(a) Water (b) Glass (c) Plastic (d) Clay

Sol. Clay is not transparent, so it cannot be used to make a lens.

Question 2 The image formed by a concave mirror is observed to be virtual, erect and larger than the object. Where should be the position of the object?

(a) Between the principal focus and centre of curvature
(b) At centre of curvature
(c) Beyond centre of curvature
(d) Between pole of the mirror and its principal focus

Sol. (d) When object is placed between pole and principal focus of a mirror, then virtual, erect and magnified image is obtained.

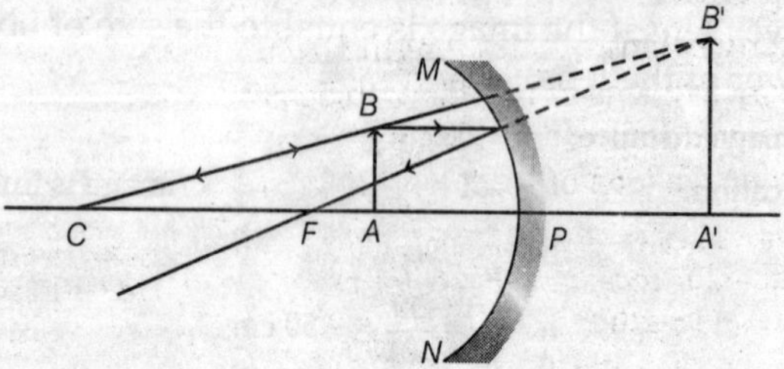

Question 3 Where should an object be placed in front of a convex lens to get a real image of the size of object?

(a) At the principal focus of the lens
(b) At twice the focal length
(c) At infinity
(d) Between the optical centre of the lens and its principal focus

Sol. (b) To obtain a real image of the size of the object, it should be placed at twice the focal length of a convex lens.

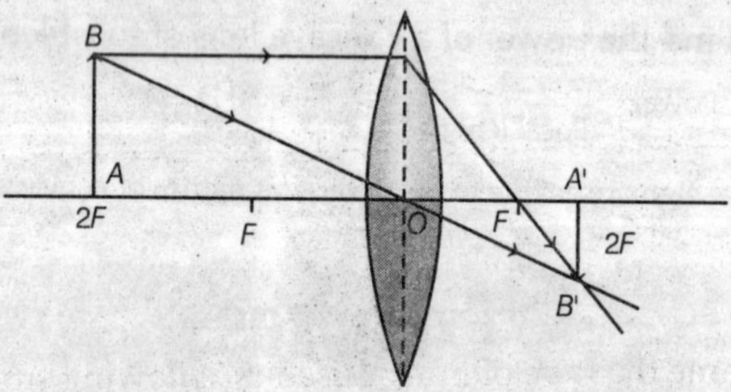

Question 4 A spherical mirror and a thin spherical lens have each a focal length of –15 cm. The mirror and lens are likely to be

(a) both concave
(b) both convex
(c) mirror is concave and lens is convex
(d) mirror is convex and lens is concave

Sol. (d) The focal length is taken as negative for both concave mirror and concave lens.

Question 5 No matter how far you stand from a mirror, your image appears erect. The mirror is likely to be

(a) only plane
(b) only concave
(c) only convex
(d) either plane or convex

Sol. (d) Plane mirrors and convex mirrors always form the erect images.

Question 6 Which of the following lenses would you prefer to use while reading small letters found in a dictionary?

(a) A convex lens of focal length 50 cm.
(b) A concave lens of focal length 50 cm.
(c) A convex lens of focal length 5 cm.
(d) A concave lens of focal length 5 cm.

Sol. (c) Convex lens is used as magnifying glass. Since, the power is the reciprocal of the focal length. So, for more power, we will use convex lens of small focal length.

Question 7 We wish to obtain an erect image of an object, using a concave mirror of focal length 15 cm. What should be the range of distance of the object from the mirror? What is the nature of image? Is the image larger or smaller than the object? Draw a ray diagram to show the image formation in this case.

Sol. The object should be kept at a distance less than 15 cm from the mirror. The image is virtual and erect. The image is larger than the object.

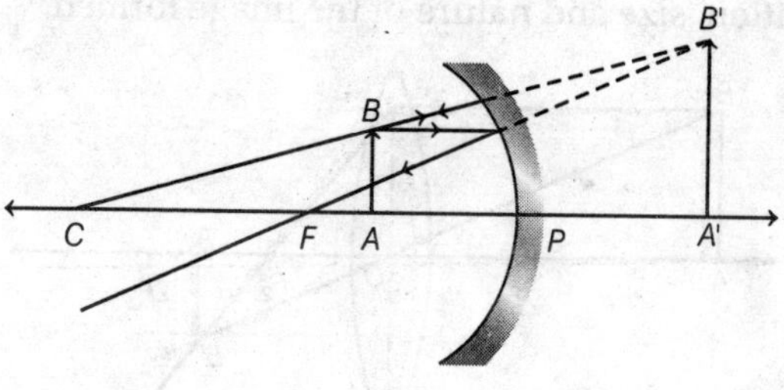

Question 8 Name the type of mirror used in following situations?

(a) Headlights of car
(b) Side/rear view mirror of a vehicle
(c) Solar furnace

Support your solution with reason.

Sol. (a) Concave mirror, to get powerful parallel beam of light.

(b) Convex mirror to get larger field of view and erect image.

(c) Concave mirror, as it can converge light of the sun in a small area.

Question 9 One-half of a convex lens is covered with a black paper. Will this lens produce a complete image of the object? Verify your solution experimentally. Explain your observations.

Sol. The lens will produce a complete image, but the image will have lower intensity and brightness because in the lower part of the lens the rays are blocked.

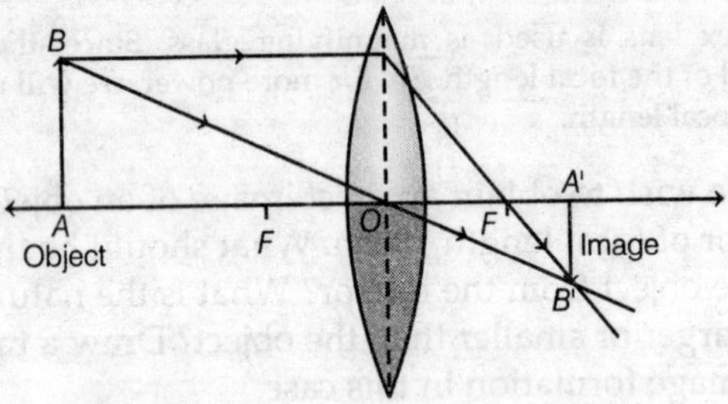

Question 10 An object 5 cm in length is placed 25 cm away from a converging lens of focal length 10 cm. Draw the ray diagram and find the position, size and nature of the image formed.

Sol.

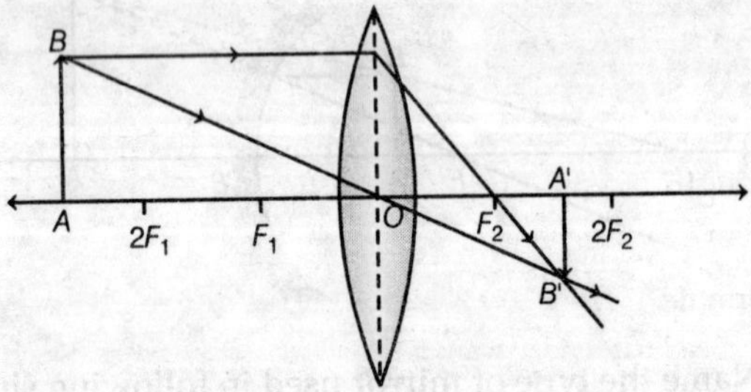

Object size, $h_0 = 5$ cm, Image size, $h_i = ?$

Object distance, $u = -25$ cm, Image distance, $v = ?$

Focal length, $f = 10$ cm

By lens formula,

$$\frac{1}{f} = \frac{1}{v} - \frac{1}{u}$$

or $\frac{1}{v} = \frac{1}{f} + \frac{1}{u} = \frac{1}{10} + \frac{1}{-25} = \frac{3}{50}$ or $v = \frac{50}{3} = 16.66$ cm from the lens.

also for a converging lens $\frac{h_i}{h_0} = \frac{v}{u}$ (from the definition of magnification)

size of image, $h_i = h_0 \times \frac{v}{u} = 5 \times \frac{50}{3 \times (-25)}$

$h_i = -3.33$ cm

(negative sign implies that diminished inverted image is formed)

The image is real in nature.

Question 11 A concave lens of focal length 15 cm forms an image 10 cm from the lens. How far is the object placed from the lens? Draw the ray diagram.

Sol. Given $f = -15$ cm

$v = -10$ cm

By lens formula, $\frac{1}{f} = \frac{1}{v} - \frac{1}{u}$

or $$\frac{1}{u} = \frac{1}{v} - \frac{1}{f} = \frac{1}{-10} - \frac{1}{-15} = \frac{1}{15} - \frac{1}{10} = \frac{-1}{30}$$

$u = -30$ cm from the lens.

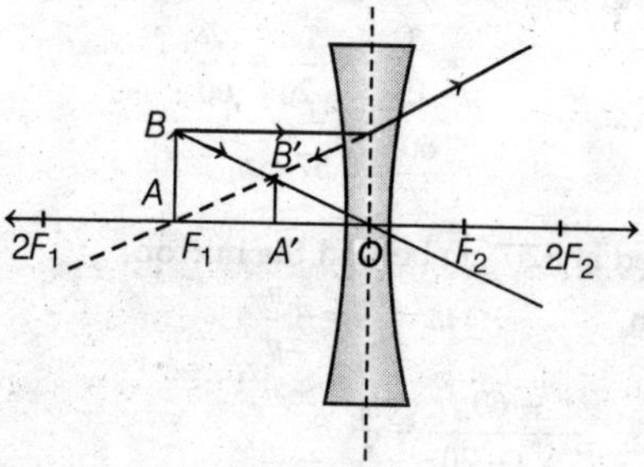

Thus, the object is placed at 30 cm from the concave lens.

Question 12 An object is placed at a distance of 10 cm from a convex mirror of focal length 15 cm. Find the position and nature of the image.

Sol. Given, $u = -10$ cm, $f = 15$ cm

By mirror formula, $$\frac{1}{f} = \frac{1}{v} + \frac{1}{u}$$

$$\Rightarrow \quad \frac{1}{v} = \frac{1}{15} - \frac{1}{(-10)}$$

$$\Rightarrow \quad \frac{1}{v} = \frac{1}{15} + \frac{1}{10} = \frac{5}{30}$$

$v = 6$ cm from the lens

Image is formed 6 cm behind the mirror.

Image is virtual and erect.

Note In the questions related to the use of mirror and lens formula, proper sign convention must be used.

Question 13 The magnification produced by a plane mirror is +1. What does it mean?

Sol. If magnification is 1, the image size is same as that of object size. Since, magnification is positive, the image is erect and virtual.

Question 14 An object 5.0 cm in length is placed at a distance of 20 cm in front of a convex mirror of radius of curvature 30 cm. Find the position of image, its nature and size.

Sol. Given, Object size, $h_0 = 5$ cm, Object distance, $u = -20$ cm

Radius of curvature = 30 cm, Focul length, $f = \frac{30}{2} = 15$ cm

Position of image (By mirror formula)

$$\frac{1}{f} = \frac{1}{u} + \frac{1}{v}$$

or $$\frac{1}{v} = \frac{1}{f} - \frac{1}{u}$$

$$= \frac{1}{15} - \frac{1}{-20} = \frac{7}{60}$$

$\Rightarrow$ $$v = \frac{60}{7} = 8.57 \text{ cm}$$

Image is formed at 8.57 cm behind the mirror.

$\therefore$ Magnification, $$m = \frac{h_i}{h_0} = -\frac{v}{u}$$

$$\frac{-60}{7 \times (-20)} = \frac{h_i}{5}$$

$$h_i = \frac{-60 \times 5}{-7 \times 20} = 2.14 \text{ cm}$$

Image is diminshed, erect and virtual.

Note Convex mirrors always form virtual, upright and diminished image, regadless of object position.

Question 15 An object of size 7.0 cm is placed at 27 cm in front of a concave mirror of focal length 18 cm. At what distance from the mirror should the screen be placed, so that a sharp focussed image can be obtained? Find the size and nature of image.

Sol. Given, $h_0 = 7$ cm,

$u = -27$ cm,

$f = -18$ cm.

By mirror formula, $$\frac{1}{v} = \frac{1}{f} - \frac{1}{u}$$

$$= \frac{1}{-18} - \frac{1}{-27} = \frac{-1}{54}$$

$$v = -54 \text{ cm}$$

Screen should be placed at 54 cm in front of the mirror.

Now, $$\frac{h_i}{h_0} = -\frac{v}{u}$$

$$\frac{h_i}{7} = -\frac{(-54)}{-27}$$

or $$h_i = -14 \text{ cm}$$

So, image is double the size of object. Also, image is real and inverted (since, h_i is negative).

Mistake Alert In this type of problem, remember to use negative values for object distance and focal length when dealing with a concave mirror.

Question 16 Find the focal length of a lens of power – 2D. What type of lens is this?

Sol. Focal length $= \frac{1}{\text{Power}} = \frac{1}{(-2)} = -0.5 \text{ m}$

Since, f is negative, lens is concave.

Question 17 A doctor has prescribed a corrective lens of power + 1.5 D. Find the focal length of the lens. Is the prescribed lens diverging or converging?

Sol. Given, power of lens, $P = +1.5$ D. Since power is positive, lens is converging or convex.

Focal length $= \frac{1}{\text{Power}} = \frac{1}{1.5} = 0.66 \text{ m}$

$\Rightarrow \quad f = 0.66 \times 100 = 66 \text{ cm}$ [1 m = 100 cm]

DIKSHA APP Questions

☐ Multiple Choice Questions

Q.1 The power of a lens of focal length 25 cm in dioptre is

(a) 0.25 D (b) 2.5 D (c) 4.0 D (d) 0.4 D

Sol. (c) The power of a lens is given by, $P \text{ (in D)} = \dfrac{1}{f \text{ (in m)}} = \dfrac{100}{f \text{ (in cm)}}$

$$\Rightarrow \quad P = \frac{100}{25} = 4 \text{ D}$$

Q.2 An object 5 cm in height is placed at 30 cm in front of a convex mirror of radius of curvature 40 cm. The nature, size and position of image is

(a) virtual erect image of 2 cm height is formed at 12 cm behind the mirror.

(b) virtual erect image of 2 cm height is formed at 12 cm in front of the mirror.

(c) real inverted image of 2 cm height is formed at 12 cm behind the mirror.

(d) real inverted image of 2 cm height is formed at 12 cm in front of the mirror.

Sol. (a) Since, the mirror is convex, it always forms a virtual, eraector and diminished image, regardless of the object's position. The image is located behind the mirror at a position closer to it than the object.

Q.3 While trying to identify convex lens from a group of glass pieces lying on a table, a student found that there is a lens that always forms a virtual and diminished image. This lens is

(a) plano convex lens (b) double concave lens

(c) double convex lens (d) plane glass sheet

Sol. (b) A double concave lens always forms a virtual and diminished image.

Q.4 A child is standing in front of a magic mirror. She finds the image of her head bigger, the middle portion of her body of the same size and that of her legs smaller. The combinations for the magic mirror from the top will be

(a) plane, convex and concave (b) convex, concave and plane

(c) concave, plane and convex (d) convex, plane and concave

Sol. (c) Concave mirrors (of large focal length) can be used to see a larger image of the head, the plane mirror for middle portion to see her body of the same size and convex mirror to see the diminished image of leg. Hence, the combinations for magic mirror from the top is concave mirror, plane mirror and convex mirror.

☐ Very Short Answer Type

Q.1 List the minimum number of rays required for locating the image formed by a concave mirror for an object?

Sol. An image can be formed with just two principal rays for any type of mirror.

Q.2 If the size of image obtained by a spherical mirror is twice the size of the object, identify the mirror.

Sol. A concave mirror can produce both magnified and diminished image of the object whereas a convex mirror can only produce a diminished image of the object. Hence, the mirror is concave mirror.

☐ Short Answer Type

Q.1 State important properties of images formed by a plane mirror.

Sol. The properties of image formed by a plane mirror are:

(i) Image formed by a plane mirror is always virtual and erect.

(ii) The size of the image is equal to the size of the object i.e. the magnification of image formed by a plane mirror is 1.

(iii) The image formed by a plane mirror is at the same distance behind the mirror as the distance of the object in front of it.

(iv) The image formed by a plane mirror is laterally inverted.

Q.2 "Power of a lens measures its convergence". Comment on this statement. Also, if two thin lens of power +3.5 D and +2 D are placed in contact, find the power of the combination.

Sol. Power of lens is given by $P = \frac{1}{f}$. If power of lens increases then focal length of the lens decreases. Hence, power of lens measures the convergence.

Power of the combination, $P = P_1 + P_2$

$$P = (+3.5) + (+2)$$

$$P = +5.5 \text{ D}$$

Q.3 A student observes that when a ray of light is incident obliquely on the face of a rectangular glass slab placed in air, it emerges from the opposite face laterally displaced parallel to the incident ray. Analyse the factors on which the lateral displacement of the emergent ray depends.

Sol. Lateral displacement depends upon

(i) thickness of the glass slab (ii) angle of incidence

(iii) refractive index of the glass slab

Q.4 Comment on the size of image and nature of image in the following cases. Also, identify the type of mirror.

(a) $m = +1$ (b) $m < +1$ (c) $m > +1$

Sol. (a) $m = +1$ implies that the image size is equal to the size of the object. Also, since the magnification is positive, this means that the image formed is erect. Only a plane mirror could form such an image.

(b) $m < +1$ implies that a diminished and erect image is formed which could only be formed by a convex mirror.

(c) $m > +1$ implies that a magnified and erect image is formed which could only be formed by a concave mirror.

Q.5 The image of a candle flame placed at a distance of 30 cm from the lens is formed on a screen placed on the other side of the lens at a distance of 60 cm from the optical centre of the lens. Identify the type of lens and calculate its focal length.

Sol. Given, Object distance, $u = -30$ cm, Image distance, $v = +60$ cm

Using lens formula, $\frac{1}{f} = \frac{1}{v} - \frac{1}{u} \Rightarrow \frac{1}{f} = \frac{1}{60} - \frac{1}{(-30)} \Rightarrow \frac{1}{f} = \frac{3}{60} \Rightarrow f = 20$ cm

Since, the focal length is positive, the lens is a convex lens.

Q.6 The incident ray makes an angle of 30° with the surface of plane mirror. Find the angle of reflection.

Sol.

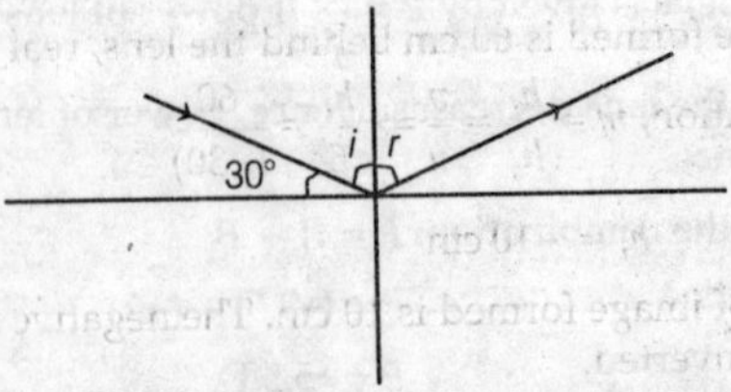

Angle of incidence, $i = 90° - 30° = 60°$

Angle of reflection, r = Angle of incidence, i (Using law of reflection) = 60°

Q.7 Comment on the size and position of the image formed by a concave mirror of focal length 15 cm when an object is placed

(i) at 20 cm

(ii) at 10 cm

(iii) at 35 cm in front of the mirror without calculations.

Sol. (i) Since, the object is placed beyond focus, between focus and centre of curvature, therefore the image formed is enlarged and beyond 2F.

(ii) Since, the object is placed between focus and pole, therefore the image formed is enlarged and behind the mirror.

(iii) Since, the object is placed beyond centre of curvature, therefore the image formed is diminished and between focus and centre of curvature.

☐ Long Answer Type

Q.1 List any two uses of convex mirrors. *A* 5 cm tall object is placed perpendicular to the principal axis of a convex lens of focal length 20 cm. The distance of the object from the lens is 30 cm. Find the nature, position and size of the image. Also, find its magnification.

Sol. The uses of convex mirrors are

(i) Convex mirrors are used as rear view mirrors in vehicles.

(ii) Convex mirrors are also used for security purposes at various places. They are placed near ATMs so that customers can check if someone is behind them.

Given, object size, $h_o = 5$ cm, Distance of object, $u = -30$ cm

Focal length, $f = 20$ cm

Using the lens formula, $\frac{1}{f} = \frac{1}{v} - \frac{1}{u} \Rightarrow \frac{1}{v} = \frac{1}{f} + \frac{1}{u}$

$\Rightarrow \quad \frac{1}{v} = \frac{1}{20} - \frac{1}{30} \Rightarrow \frac{1}{v} = \frac{1}{60}$

$\Rightarrow \quad v = 60$ cm

The image formed is 60 cm behind the lens, real and inverted.

Magnification, $m = \frac{h_i}{h_o} = \frac{v}{u} \Rightarrow \frac{h_i}{5} = \frac{60}{(-30)}$

$\Rightarrow \quad h_i = -10$ cm

The size of image formed is 10 cm. The negative sign indicated that the image is inverted.

Also, the magnification, $m = \frac{h_i}{h_o} = -\frac{10}{5} = -2$

Q.2 Define refractive index of a medium. On what factors does the refractive index of a medium depend?
With respect to air, the refractive index of ice is 1.31 and that of rock salt is 1.54. Calculate the refractive index of rock salt with respect to ice.

Sol. Refractive index is the measure of the extent of deviation in the path of a light ray when it passes from one medium to another.

The refractive index for a given pair of media depends upon the speed of light in the two media, wavelength of light and density of the media.

Now, refractive index of ice with respect to air, ${}^a\mu_i = 1.31$

and refractive index of rock salt with respect to air, ${}^a\mu_r = 1.54$

The refractive index of rock salt with respect to ice,

$$ {}^i\mu_r = \frac{{}^a\mu_r}{{}^a\mu_i} $$

$$ {}^i\mu_r = \frac{1.54}{1.31} = 1.176 $$

Q.3 (i) The radius of curvature of concave mirror is 50 cm. Where should an object be placed from the mirror so as to form its image at infinity? Justify your answer.

(ii) An object is placed at 25 cm in front of a concave mirror of focal length 15 cm. At what distance from the mirror a screen be placed in order to obtain a sharp image?

Sol.

(i) Radius of curvature, $R = 50$ cm

Focal length, $f = \frac{R}{2} = \frac{50}{2} = 25$ cm

Since, an object placed at the focus forms the image at infinity, therefore, the object must be placed at focus, *i.e.*, $u = -25$ cm

(ii) $u = -25$ cm, $f = -15$ cm

Using mirror formula, $\frac{1}{f} = \frac{1}{v} + \frac{1}{u}$

$$ \Rightarrow \quad \frac{1}{-15} = \frac{1}{v} + \frac{1}{-25} $$

$$ \Rightarrow \quad \frac{1}{-15} + \frac{1}{25} = \frac{1}{v} $$

$$ \Rightarrow \quad \frac{1}{v} = \frac{1}{25} - \frac{1}{15} $$

$$\Rightarrow \quad \frac{1}{v} = \frac{3-5}{75}$$

$$\Rightarrow \quad v = -37.5 \text{ cm}$$

Hence, a screen must be placed at 37.5 cm from the mirror in the same side as that of the object.

Q.4 Justify why is convex lens called converging lens and concave lens a diverging lens?

With the help of ray diagrams, explain the formation of images by a concave lens for the following positions of the object

(i) object at infinity

(ii) object between infinity and optical centre of the lens

Sol. A convex lens is called a converging lens because when parallel rays of light fall on such a lens, the rays get refracted and after refraction they converge at a point some distance away from the lens called focal point.

A concave lens is called a diverging lens because when parallel rays of light fall on such a lens, the rays get refracted and after refraction they diverge and they seem to appear to be coming from a point called focal point.

When an object is placed at infinity, concave lens will form virtual, erect, point sized image at the f.

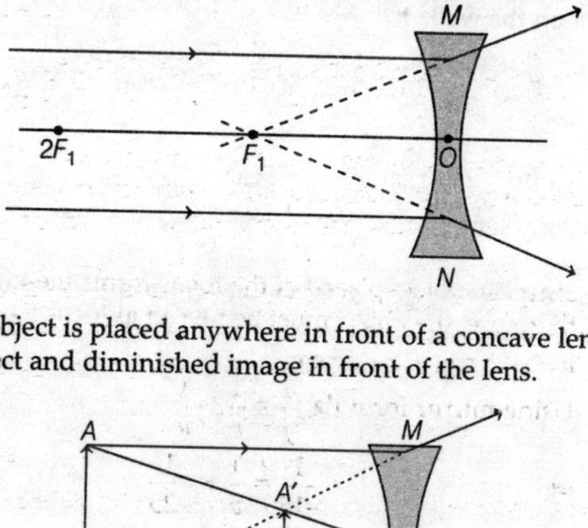

When an object is placed anywhere in front of a concave lens, it forms virtual, erect and diminished image in front of the lens.

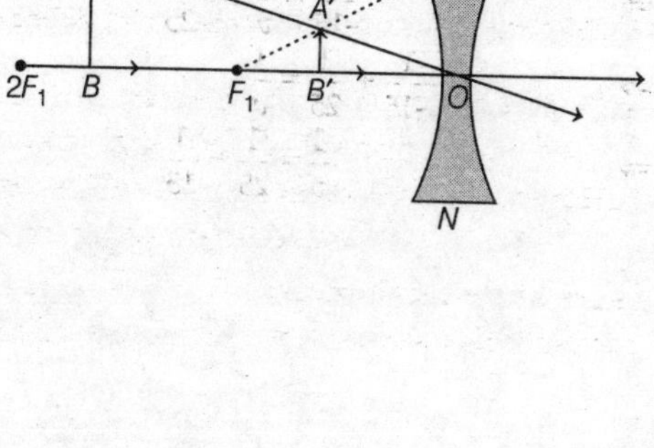

Q.5 A student wants to project the image of a candle flame on the walls of school lab by using a mirror. Which type of mirror should he use and why? At what distance in terms of focal length of the mirror should he place the candle flame so as to get the magnified image on the wall?
Draw a ray diagram to show the formation of image in this case. Can he use this mirror to project a diminished image of the candle flame on the same wall. Explain your answer.

Sol. A concave mirror should be used, as only a concave mirror produces real image of an object that can be obtained on the screen, in this case.

The object should be placed between *F* and 2*F*, so as to get a magnified image on the wall.

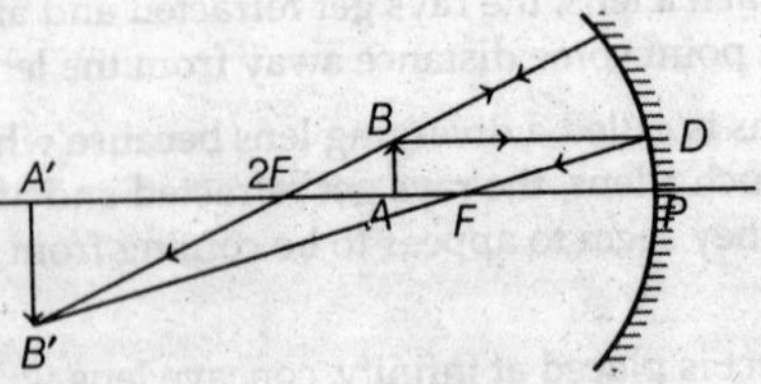

When the candle flame is placed beyond 2*F*, a diminished real image will be formed on the wall.

The Human Eye and the Colourful World

CHAPTER 10

Important Points

01 Human Eye Human eye is one of the most valuable and sensitive sense organs. It enables us to see the wonderful world and the colour around us. The detailed structure of human eye is shown below.

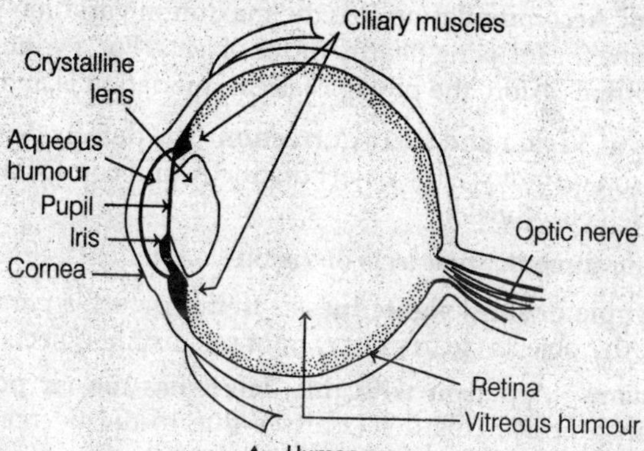

▲ Human eye

02 Accommodation It is the ability or the property of the eye lens to adjust its focal length. However, the focal length cannot be decreased or increased below a certain limit, due to which a healthy person cannot view clearly, if the object is held too close (*i.e.,* less than 25 cm).

For distant objects

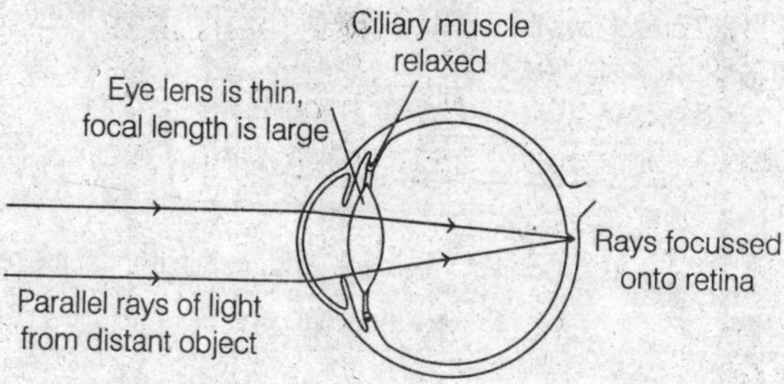

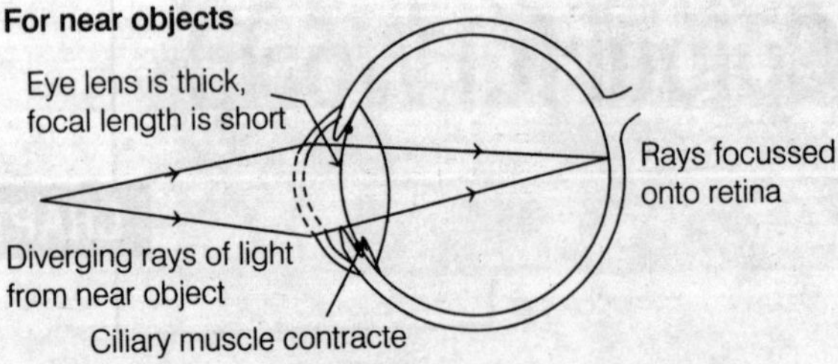

03 The ciliary muscles help in accommodation by changing the curvature of the lens. When muscles are relaxed, the lens becomes thin and its focal length is increased. This enables us to see distant object clearly. While viewing nearby objects, the ciliary muscles contract, the lens becomes thicker and its focal length decreases.

04 **Power of Accommodation** It is the maximum variation in power of eye lens for focusing nearby or far objects. For a young adult with normal vision, the power of accommodation is about 4D.

05 **Defects of Vision and their Correction** The defects due to which the person cannot see the object distinctly and comfortably, are called defects of vision.

There are three main defects of vision

(i) **Myopia or short sightedness** In this defect, a person can see nearby objects clearly but cannot see distant objects clearly.

Causes A person with this defect has the far point nearer than infinity. This defect arises due to the decrease in focal length of the lens due to either

(a) excessive curvature of eye lens.

(b) elongation of the eye ball, as a result the image is formed before retina.

Remedy This defect can be corrected by using concave lens of appropriate power.

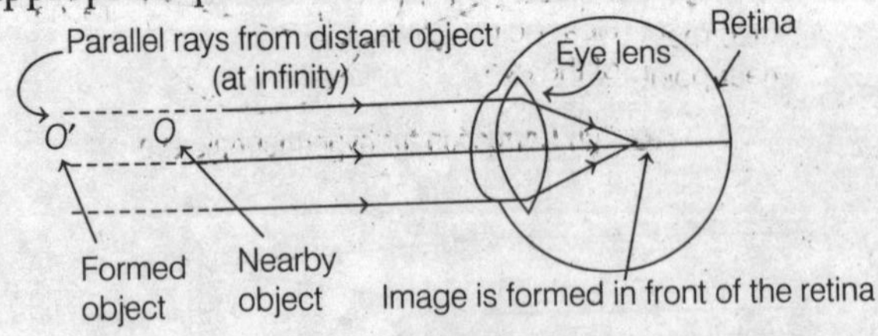

▲ (i) Myopic eye

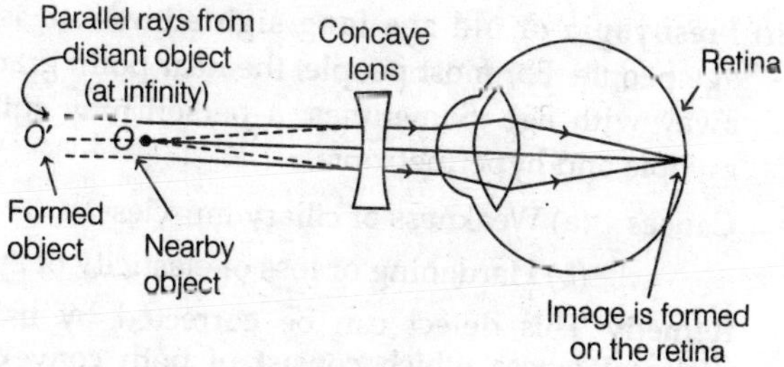

▲ (ii) Correction for myopic eye

(ii) **Hypermetropia or long sightedness** In this defect, a person can see distant objects clearly but cannot see nearby objects clearly. A person with this defect has the near point farther away from normal near point (25 cm).

Causes This defect arises due to following reasons

(a) Focal length of eye lens become large,

(b) Eye ball become too short so that the image is formed behind retina.

Remedy This defect can be corrected by using convex lens of appropriate power.

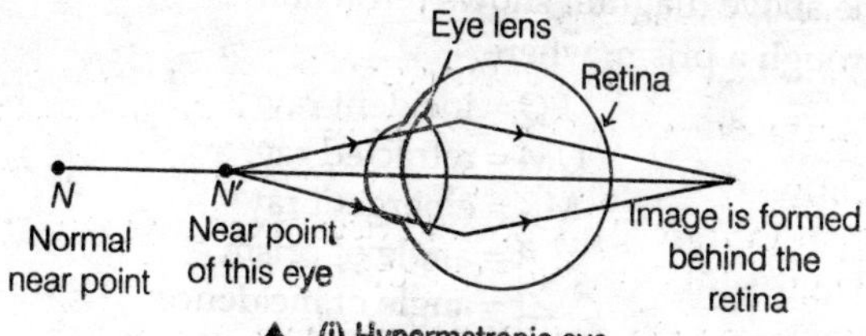

▲ (i) Hypermetropic eye

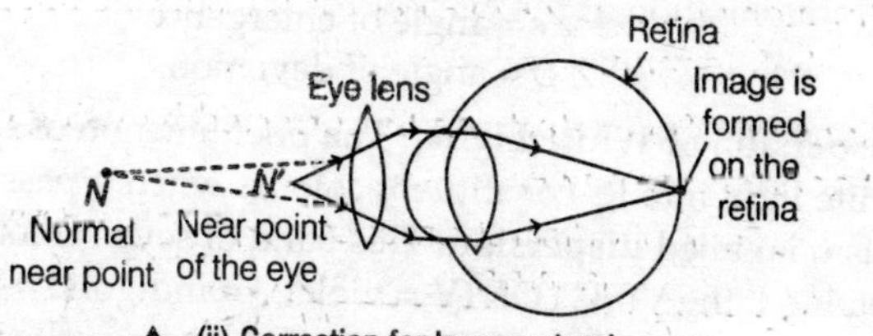

▲ (ii) Correction for hypermetropic eye

(iii) **Presbyopia or old age long sightedness** It is found in old age people. For most people, the near point gradually recedes away with age. Sometimes, a person may suffer from both myopia and hypermetropia.

Causes (a) Weakness of ciliary muscles

(b) Hardening or loss of elasticity of eye lens.

Remedy This defect can be corrected by using bifocal or varifocal lenses which consist of both convex and concave lenses. The upper portion consists of a concave lens and lower portion consist of convex lens.

06 Refraction of Light through a Prism Prism is a transparent refracting medium bounded by atleast two lateral surfaces, inclined to each other at a certain angle (60° or 45°). It has two triangular bases and three rectangular lateral surfaces.

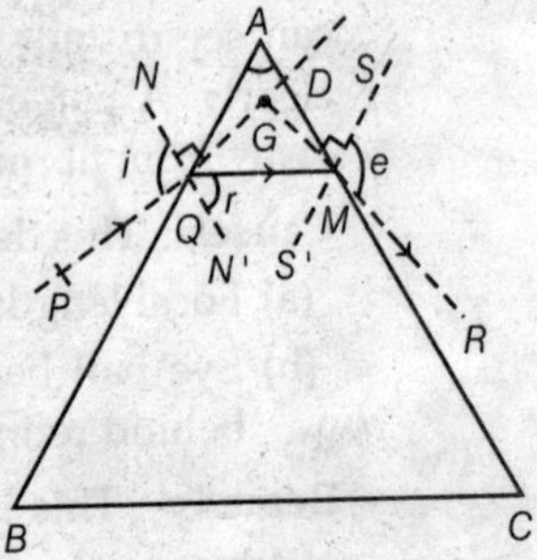

The angle between two lateral surfaces is called angle of prism (A).

The above diagram shows refraction through a prism, where;

PQ = incident ray
QM = refracted ray
MR = emergent ray
$\angle A$ = angle of prism
$\angle i$ = angle of incidence
$\angle r$ = angle of refraction
$\angle e$ = angle of emergence
$\angle D$ = angle of deviation.

07 Dispersion of White Light The phenomenon of splitting of white light into its constituent colours when it passes through a prism is called **dispersion.** This band of seven colours so obtained, the VIBGYOR (V = violet, I = indigo, B = blue, G = green, Y = yellow, O = orange, R = red) is called **spectrum.**

Isaac Newton was the first one to use a glass prism to obtain the spectrum of light.

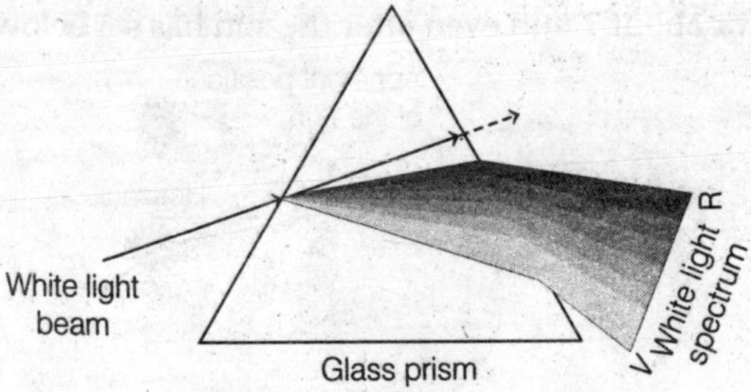

▲ Dispersion of white light by a glass prism

08 Atmospheric Refraction The earth's atmosphere is not uniform throughout, its density goes on changing as we move up or down. It can be considered to be consisting of layers of different densities, which act as rarer or denser medium with respect to each other. Due to this, when the light rays pass through the earths atmosphere, they undergo refraction. The refraction of light due to these layers is called atmospheric refraction.

Some phenomena based on atmospheric refraction are

(i) **Twinkling of stars** The twinkling of a star is due to atmospheric refraction of starlight. As the light from the star enters the earth's atmosphere, it undergoes refraction due to varying optical densities of air at various altitudes. The continuously changing atmosphere refracts the light by different amounts. In this way, the starlight reaching our eyes increases and decreases continuously and the star appears to twinkle at night.

(ii) **Advance sunrise and delayed sunset** This is because of atmospheric refraction. When the sun is slightly below the horizon, the sun's light coming from less dense to more dense air, is refracted downwards. Because of this, the sun appears to be raised above the horizon and so the rising sun can be seen about 2 min before actual sunrise.

Similarly, due to atmospheric refraction the sun can be seen for about 2 min even after the sun has set below horizon.

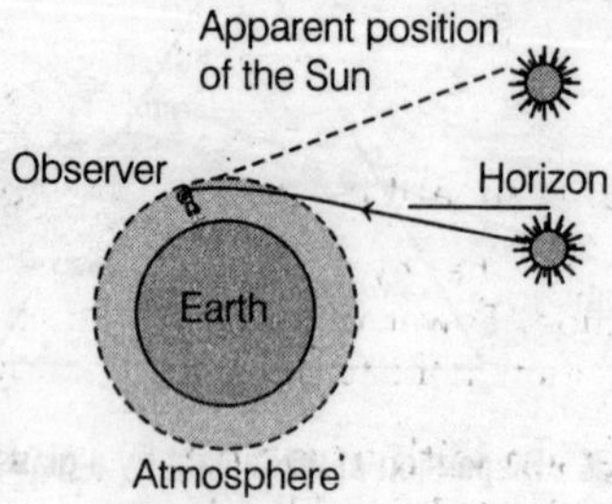

▲ Atmospheric refraction effect at sunrise and sunset

09 Scattering of Light Scattering of light refers to the process by which small particles or molecules in the atmosphere cause light to change its direction. The colour of scattered light depends on the size of scattering particles. Very fine particles scatter mainly blue light while particles of larger size scatter light of longer wavelengths.

Some phenomena based on scattering of light are given below.

(i) **Tyndall effect** The path of a beam of light through a true solution is not scattered.

The scattering of light when it passes through a colloidal solution is called **Tyndall effect**. The earth's atmosphere is a heterogenous mixture of minute particles of smoke, tiny water droplets, suspended particles of dust and molecules of air, which becomes visible due to scattering of light.

(ii) **Colour of the sky** During the day time, sky appears blue. This is because the size of the particles in the atmosphere is smaller than the wavelength of visible light, so they scatter the light of shorter wavelengths (blue end of spectrum) and hence, the sky appears blue. It should be noted that the sky appears black to the passengers flying at higher altitudes because scattering of light is not prominent at such height due to the absence of particles.

(iii) **Colour of sun at sunrise and sunset** At sunrise and sunset, the sun appear red. Light from the sun near the horizon passes through thicker layers of air and covers larger distance in the atmosphere before reaching our eyes. Near the horizon most of the blue light and shorter wavelength is scattered away by the particles. Therefore, the light that reaches our eyes is of longer wavelength. This give rise to the reddish appearance.

Intext Questions

On Page 164

Question 1 What is meant by power of accommodation of the eye?

Sol. The ability of the eye lens to adjust its focal length is called accommodation. Power of accommodation of the eye is the maximum possible variation in the focal length of eye lens.

Question 2 A person with myopic eye cannot see objects beyond 1.2 m distinctly. What should be the type of the corrective lens used to restore proper vision?

Sol. To correct the defect, the lens should be used to form the images at 1.2 m

So, $v = -1.2$ m, $u = -\infty$

From lens formula, $$\frac{1}{f} = \frac{1}{v} - \frac{1}{u}$$

or $$\frac{1}{f} = \frac{1}{(-1.2)} - \frac{1}{(-\infty)}$$

$$f = -1.2 \text{ m}$$

Since the total length is negative, a concave lens is to be used

$$\text{Power} = \frac{1}{f}$$

$$= \frac{1}{-1.2} = -0.83 \text{ D}$$

Question 3 What is the far point and near point of the human eye with normal vision?

Sol. Far point = Infinity; Near point = 25 cm

Question 4 A student has difficulty reading the blackboard while sitting in the last row. What could be the defect the child is suffering from? How can it be corrected?

Sol. He is suffering from myopia/near sightedness because he is not able to see the distant objects properly. This defect can be corrected by using a concave lens of suitable power.

Mistake Alert In this problem, don't confuse myopia (where distant objects appear blurry) with hypermetropia (where near objects appear blurry).

Exercises

Question 1 The human eye can focus on objects at different distances by adjusting the focal length of the eye lens. This is due to

(a) presbyopia
(b) accommodation
(c) near sightedness
(d) far sightedness

Sol. (b) Accomodation is the ability of eye lens to focus both near and distant objects by adjusting its focal length.

Question 2 The human eye forms the image of an object at its

(a) cornea
(b) iris
(c) pupil
(d) retina

Sol. (d) Retina is the light sensitive surface of eye which acts like screen on which the image is formed.

Question 3 The least distance of distinct vision for a young adult with normal vision is about

(a) 25 m
(b) 2.5 cm
(c) 25 cm
(d) 2.5 m

Sol. (c) The minimum distance at which an object can be seen most distinctly without any strain is 25 cm.

Question 4 The change in focal length of an eye lens is caused by action of the

(a) pupil
(b) retina
(c) ciliary muscles
(d) iris

Sol. (c) Ciliary muscles contract and expand in order to change the lens shape for focusing image at retina.

Question 5 A person needs a lens of power – 5.5 dioptres for correcting his distant vision. For correcting his near vision he needs a lens of power + 1.5D. What is the focal length of the lens required for correcting (i) distant vision (ii) near vision?

Sol. (i) Focal length $= \dfrac{1}{\text{Power}}$

$$= -\frac{1}{5.5}$$

$$= -0.18 \text{ m}$$

$$= -18 \text{ cm (concave lens)}$$

(ii) Focal length $= \dfrac{1}{\text{Power}}$

$$= +\frac{1}{1.5}$$

$$= 0.66 \text{ m}$$

$$= 66 \text{ cm (convex lens)}$$

Mistake Alert In this type of problem, ensure you use the correct sign for power negative for concave lenses and positive for convex lenses.

Question 6 The far point of a myopic person is 80 cm in front of the eye. What is the nature and power of the lens required to correct the problem?

Sol. For correcting myopia, concave lens is required.

The image of a distant object should be formed at 80 cm by the concave lens.

$\therefore$ $u = -\infty,$

$v = -80$ cm

By lens formula, $\dfrac{1}{f} = \dfrac{1}{v} - \dfrac{1}{u}$

$$= \frac{1}{-80} - \frac{1}{\infty} = \frac{-1}{80}$$

$$\text{Power} = \frac{1}{\text{Focal length}}$$

$$= \frac{1}{0.8 \text{ m}}$$

$$= 1.25 \text{ D} \quad (80 \text{ cm} = 0.8 \text{ m})$$

Concave lens has negative power = – 1.25 D

Question 7 Make a diagram to show how hypermetropia is corrected. The near point of a hypermetropic eye is 1 m. What is the power of the lens required to correct this defect? Assume that near point of the normal eye is 25 cm.

Sol. Here, Objects distance, $u = -25$ cm

Image distance, $v = -100$ cm

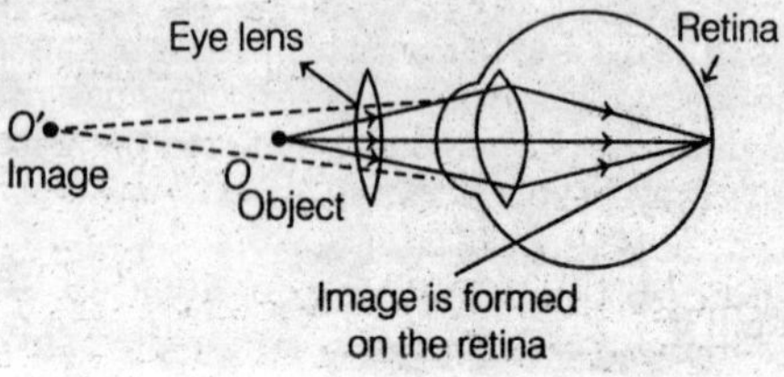

($\therefore$ For correcting image should be formed at 25 cm)

From lens formula, $\frac{1}{f} = \frac{1}{v} - \frac{1}{u}$

$$\frac{1}{f} = \frac{1}{-100} - \frac{1}{-25} = \frac{-1+4}{100}$$

$$\Rightarrow \quad f = \frac{100}{3} \text{ cm} = \frac{1}{3} \text{ m}$$

$$\text{Power} = \frac{1}{f} = \frac{3}{1} = +3.0 \text{ D}$$

Question 8 Why is a normal eye not able to see clearly the objects placed closer than 25 cm?

Sol. The nearest distant of an object from retina to form a sharp image is 25 cm. The focal length of eye lens can't be further reduced. So, at object distance less than 25 cm, blurred image of object is formed on retina.

Question 9 What happens to the image distance in the eye when we increase the distance of an object from the eye?

Sol. The image distance remains the same because the focal length of the eye lens gradually changes to maintain the position of image on the retina of the eye.

Question 10 Why do stars twinkle?

Sol. The twinkling of stars is due to atmosphere refraction of star light. The atmosphere is made of several layers and the refractive index which keep on charging continuously due to this path of light rays from the star keep on changing their path continuously. As a consequence, the number of rays entering, the pupil of the eye goes on changing with time and the stars appear twinkling.

Question 11 Explain why the planets do not twinkle?

Sol. Planets are much closer to earth and are thus seen as extended sources. So,they are considered as a collection of large number of point sized sources of light, the total variation in amount of light entering the eye from all sources average out to zero. This nullifies the twinkling effect. So, planets do not twinkle.

Question 12 Why does the Sun appear reddish early in the morning?

Sol. In the morning, sun is far away from us. So, light has to travel a longer distance through the atmosphere to reach our eyes. Blue light gets scattered during this cause. Red colour is scattered the least. So, more red light reaches our eyes and sun appears reddish.

Question 13 Why does the sky appear dark instead of blue to an astronaut?

Sol. Sunlight gets scattered in the atmosphere of earth. However, in space, there is no atmosphere. So, no sunlight gets scattered in space and sky appears dark.

Electricity

CHAPTER 11

Important Points

01 Electric Current Electric current is defined as the rate of flow of electric charge.

$$\text{Current}\,(I) = \frac{\text{Charge}\,(Q)}{\text{Time}\,(t)}$$

- Its SI unit is ampere. When one coulomb of charge flows through any area in one second, current flowing is 1 A.
- Electric current is measured by the ammeter. Ammeter has very low resistance and is always connected in series.

02 Electric Circuit A continuous path of electric current comprising of a source of power, conducting wires, switch or key, resistor (or a bulb, etc.), ammeter, etc. is called an electric circuit.

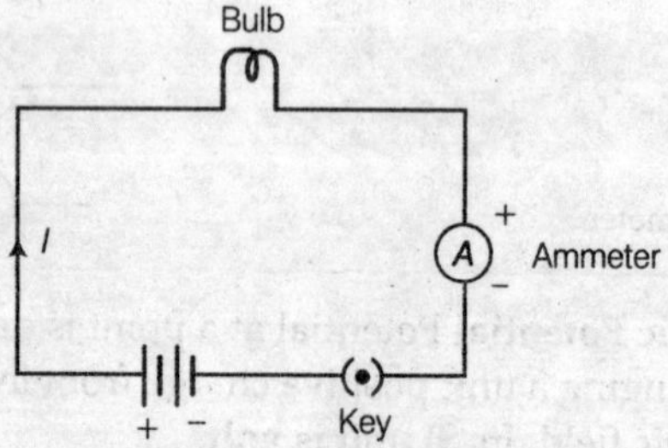

A switch is a device which makes a conducting link between the cell and bulb (or any other electrical appliance).

Symbols of Some Commonly used Components in Circuit diagrams.

S. No.	Component	Symbols
1.	An electric cell	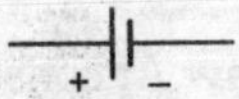
2.	A battery or a combination of cells	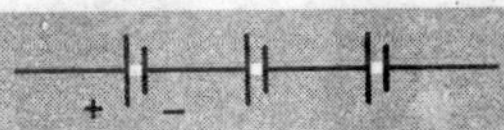
3.	Plug key or switch (open)	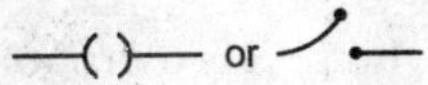
4.	Plug key or switch (closed)	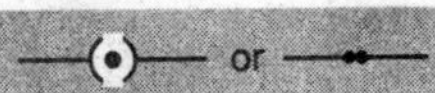
5.	Wire joint	
6.	Wires crossing without joining	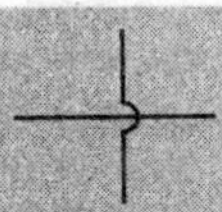
7.	Electric bulb	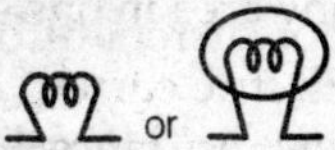
8.	Resistor or resistance	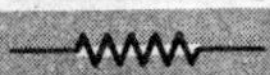
9.	Variable resistance or rheostat	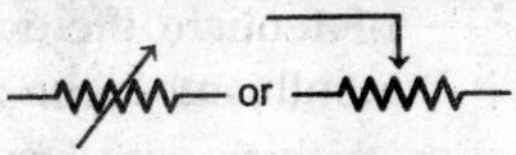
10.	Ammeter	
11.	Voltmeter	

03 Electrostatic Potential Potential at a point is defined as the work done in bringing a unit positive charge from infinity to that point in an electric field. Its SI unit is **volt.**

04 Potential Difference Potential difference between two points is defined as the amount of work done in moving a unit positive charge from one point to another in an electric field.

$$\text{Potential difference } (V) = \frac{\text{Work done } (W)}{\text{Charge } (Q)}$$

Potential difference is measured by a **voltmeter.** A voltmeter has a very high resistance and is always connected in parallel. SI unit of potential difference is **volt.**

$$1\,V = \frac{1\,J}{1\,C}$$

05 **Ohm's Law** At constant temperature, the current flowing through a conductor is directly proportional to the potential difference across its ends.

i.e., $I \propto V$ or $V \propto I$ or $V = R \times I$

where, R is a proportional constant and is called resistance of the conductor.

V-I graph for a metal conductor is shown below

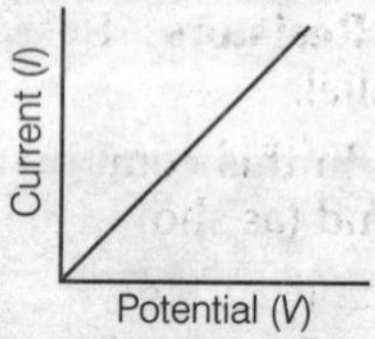

06 **Resistance** It is the property of a conductor to opposes/resists the flow of current through it. Its SI unit is **ohm** (Ω).

$$\text{Resistance}\,(R) = \frac{V}{I} \Rightarrow 1\,\Omega = \frac{1\,V}{1\,A}$$

- If one ampere of current flows through a conductor on applying a potential difference of one volt across it, then resistance of the conductor is one ohm.
- A thick wire has less resistance whereas a thin wire has more resistance.

07 **Factors Affecting Resistance**

- Resistance (R) is directly proportional to the length of the conductor (l).
- Resistance is inversely proportional to the cross-sectional area (A) of the conductor.
- Resistance of conductors increase with increase in the temperature of the conductor.
- Resistance of a semiconductor decreases with increase in its temperature.

$$\text{Mathematically, } R = \frac{\rho l}{A} = \frac{\rho l}{\pi r^2}$$

where, ρ = resistivity of the conductor and r = radius of conductor.

08 Resistivity or Specific Resistance

- Resistivity (ρ) of a substance is defined as the resistance of a wire of length one metre and cross-sectional area $1\,m^2$. Its SI unit is **ohm-metre.**
- Resistivity of a substance does not depend upon its length or thickness. It depends only on the nature of substance. Both resistivity and resistance of a material vary with temperature.
- Metals have low resistivity (low resistance), so they are used as conducting wires, whereas alloys have comparatively higher resistivity, so they are used in making heating elements.

09 Resistance of a System of Resistors Resistors are combined in two ways - series and parallel.

(i) **Series Combination** In this combination, different resistors are connected end to end (as shown in figure).

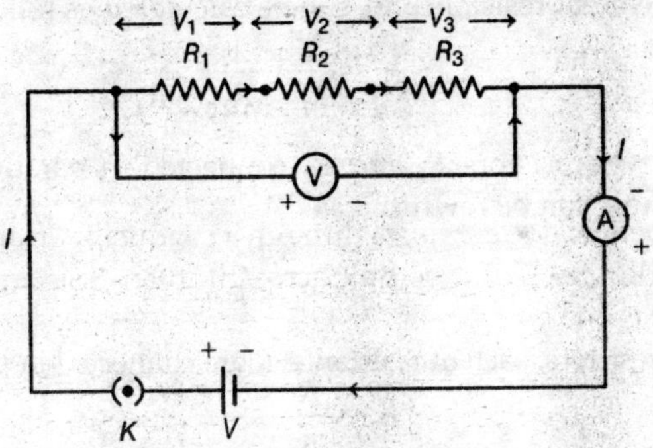

▲ Series Combination of Resistors

In series connection, equivalent resistance R_S is given by

$$R_S = R_1 + R_2 + R_3 + \ldots$$

Sum of all the potential differences is equal to the applied potential difference.

i.e., $$V = V_1 + V_2 + V_3$$

Current through each resistor is same

i.e., $$I = I_1 = I_2 = I_3$$

(ii) **Parallel Combination** In this combination, first ends of all the resistor are connected to one point and last ends to the other point (as shown in figure).

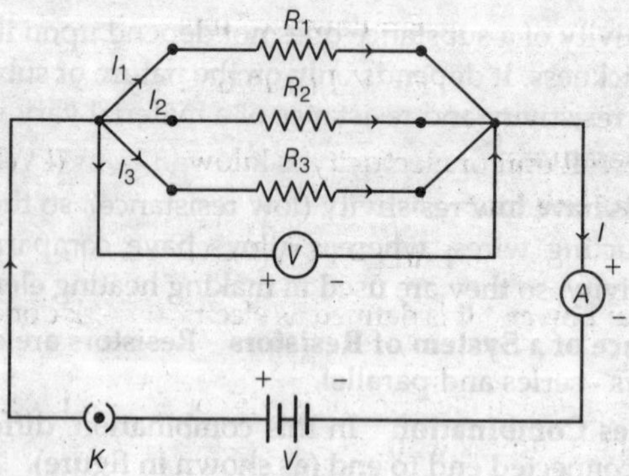

Equivalent resistance R_p can be calculated as follows

$$\frac{1}{R_p} = \frac{1}{R_1} + \frac{1}{R_2} + \frac{1}{R_3} + \ldots$$

For two resistors R_1 and R_2 connected in parallel, the above formula can be rewritten as

$$R_p = \frac{R_1 R_2}{R_1 + R_2}$$

If n resistors, each of resistance R are connected in parallel, then

$$R_p = \frac{R}{n}$$

In parallel combination, potential differences across each resistor are same.

$$V_1 = V_2 = V_3$$

and $$I = I_1 + I_2 + I_3 \ldots$$

10 Heating Effect of Electric Current On passing electric current, a conductor becomes hot after some time. This effect is known as heating effect of electric current.

Heat produced in a conductor is given by

$$H = I^2 Rt = VIt = \frac{V^2}{R} t \text{ joule}$$

$$H = \frac{I^2 Rt}{4.2} = \frac{VIt}{4.2} = \frac{V^2}{R} \frac{t}{4.2} \text{ cal}$$

Here, symbols have their usual meaning.

11 **Electrical Energy (*E*)** The work done by the source of electricity in maintaining the flow of current through the circuit is called electric energy.

Formula used

$$E = \text{Power} \times \text{Time}$$

$$\therefore \quad E = V\,I\,t = I^2Rt = \frac{V^2}{R}t$$

12 Commercial unit of electricity is kilowatt hour (kWh) commonly known as **one unit.**

$$1 \text{ unit} = 1 \text{ kWh} = 3.6 \times 10^6 \text{ J}$$

13 **Electrical Power** It is defined as electrical work done per unit time.

or

The rate at which electric energy is consumed is called electrical power. Its SI unit is **watt.**

$$\text{Power} = \frac{\text{Work}}{\text{Time}},$$

$$\therefore \quad 1\text{ W} = \frac{1\text{ J}}{1\text{ s}}$$

Formula for calculating power, $P = VI = I^2R = \frac{V^2}{R}$ $\left[\text{putting } I = \frac{V}{R}\right]$

Note Bigger units of power are as given below

- 1 kilowatt (kW) = 10^3 W
- 1 megawatt (MW) = 10^6 W
- 1 gigawatt (GW) = 10^9 W

Intext Questions

On Page 172

Question 1 What does an electric circuit mean?

Sol. A closed and continuous path of electric current is known as electric circuit.

Question 2 Define the unit of current.

Sol. The SI unit of electric current is ampere (A). The current flowing through a conductor is 1 A, if a charge of 1 C flows through it in 1 s.

or $$1\text{ A} = \frac{1\text{C}}{1\text{s}}.$$

Question 3 Calculate the number of electrons constituting one coulomb of charge.

Sol. Charge on one electron = 1.6×10^{-19} C

If 1.6×10^{-19} C is on one electron, then 1 C charge is on $\frac{1}{1.6 \times 10^{-19}}$ electrons.

$= 6.25 \times 10^{18}$ electrons

On Page 174

Question 1 Name a device that helps to maintain a potential difference across a conductor.

Sol. Electric cell or battery is a device that helps to maintain a potential difference across a conductor.

Question 2 What is meant by saying that the potential difference between two points is 1 V?

Sol. The potential difference between two points is 1 V when 1 J of work is done in moving a charge of 1 C from one point to another.

Question 3 How much energy is given to each coulomb of charge passing through a 6 V battery?

Sol. $Q = 1\text{C}, V = 6\text{ V},$

$W = VQ = 6 \times 1 = 6\text{ J}$

6 J is given to each coulomb of charge passing through a 6 V battery.

On Page 181

Question 1 On what factors does the resistance of a conductor depend?

Sol. The resistance of a conductor depends on the following factors

(a) Length of the conductor

(b) Area of cross-section of the conductor.

(c) Nature of material of the conductor.

Question 2 Will current flow more easily through a thick wire or a thin wire of the same material, when connected to the same source? Why?

Sol. Resistance is inversely proportional to the area of cross-section of the wire. Since, thick wire has a large area of cross section, its resistance will be less. Thus current will flow more easily through a thick wire.

Question 3 Let the resistance of an electrical component remains constant while the potential difference across the two ends of the component decreases to half of its former value. What change will occur in the current through it?

Sol. Let the resistance be R. Potential difference 'V' across the two ends becomes $V/2$.

Since $$I = \frac{V}{R}$$

As $V \to V/2$, $$I' = \frac{V}{2R} = \frac{1}{2}I$$

In other words, current through the component becomes half of its original value.

Question 4 Why are coils of electrical toasters and electric irons made of an alloy rather than a pure metal?

Sol. Alloys have a higher resistivity than their constituent metals. Alloys do not oxidise or burn at higher temperatures as they have high melting point. Thus, they are used to make coils of electrical toasters and electric irons rather than pure metals.

Question 5 Use the data of given table to answer the questions.

Electrical resistivity of some substances at 20°C

	Material	Resistivity (Ω - m)
Conductors	Silver	1.60×10^{-8}
	Copper	1.62×10^{-8}
	Aluminium	2.63×10^{-8}
	Tungsten	5.20×10^{-8}
	Nickel	6.84×10^{-8}
	Iron	10×10^{-8}
	Chromium	12.9×10^{-8}
	Mercury	94×10^{-8}
	Manganese	1.84×10^{-6}
Alloys	Constantan (Cu + Ni)	49×10^{-6}
	Manganin (Cu + Mn + Ni)	44×10^{-6}
	Nichrome (Ni + Cr + Mn + Fe)	100×10^{-6}
Insulators	Glass	$10^{10} - 10^{14}$
	Hard rubber	$10^{13} - 10^{16}$
	Ebonite	$10^{15} - 10^{17}$
	Diamond	$10^{12} - 10^{13}$
	Dry paper	10^{12}

(a) Which among iron and mercury is a better conductor?

(b) Which material is the best conductor?

Sol. The substance which has less resistivity is a better conductor.

(a) Iron is a better conductor than mercury.

(b) Silver is the best conductor as it has the least resistivity.

On Page 185

Question 1 Draw a schematic diagram of a circuit consisting of a battery of three cells of 2 V each, a 5 Ω resistor, an 8 Ω resistor and a 12 Ω resistor and a plug key, all connected in series.

Sol. To draw the schematic diagram of the circuit, use the standard symbols for different components of the circuit.

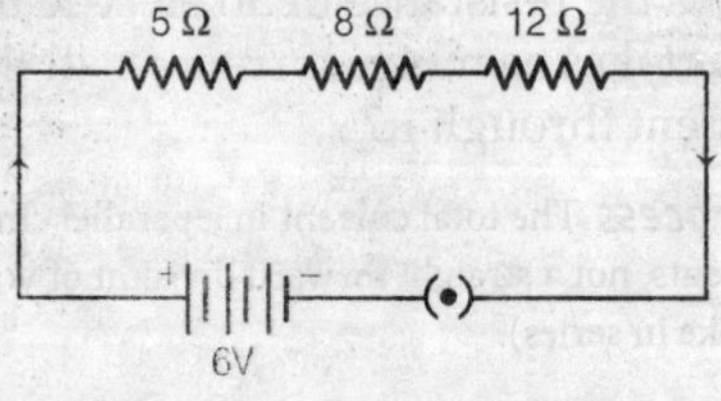

Question 2 Redraw the above circuit, putting an ammeter to measure the current through the resistors and a voltmeter to measure the potential difference across 12 Ω resistor. What would be the readings in ammeter and voltmeter?

Sol.

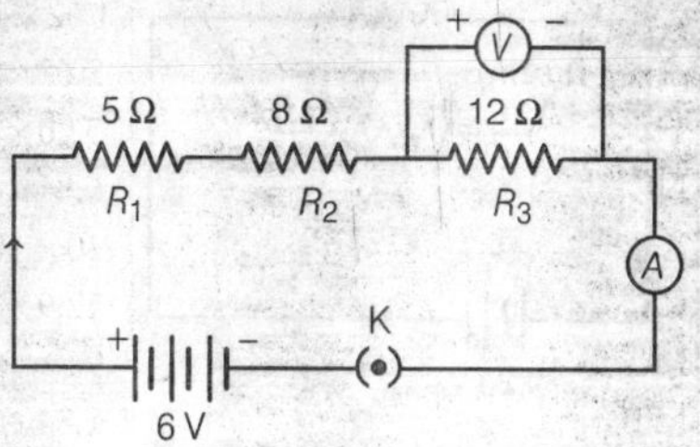

Equivalent resistance of the circuit $= R_1 + R_2 + R_3$ (in series)

$= 5\ \Omega + 8\ \Omega + 12\ \Omega = 25\ \Omega$

In series combination, current flowing through all the resistance is same and equal to the total current flowing through the circuit.

$\therefore$ Current in the resistors, $I = \frac{V}{R} = \frac{6}{25} = 0.24$ A

$\therefore$ Ammeter reading = 0.24 A

Potential across 12 Ω resistance, $V = IR = 0.24 \times 12 = 2.88$ V

$\therefore$ Voltmeter reading is 2.88 V.

On Page 188

Question 1 Judge the equivalent resistance when the following are connected in parallel (a) 1 Ω and 10^6 Ω (b) 1 Ω, 10^3 Ω and 10^6 Ω.

Sol. (a) 1 Ω (b) 1 Ω

When resistors are connected in parallel, than the equivalent resistance is less than the least resistance connected in the combination. In both the above cases, the equivalent resistance is less than 1 Ω but is approximately 1 Ω.

Question 2 An electric lamp of 100 Ω, a toaster of resistance 50 Ω and a water filter of resistance 500 Ω are connected in parallel to a 220 V source. What is the resistance of an electric iron connected to the same source that takes as much current as all three appliances and what is the current through it?

◎ ***Thinking Process*** The total current in a parallel circuit is the sum of individual currents, not a straight forward division of voltage by combined resistance (unlike in series).

Sol. Let resistance of lamp be $R_1 = 100\ \Omega$

Resistance of toaster be $R_2 = 50\ \Omega$

Resistance of filter be $R_3 = 500\ \Omega$

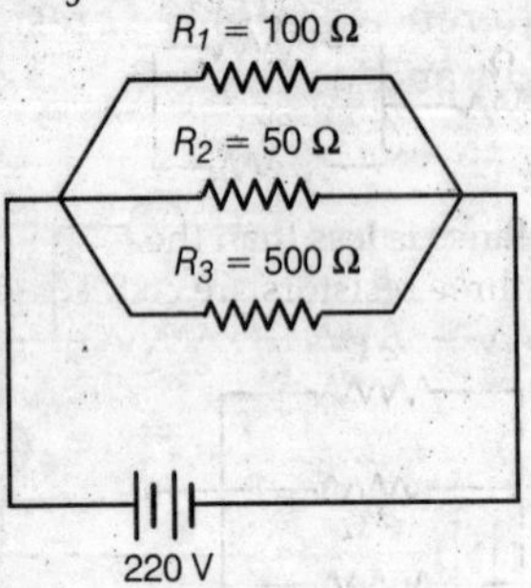

Net resistance

$$\frac{1}{R} = \frac{1}{R_1} + \frac{1}{R_2} + \frac{1}{R_3} \text{ (parallel combination)}$$

$$\frac{1}{R} = \frac{1}{100} + \frac{1}{50} + \frac{1}{500} = \frac{16}{500}$$

or $$R = \frac{500}{16} = 31.25\ \Omega$$

So, resistance of iron that takes same current as drawn by all the appliances should be $31.25\ \Omega$

Current through circuit, $I = \frac{V}{R} = \frac{220}{31.25} = 7.04$ A

Thus, current through iron = 7.04 A

Question 3 What are the advantages of connecting electrical devices in parallel with the battery instead of connecting them in series?

Sol. Following are the advantages of connecting electrical devices in parallel with the battery

(a) The current is divided through the electrical devices. The total resistance in the circuit is decreased and devices work properly.

(b) If one of the devices in a parallel combination fuses or fails, the other devices keep working without being affected.

Question 4 How can three resistors of resistances $2\ \Omega$, $3\ \Omega$ and $6\ \Omega$ be connected to give a total resistance of

(a) $4\ \Omega$ (b) $1\ \Omega$

Sol. (a) If 3Ω and 6Ω are connected in parallel, thus equivalent resistance of parallel combination

$$= \frac{1}{\frac{1}{3} + \frac{1}{6}} = 2\Omega$$

If this combination is connected in series with 2Ω resistance, then total equivalent resistance = 2Ω + 2Ω = 4Ω. The resistors connection is shown below

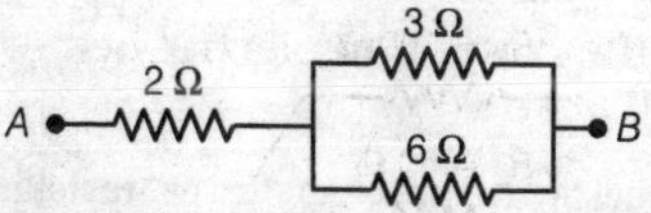

(b) Since equivalent resistance is less than the least value of resistance (i.e., 2Ω), it means all three resistors are connected in parallel.

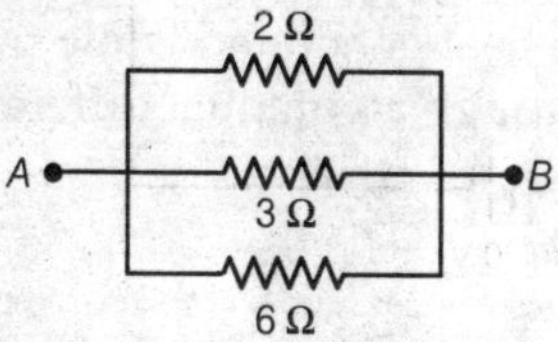

$$\text{Equivalent resistance} = \frac{1}{\frac{1}{2}+\frac{1}{3}+\frac{1}{6}} = 1\ \Omega$$

Mistake Alert In this type of problems, be careful in choosing between series and parallel arrangements; the resistance decreases in parallel but increases in series.

Question 5 What is (a) the highest and (b) the lowest resistance that can be secured by combinations of four coils of resistance 4 Ω, 8 Ω, 12 Ω, 24 Ω?

Sol. (a) The overall resistance is increased in a series combination.

∴ Highest equivalent resistance

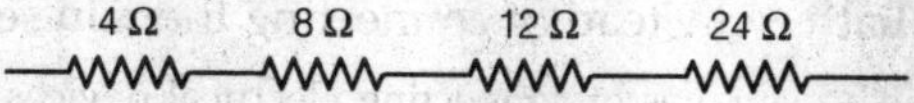

$$= R_1 + R_2 + R_3 + R_4$$

$$= 4\Omega + 8\Omega + 12\Omega + 24\Omega = 48\Omega$$

(b) The overall resistance is reduced in a parallel combination.

∴ Lowest equivalent resistance

$$= \frac{1}{\frac{1}{R_1}+\frac{1}{R_2}+\frac{1}{R_3}+\frac{1}{R_4}}$$

$$= \frac{1}{\frac{1}{4}+\frac{1}{8}+\frac{1}{12}+\frac{1}{24}}$$

$$= \frac{1}{\frac{12}{24}} = 2\ \Omega$$

On Page 190

Question 1 Why does the cord of an electric heater not glow while the heating elements does?

Sol. The cord of an electric heater has lesser resistance than its heating element. So, more heat is produced in the heating element than the cord and it glows.

Question 2 Compute the heat generated while transferring 96000 C of charge in one hour through a potential difference of 50 V.

Sol. Given, $Q = 96000\text{ C}, t = 1\text{ h} = 3600\text{ s}, V = 50\text{ V}$

Heat generated, $H = VIt = \frac{V\,Q\,t}{t} = VQ$

$= 50 \times 96000$

$= 4800000\text{ J} = 4800\text{ kJ}$

4800 kJ is generated while transferring 96000C of charge.

Question 3 An electric iron of resistance 20 Ω takes a current of 5A. Calculate the heat developed in 30 s.

Sol. Given,

$R = 20\,\Omega, I = 5\text{ A}, t = 30\text{ s}$

Heat developed, $H = I^2 Rt$

$= (5)^2 \times 20 \times 30 = 5 \times 5 \times 20 \times 30$

$= 15000\text{ J} = 15\text{ kJ}$

15 kJ heat is developed in 30 s.

On Page 192

Question 1 What determines the rate at which energy is delivered by the current?

Sol. Electric power determines the rate at which energy is delivered by a current.

Question 2 An electric motor takes 5 A from a 220 V line. Determine the power of motor and energy consumed in 2 h.

Sol. Given, $I = 5\text{ A}, V = 220\text{ V}, t = 2\text{ h}$

Power of motor, $P = VI$

$= 220 \times 5 = 1100\text{ W} = 1.1\text{ kW}$

Energy consumed, $E = Pt$

$= 1.1 \times 2 = 2.2\text{ kWh}$

$\therefore$ Power = 1.1 kW and Energy consumed = 2.2 kWh

Exercises

Question 1 A piece of wire of resistance R is cut into five equal parts. These parts are then connected in parallel. If the equivalent resistance of this combination is R', then the ratio R/R' is

(a) $\frac{1}{25}$ (b) $\frac{1}{5}$ (c) 5 (d) 25

Sol. (d) Resistance of complete wire is R. If it is cut into 5 equal parts, then resistance of each part will be $\frac{R}{5}$.

Five parts of resistance $\frac{R}{5}$ each are connected in parallel.

Equivalent resistance

$$R' = \frac{1}{\left(\frac{1}{\frac{R}{5}}\right)+\left(\frac{1}{\frac{R}{5}}\right)+\left(\frac{1}{\frac{R}{5}}\right)+\left(\frac{1}{\frac{R}{5}}\right)+\left(\frac{1}{\frac{R}{5}}\right)} = \frac{1}{\frac{25}{R}} = \frac{R}{25}$$

$$\text{Ratio } \frac{R}{R'} = \frac{R}{\frac{R}{25}} = 25$$

Question 2 Which of the following terms does not represent electric power in a circuit?

(a) I^2R (b) IR^2 (c) VI (d) V^2/R

Sol. (b) Electric power $= VI = IR \times I = I^2R$ $[\because V = IR]$

$$= \left(\frac{V}{R}\right)^2 R = \frac{V^2}{R} \qquad \left[\because I = \frac{V}{R}\right]$$

So, IR^2 does not represent electric power.

Question 3 An electric bulb is rated 220 V and 100 W. When it is operated on 110 V, the power consumed will be

(a) 100 W (b) 75 W (c) 50 W (d) 25 W

Sol. (d) Given, $V = 220$ V, $P = 100$ W

Since, $P = \frac{V^2}{R}$

Resistance of bulb, $R = \frac{V^2}{P} = \frac{220 \times 220}{100} = 484\ \Omega$

Now, when $V = 110$ V

Power consumed, $P = \frac{V^2}{R} = \frac{110 \times 110}{484} = 25$ W

Question 4 Two conducting wires of same material and of equal lengths and equal diameters are first connected in series and then parallel in a circuit across the same potential difference, the ratio of heat produced in series and parallel combinations would be

(a) 1 : 2 (b) 2 : 1 (c) 1 : 4 (d) 4 : 1

Sol. (c) Let R be the resistance of each wire (Resistance of both the wires will be same because they are of same material and have same length and same cross-sectional area)

Equivalent resistance in series = $R + R = 2R$,

Heat produced, $H = \dfrac{V^2 t}{R}$

If wires are connected in series, $H_s = \dfrac{V^2 t}{2R}$

Equivalent resistance in parallel = $\dfrac{R}{2}$

Heat produced, $H_p = \dfrac{2V^2 t}{R}$

$\because$ Ratio of heat produced,

$$\frac{H_s}{H_p} = \frac{\frac{V^2 t}{2R}}{\frac{2V^2 t}{R}} = 1 : 4$$

Thus, the ratio of H_s and H_p is 1 : 4.

Question 5 How is a voltmeter connected in the circuit to measure the potential difference between two points?

Sol. A voltmeter is connected in parallel in the circuit across the points between which potential difference is to be measured.

Question 6 A copper wire has diameter 0.5 mm and resistivity of 1.6×10^{-8} Ωm. What will be the length of this wire to make its resistance 10 Ω? How much does the resistance change if diameter is doubled?

Sol. Given, Radius of wire = diameter/2 = $\dfrac{0.5}{2}$ = 0.25 mm = 0.25×10^{-3} m.

$$p = 1.6 \times 10^{-8}\ \Omega\text{-m},$$
$$R = 10\ \Omega$$

We know that, $R = \dfrac{\rho l}{A} = \dfrac{\rho l}{\pi r^2}$ $[\because A = \pi r^2]$

Or $l = \dfrac{R\pi r^2}{\rho} = \dfrac{10 \times 3.14 \times 0.25 \times 0.25 \times 10^{-6}}{1.6 \times 10^{-8}} = 122.77$ m

If diameter is doubled, then resistance becomes $\dfrac{1}{4}$ th of its original value.

Question 7 The values of current I flowing in a given resistor for the corresponding values of potential difference V across the resistor are given below

I (amperes)	0.5	1.0	2.0	3.0	4.0
V (volts)	1.6	3.4	6.7	10.2	13.2

Plot a graph between V and I and calculate resistance of that resistor.

Sol.

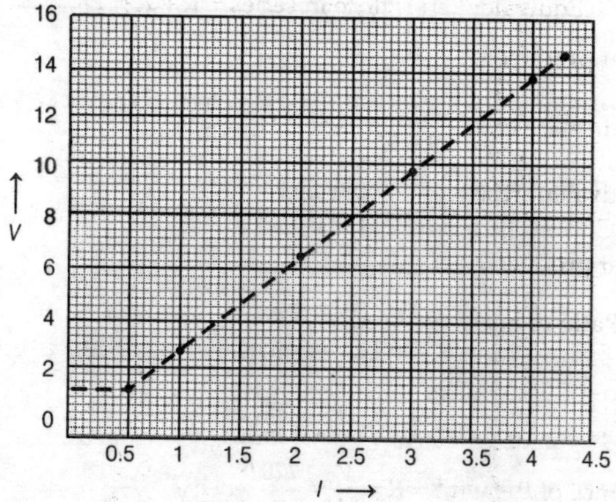

$$R = \text{Slope of } V\text{-}I \text{ graph} = \frac{13.2-6.7}{4.0-2.0} = \frac{6.5}{2} = 3.25\ \Omega$$

Mistake Alert Ensure that V is plotted on the Y-axis and I on the X-axis. If the points do not form a straight line, there might be an error in measurement or plotting.

Question 8 When a 12 V battery is connected across an unknown resistor, there is a current of 2.5 mA in the circuit. Find the value of resistance of the resistor.

Sol. Given, $V = 12$ V,

$$I = 2.5 \text{ mA} = 2.5 \times 10^{-3} \text{ A}$$

$$R = \frac{V}{I} = \frac{12}{2.5 \times 10^{-3}} = 4800\ \Omega$$

$$= 4.8 \times 10^{3}\ \Omega$$

Question 9 A battery of 9 V is connected in series with resistors of 0.2 Ω, 0.3 Ω, 0.4 Ω, 0.5 Ω and 12 Ω respectively. How much current will flow through 12 Ω resistor?

Sol. The circuit diagram for the given system of resistors can be drawn as below

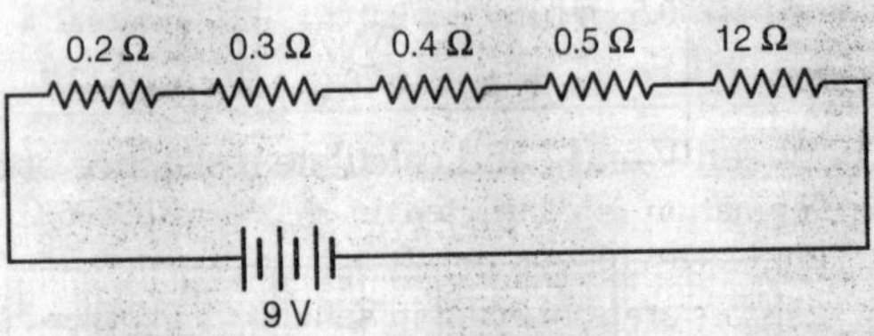

Total resistance, $R = 0.2\ \Omega + 0.3\ \Omega + 0.4\ \Omega + 0.5\ \Omega + 12\ \Omega$

$= 13.4\ \Omega$

Current through all resistors in series is the same.

$\therefore$ Current through 12 Ω resistor $= \frac{V}{R} = \frac{9}{13.4}$

$= 0.67$ A

Question 10 How many 176 Ω resistors (in parallel) are required to carry 5 A on a 220 V line?

Sol. Given, $V = 220$ V, $I = 5$ A

Resistance of the wire $= R = \frac{V}{I} = \frac{220}{5} = 44\ \Omega$

The net resistance 44 Ω is less than the individual resistance 176 Ω, so individual resistances are to be connected in parallel.

In parallel connection, equivalent resistance $= \frac{1}{\frac{1}{R} + \frac{1}{R} + \frac{1}{R}}$

$$= \frac{1}{\frac{n}{R}} = \frac{R}{n}$$

$\therefore$ $$44\ \Omega = \frac{176\ \Omega}{n}$$

or $$n = \frac{176}{44} = 4 \text{ resistors}$$

Question 11 Show how would you connect three resistors, each of resistance 6Ω, so that the combination has a resistance of

(a) 9 Ω (b) 4 Ω

Sol. (a) If two 6 Ω resistors are connected in parallel, then the equivalent resistance is $\left(\frac{6}{2}\right) = 3\ \Omega$

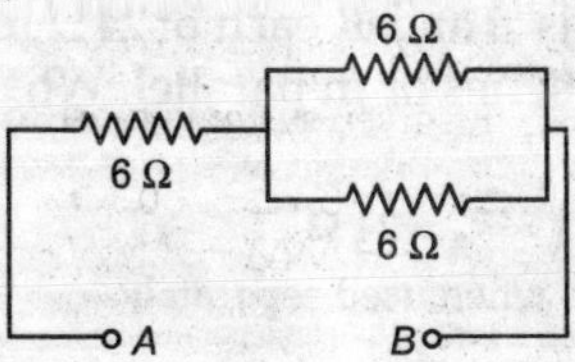

This combination is connected in series with a 6 Ω resistor to get overall equivalent resistance is (6 + 3 =) 9 Ω

(b) If two resistors are connected in series and another resistor of 6 Ω is connected in parallel to them, then the total equivalent resistance is 4 Ω.

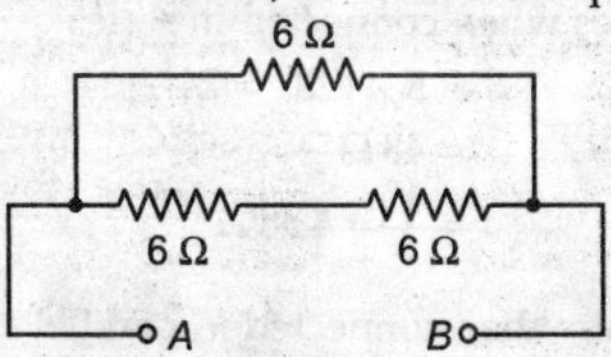

Equivalent resistance of 6 Ω resistances connected in series, R′ = 6 + 6 = 12 Ω. Now 12 Ω and 6 Ω are connected in parallel.

Equivalent resistance $R_{eq} = \frac{12 \times 6}{12 + 6} = \frac{72}{18} = 4\ \Omega$

Question 12 Several electric bulbs designed to be used on a 220 V electric supply line, are rated 10 W. How many lamps can be connected in parallel with each other across the two wires of 220 V line if the maximum allowable current is 5 A?

Thinking Process To solve this problem, use the formula $P = VI$ to calculate the power conscum by each bulb and then divide the total allowable power by the power of each bulb. Since the bulbs are connected in parallel, each bulb operates at the same voltage (220V).

Sol. Given, $V = 220$ V, $P = 10$ W, $I = 5$ A

Resistance of bulb, $R' = \frac{V^2}{P} = \frac{220 \times 220}{10} = 4840\ \Omega$

Since, bulbs are connected in parallel,

Equivalent resistance, $R = \frac{\text{Individual resistance } (R')}{\text{Number of bulbs } (n)}$

$\Rightarrow \qquad R = \frac{4840}{n}\ \Omega$

Now, $\qquad V = IR,\ 220 = \frac{5 \times 4840}{n}$

$$n = \frac{5 \times 4840}{220} = 110 \text{ bulbs}$$

Question 13 A hot plate of an electric oven connected to a 220 V line has two resistance coils *A* and *B*, each of 24 Ω resistance, which may be used separately in series or in parallel. What are the currents in three cases?

Sol. Given, $V = 220$ V, $R_A = R_B = 24\ \Omega$

(a) Current in plates when used separately

$$I = \frac{V}{R_A} = \frac{V}{R_B}$$

$$= \frac{220}{24} = 9.16\text{ A}$$

(b) Current in plates when connected in series

$$R = R_A + R_B = 24 + 24$$

$$= 48\ \Omega$$

$$I = \frac{V}{R} = 4.58\text{ A}$$

(c) Current in plates when connected in parallel

$$R = \frac{R_A R_B}{R_A + R_B} = \frac{24 \times 24}{48} = 12\ \Omega$$

$$\therefore \text{Current flowing } I = \frac{V}{R} = \frac{220}{12} = 18.33\text{ A}$$

Question 14 Compare the power used in 2 Ω resistor in each of the following circuits.

(a) A 6 V battery in series with 1 Ω and 2 Ω resistors

(b) A 4 V battery in parallel with 12 Ω and 2 Ω resistors

Sol. (a) The circuit is shown alongside. Current through 2 Ω resistor,

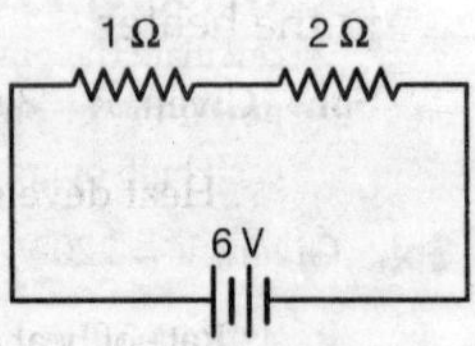

$$I_1 = \frac{V}{R_1 + R_2}$$

$$= \frac{6\text{ V}}{3\ \Omega} = 2\text{ A}$$

Power used $= I_1^2 R = 2 \times 2 \times 2 = 8$ W

(b) The circuit is shown alongside.

Potential across 2 Ω resistor $V = 4$ V

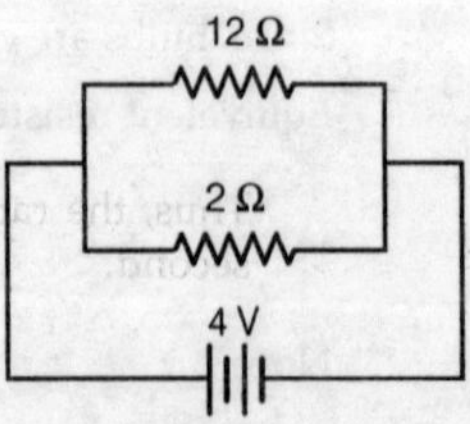

$$\text{Power used} = \frac{V^2}{R}$$

$$= \frac{4 \times 4}{2} = 8\text{ W}$$

Power used is same in both the cases.

Question 15 Two lamps, one rated 100 W at 220 V and the other 60 W at 220 V, are connected in parallel to electric mains supply. What current is drawn from the line if the supply voltage is 220 V ?

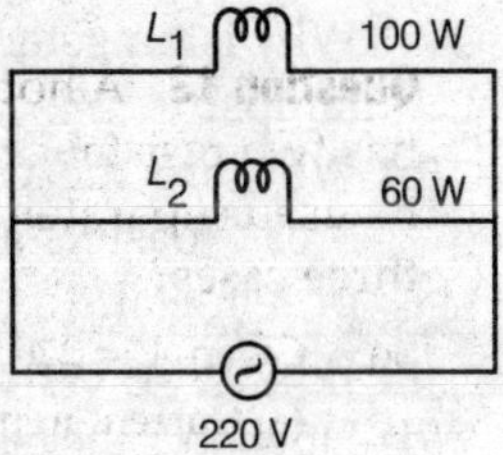

Sol. Given,

Potential, $V = 220$ V

Power, $P_1 = 100$ W, $P_2 = 60$ W

Current, $I_1 = \frac{P_1}{V} = \frac{100}{220} = 0.45$ A

Current, $I_2 = \frac{P_1}{V} = \frac{60}{220} = 0.27$ A

$\therefore$ Total current drawn, $I = I_1 + I_2$

$= 0.45 + 0.27 = 0.72$ A

Question 16 Which uses more energy, a 250 W TV set in 1 h or a 1200 W toaster in 10 min?

Sol. Given, $P_1 = 250$ W $P_2 = 1200$ W

$t_1 = 1$ h $= 3600$ s,

$t_2 = 10$ min $= 600$ s

Energy, $Q_1 = P_1 t_1 = 250 \times 3600 = 900000$ J $= 900$ kJ

and $Q_2 = P_2 t_2 = 1200 \times 600 = 720000$ J $= 720$ kJ

Thus, TV set uses more energy.

Question 17 An electric heater of resistance 8 Ω draws 15 A from the service mains for 2 h. Calculate the rate at which heat is developed in the heater.

Sol. Given, $R = 8\ \Omega$, $I = 15$ A, $t = 2$ h $= 7200$ s

$\therefore$ Heat developed, $H = I^2 R t$

$= 15 \times 15 \times 8 \times 7200$ J

$\therefore$ Rate of heat development, $P - H/t$

$= \frac{15 \times 15 \times 8 \times 7200}{7200}$

$= 1800$ W or 1800 J/s

Thus, the rate at which heat is developed in the heater is 1800 joule per second.

Question 18 Explain the following questions

(a) Why is tungsten used almost exclusively for filament of electric lamps?

(b) Why are the conductors of electric heating devices, such as bread toasters and electric irons, made of an alloy rather than a pure metal?

(c) Why is the series arrangement not used for domestic circuits?

(d) How does the resistance of a wire vary with its area of cross section?

(e) Why are copper and aluminum wires usually employed for electricity transmission?

Sol. (a) Tungsten has a high melting point (3380°C). It does not melt at high temperatures. It retains as much of heat generated, so that it becomes very hot and emits light. This is the reason why tungsten is used as filament of electric lamps.

(b) Conductors of electric heating devices are made of alloys because alloys do not oxidise (burn) readily at high temperatures, unlike metals. Also alloys have a greater resistivity (generally) as compared to their constituent pure metals.

(c) Series arrangement is not used in domestic circuits because if one component fails, the circuit is broken and none of the other components will work. Also, components need currents of widely different values to operate properly. But in a series circuit, the current is constant throughout the electric circuit.

(d) Resistance is inversely proportional to the area of cross-section of the wire. Thus, if the wire is thick (large area of cross-section), then resistance is less. If the wire is thin (less area of cross-section), then resistance is large.

(e) Copper and aluminium wires are used for transmission of electricity because they have low resistivity. So, they conduct the electric current without heavy heat losses. Also, they are quite cost effective, as compared to silver.

DIKSHA APP Questions

☐ Very Short Answer Type

Q.1 When do we say that the potential difference between two points of a circuit is 1 volt?

Sol. Potential difference between two points of an electric circuit is said to be 1 volt when a work of 1 J is to be done in moving a charge of 1 C between the two points.

Q.2 Two bulbs having power of 50 W and 25 W respectively are connected with the same source. Which has higher resistance? What is their ratio?

Sol. $\because$ $$P = \frac{V^2}{R}$$

$\Rightarrow$ $$R = \frac{V^2}{P}$$

So, $$R_1 = \frac{V^2}{50}\ \Omega$$

and $$R_2 = \frac{V^2}{25}\ \Omega$$

$$\frac{R_1}{R_2} = \frac{25}{50} = \frac{1}{2}$$

Clearly, resistance of 25 W bulb is more.

Q.3 A wire of resistance 5 Ω is bent in the form of a closed circle. Find the resistance across the diameter of the circle?

Sol. Consider two semicircular elements connected across the diameter as shown

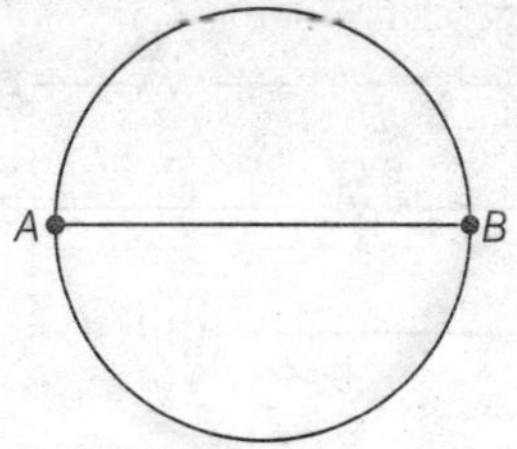

Total resistance = 5 Ω

Resistance of each of the two semicircular elements = $\frac{5}{2}\,\Omega$.

As, both the elements are connected in parallel,

$$\therefore \quad \frac{1}{R} = \frac{1}{R_1} + \frac{1}{R_2}$$

$$= \frac{2}{5} + \frac{2}{5}$$

$$= \frac{4}{5}\,\Omega$$

$$\Rightarrow \quad R = \frac{5}{4}\,\Omega$$

Q.4 The electric power consumed by a device may be calculated by either of the two expressions $P = I^2 R$ or $P = \frac{V^2}{R}$. The first expression indicates that it is directly proporional to R whereas the second expression indicates inverse proportionality. How can the seemingly different dependence of P on R in these expressions be explained?

Sol. $P = I^2 R$ is used to calculate electric power when the current flowing through the circuit is constant (Series combination).

$P = \frac{V^2}{R}$ is used to calculate electric power when the potential difference flowing through the circuit is constant (Parallel combination).

☐ Short Answer Type

Q.1 In the circuit shown below, solve and calculate

(i) Total resistance in the arm CE.

(ii) Total current drawn from the battery.

(iii) Current in each arm,

i.e., AB and CE of the circuit.

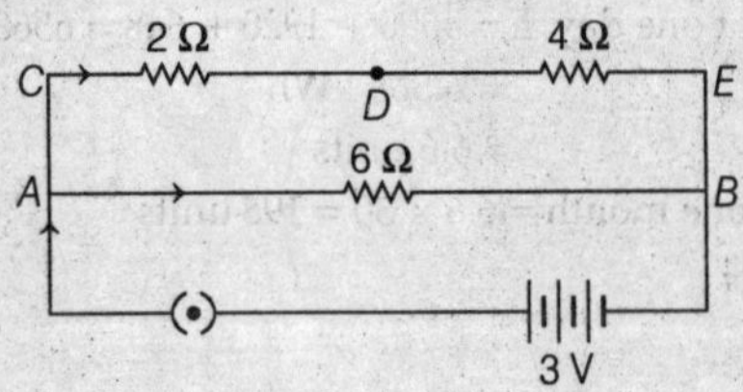

Sol. (i) Total resistance in arm *CE*, $R_{CE} = 2 + 4 = 6\ \Omega$

(ii) Total resistance of circuit

$$\frac{1}{R} = \frac{1}{R_1} + \frac{1}{R_2}$$

$$\Rightarrow \quad \frac{1}{R} = \frac{1}{6} + \frac{1}{6}$$

$$\Rightarrow \quad \frac{1}{R} = \frac{2}{6}$$

so $$R = \frac{6}{2} = 3\ \Omega$$

Now, $V = IR$ (Ohm's law)

$$\Rightarrow \quad I = \frac{V}{R} = \frac{3}{3} = 1\ \text{A}$$

$$I_{AB} = \frac{V}{R_{AB}} = \frac{3}{6} = 0.5\ \text{A}$$

and, $$I_{CE} = \frac{V}{R_{CE}} = \frac{3}{6} = 0.5\ \text{A}$$

Q.2 A household uses the following electrical appliances

(i) Refrigerator of rating 400 W for ten hours each day.

(ii) Two electric fans of rating 80 W each for twelve hours each day.

(iii) Six electric tubes of rating 18 W each for 6 hours each day.

Predict the amount of electricity bill of the household for month of June if cost is Rs. 3.00/unit.

Sol. June month has 30 days

So, according to the data given in the question,

$$E = P \times t$$

(i) The electricity consumption of one day is

One refrigerator, $E_1 = 400 \times 10 = 4000$ Wh

(ii) Two fans, $E_2 = 2 \times 80 \times 12 = 1920$ Wh

(iii) Six electric tubes, $E_3 = 6 \times 18 \times 6 = 648$ Wh

Total energy consumption of one day, $E = 4000 + 1920 + 648 = 6568$ Wh

$= 6.568$ kWh

$= 6.6$ units

Electricity consumption of one month $= 6.6 \times 30 = 198$ units

Total cost $= 198 \times 3 =$ Rs. 594

Q.3 A wire of resistance 10 Ω is drawn out so that its length is thrice its original length. Find resistance of the new wire.

Sol. Resistance (R) = Resistivity $(\rho) \times$ Length (l) /Area (A)

i.e., $$R = \rho \frac{l}{A}$$

When the length increases by three times, the cross-section area will reduce by three times.

Hence, $l' = 3l$

and, $$A' = \frac{A}{3}$$

$\therefore$ $$R' = \rho \frac{l'}{A'}$$

$\Rightarrow$ $$R' = \rho \frac{(3l)}{\left(\frac{A}{3}\right)}$$

$\Rightarrow$ $$R' = \frac{9\rho l}{A}$$

$\Rightarrow$ $$R' = 9R$$

$\Rightarrow$ $$R' = 9 \times 10 \qquad (\because R = 10\ \Omega)$$

$\Rightarrow$ $$R' = 90\ \Omega$$

$\therefore$ New resistance is 90 Ω.

☐ Long Answer Type

Q.1 (i) Define the term resistivity of a conductor. Give its SI unit.

(ii) A copper wire of resistivity ρ is stretched to reduce its diameter to half of its previous value. What will be its new resistivity?

(iii) Find the resistance of a wire 1.1 m long and 0.2 mm in diameter. Given, resistivity of wire = $49 \times 10^{-8}\ \Omega$ m. Also, what is the current flowing through the wire, when a potential difference of 1 V is applied across its ends?

Sol. (i) Resistivity is the characteristic property or nature of a conductor to resist the electricity to flow. Resistivity of conductor is the resistance of conductor of unit length and unit area of cross-section. Its unit is ohm-metre.

(ii) There will be no change in resistivity of the copper wire as resistivity does not depend on length and area.

(iii) Length, $l = 1.1$ m

Diameter, $d = 0.2$ mm $\qquad \left(\because r = \frac{d}{2}\right)$

$\therefore$ Radius, $r = 0.1$ mm

Resistivity, $\rho = 49 \times 10^{-8}\ \Omega$ m

We know, $R = \rho \dfrac{l}{A}$

$$\Rightarrow \quad R = \frac{49 \times 10^{-8} \times 1.1}{\pi \times (0.1 \times 10^{-3})^2} \qquad [A = \pi r^2 \text{ and } r = 0.1 \times 10^{-3} \text{ m}]$$

$$\Rightarrow \quad R = 17.15\ \Omega$$

Now, current, $I = \dfrac{V}{R}$

$$\Rightarrow \quad I = \frac{1}{17.15} = 0.06 \text{ A}$$

Q.2 Two resistors of resistances 3 Ω and 6 Ω respectively are connected to a battery of 6 V, so as to have (a) minimum resistance, (b) minimum current.

(i) How will you connect the resistances in each case and find the value of equivalent resistance in each case?

(ii) Calculate the strength of the current in the circuit in both cases.

Sol. (i) For minimum resistance, the resistors should be connected in parallel

$$\frac{1}{R} = \frac{1}{R_1} + \frac{1}{R_2}$$

$$\Rightarrow \quad \frac{1}{R} = \frac{1}{3} + \frac{1}{6}$$

$$\Rightarrow \quad \frac{1}{R} = \frac{3}{6}$$

$$\Rightarrow \quad R = 2\ \Omega$$

For minimum current, resistance should be maximum. So, resistor would be connected in series.

$$R = R_1 + R_2$$

$$= 3 + 6 = 9\ \Omega$$

(ii) Current when resistance is minimum

$$I = \frac{V}{R}$$

$$\Rightarrow \quad I = \frac{6}{2} = 3 \text{ A}$$

Current when resistance is maximum

$$I = \frac{V}{R}$$

$$\Rightarrow \quad I = \frac{6}{9} = \frac{2}{3} \text{ A}$$

Q.3 (i) Examine what determines the rate at which energy is delivered by a current?

(ii) An electrical geyser has a rating 2000 W, 200 V marked on it. Predict the value of fuse wire that may be required for safe use with this geyser.

(iii) Estimate which will use more energy, a 250 W TV set in 1 hour or a 1200 W toaster in 10 minutes?

Sol. (i) Electrical power determines the rate at which the energy is delivered by a current.

As electric power is the ratio of electrical energy to time.

(ii)
$$P = V \times I$$
$$\Rightarrow \quad I = \frac{P}{V}$$
$$\Rightarrow \quad I = \frac{2000}{200} = 10 \text{ A}$$

Fuse wire of rating 11 A should be used.

(iii)
$$E = P \times t$$
$$E_{TV} = 250 \times 1 = 250 \text{ Wh}$$
$$E_{Toaster} = 1200 \times \frac{10}{60}$$
$$= \frac{1200}{6} = 200 \text{ Wh}$$

$\therefore$ TV uses more energy.

Q.4 (i) Discuss what will happen when voltmeter is connected in series and ammeter is connected in parallel in a circuit?

(ii) Calculate the value of each resistance of two resistors which when connected in parallel give resultant value of 2 Ω and when connected in series the resultant value becomes 9 Ω.

Sol. (i) If voltmeter is connected in series, then due to its high resistance no current will flow through circuit, so no voltage drop will occur. Voltage in same line will be zero and voltmeter will indicate zero and on the other hand if ammeter is connected in parallel due to its low resistance, it will act like short circuit, so chances of ammeter getting damaged are high.

(ii) Let R_1 and R_2 be the two resistances. When they are in parallel, resultant resistance R_p is given by

$$\frac{1}{R_p} = \frac{1}{R_1} + \frac{1}{R_2}$$

$$\Rightarrow \quad R_p = \frac{R_1R_2}{R_1 + R_2}$$

$$\Rightarrow \quad 2 = \frac{R_1R_2}{R_1 + R_2} \qquad (\because R_p = 2\,\Omega, \text{given})$$

$$R_1R_2 = 2(R_1 + R_2) \qquad \text{...(i)}$$

When they are in series, resultant resistance R_s is given by

$$R_s = R_1 + R_1 \qquad (R_s = 9\,\Omega, \text{ given})$$

$$R_1 + R_2 = 9 \qquad \text{...(ii)}$$

From Eq. (i)

$$R_1R_2 = 18 \qquad \text{...(iii)}$$

We know that

$$(R_1 - R_2)^2 = (R_1 + R_2)^2 - 4R_1R_2$$

$$= (9)^2 - 5 \times 18 = 81 - 72 = 9$$

$$R_1 - R_2 = 3 \qquad \text{...(iv)}$$

$$R_1 + R_2 = 9$$

$$R_1 - R_2 = 3$$

$$2R_1 = 12$$

$$\Rightarrow \quad R_1 = 6\,\Omega$$

From Eq. (ii)

$$R_2 = 9 - R_1$$

$$\Rightarrow \quad R_2 = 9 - 6 = 3\,\Omega$$

Hence, two resistors are of resistance value 6 Ω and 3 Ω.

Magnetic Effects of Electric Current

CHAPTER 12

Important Points

01 **Magnetic Field** The space around a magnet in which its effect can be experienced is called **magnetic field**. Magnetic field is a vector quantity and SI unit is tesla.

02 **Magnetic Lines of Force** These are the lines in a magnetic field along which a magnetic north pole would move under the influence of the field. These are also called **field lines.**

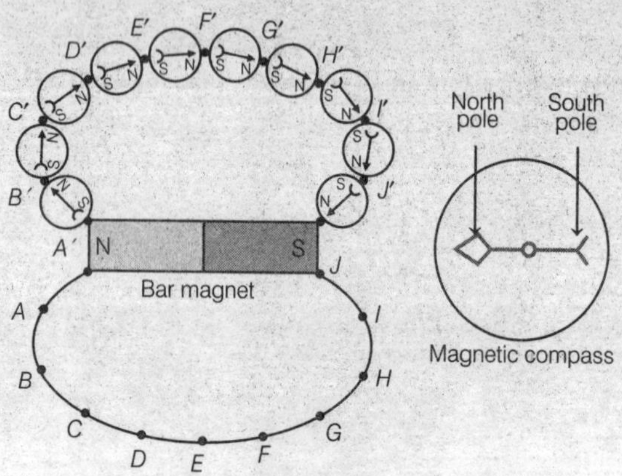

▲ Magnetic lines of force obtained by joining various positions of north pole of plotting compass

03 Magnetic lines of force can be plotted by using a magnetic compass.

Characteristics of Magnetic Lines of Force

(a) The magnetic lines of force originate from north pole of a magnet and end at its south pole.

(b) The magnetic lines of force come closer to one another near the poles but they are widely separated away from the pole.

(c) These lines are closed and continuous curves.

(d) The magnetic lines of force do not intersect one another. (Any point on magnetic lines of force indicate the direction of force on a north pole kept there. If two lines meet, it means that force is acting in two directions at that point which is not possible).

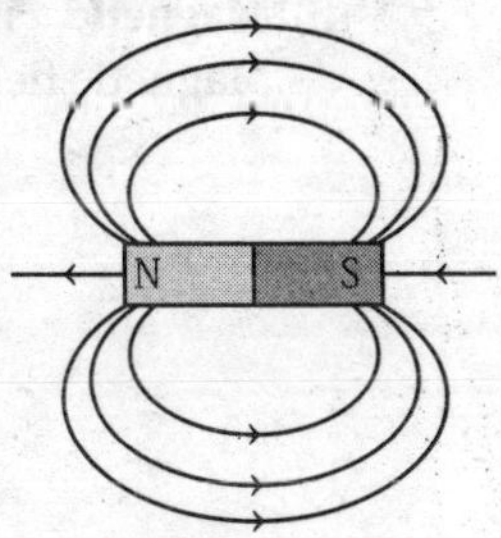

▲ Magnetic lines of force due to a bar magnet

(e) **Magnetic Field due to a Current Carrying Conductor** When an electric current passes through a metallic conductor, it produces a magnetic field around it.

(f) **Magnetic Field due to a Current through a Straight Conductor** The magnetic field lines of force due to a straight wire are the concentric circles with their common centre on the conductor.

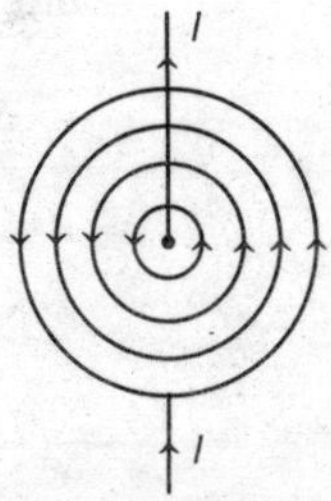

▲ Concentric field lines around a straight conductonr

(g) **Maxwell's Right Hand Thumb Rule or Maxwell's Cork Screw Rule** Direction of the magnetic field produced by a current carrying conductor is given by **Maxwell's right hand thumb rule.**

"Imagine holding the current carrying conductor in your right hand such that the thumb points in direction of the current, then the direction in which the fingers encircle, gives the direction of magnetic field lines."

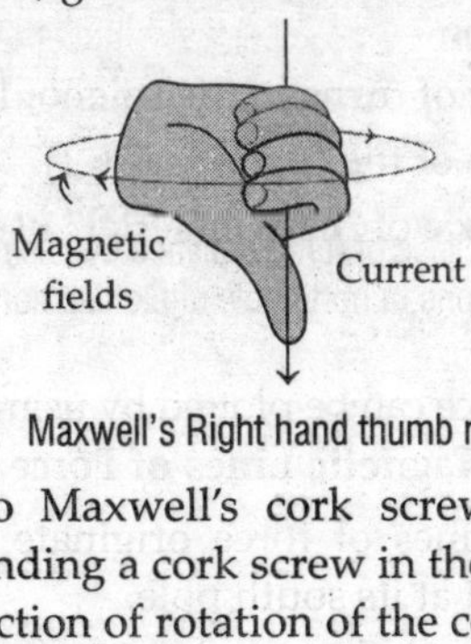

▲ Maxwell's Right hand thumb rule

According to Maxwell's cork screw rule, "If we consider ourselves winding a cork screw in the direction of the current, then the direction of rotation of the cork screw is the direction of the magnetic field lines".

(h) **Magnetic Field due to a Current through a Circular Loop** Magnetic field lines due to a circular coil is shown below.

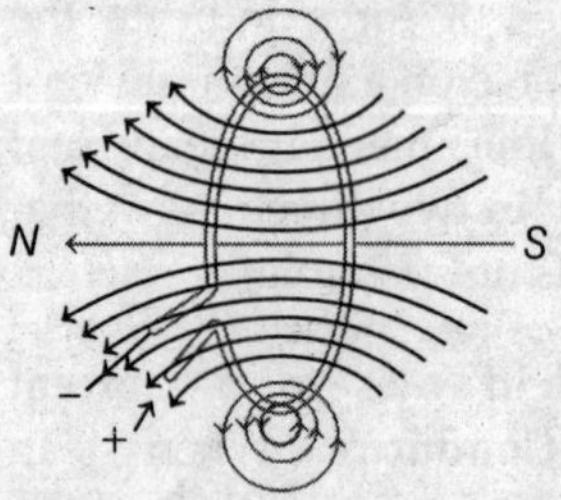

▲ Magnetic fields due to a circular coil

(i) **Magnetic Field due to a Current in a Solenoid** Magnetic field lines due to current carrying solenoid is shown below.

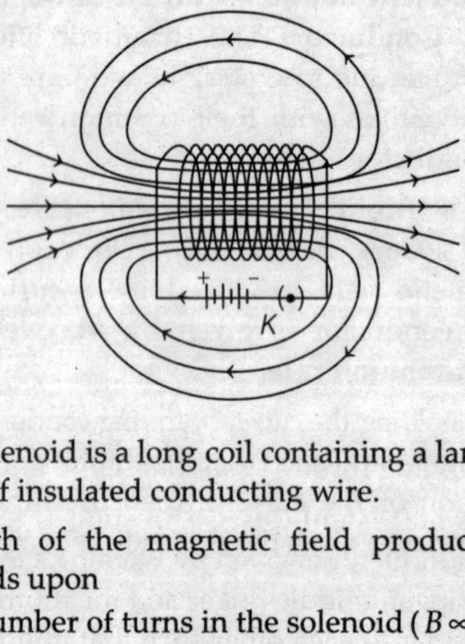

- The solenoid is a long coil containing a large number of close turns of insulated conducting wire.
- Strength of the magnetic field produced by a solenoid depends upon
  - (a) Number of turns in the solenoid ($B \propto N$)
  - (b) Strength of the current ($B \propto I$)
  - (c) The nature of "core material" used in making solenoid.

- The polarity of the ends of solenoid can be checked as follows.

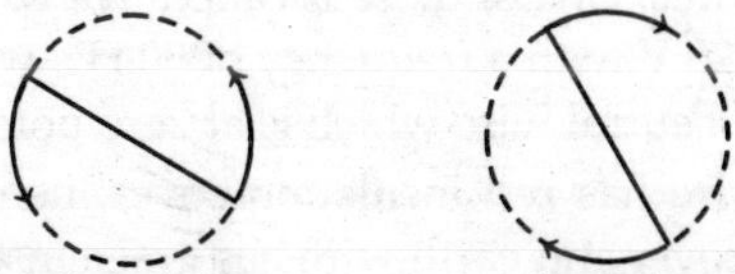

Note If the current in a circular loop (or coil) is in anti-clockwise direction, then it behaves like a North pole. If the current in a circular loop (or coil) is in clock wise direction, then it behaves like south pole.

04 **Force on a Current Carrying Conductor in a Magnetic Field** When a current carrying conductor is placed in a magnetic field, a mechanical force is exerted on the conductor which tends to make it move.

Direction of force acting on a current carrying wire placed in magnetic field is

(i) perpendicular to the direction of the current

(ii) perpendicular to the direction of the magnetic field. Mathematically,

$$F = Bil \sin \theta$$

Maximum force acts on a wire, when it is perpendicular to the field ($\because \theta = 90°$ and $\sin 90° = 1$, maximum) and no force acts on it when it is parallel to the field ($\because \theta = 0°$ and $\sin 0° = 0$).

Direction of force can be reversed by reversing the direction of current flowing through the conductor.

05 **Fleming's Left Hand Rule** Direction of force acting on a current carrying conductor is given by Fleming's left hand rule, "Spread the indexfinger, middle finger and the thumb of left hand mutually perpendicular to each other such that middle finger points in the direction of current, indexfinger points in the direction of magnetic field, then the thumb gives the direction of the force."

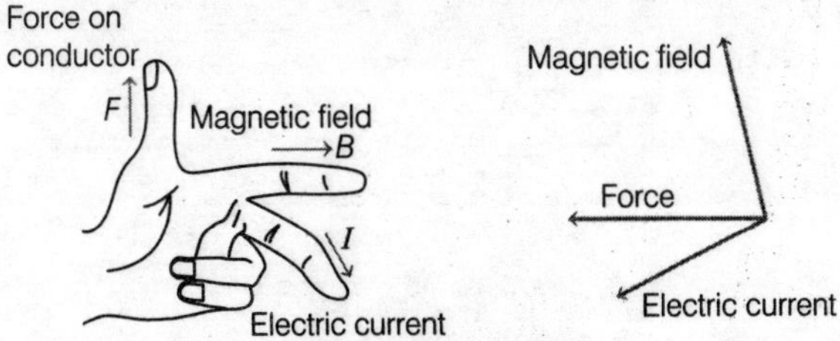

▲ **Fleming's left hand rule**

06 Domestic Electric Circuits Electricity generated at the power station is brought to our homes by two thick copper or aluminium wires. One of these is called live wire which is at a potential of 220 V with a frequency of 50 Hz, whereas the other wire is called neutral wire which is at zero potential.

- The **live wire** has red insulation cover, neutral wire has black insulation cover and earth wire has green insulation cover.
- Another wire called **earth wire** is used as a safety measure and is usually connected to a metal plate deep in the earth near the house.
- The fuse is put in the live wire.
- Usually, there are two separate circuits in a house, the lighting circuit with a 5 A fuse and the power circuit with a 15 A fuse.
- Each distribution circuit is provided with a separate fuse so that, if a fault like short circuiting occurs in one circuit, its corresponding fuse blows off but the other circuits remain unaffected.
- Various distribution circuits are connected in parallel. All the electrical appliances like bulb, fans and sockets, etc., are connected in parallel across the live wire and neutral wire.

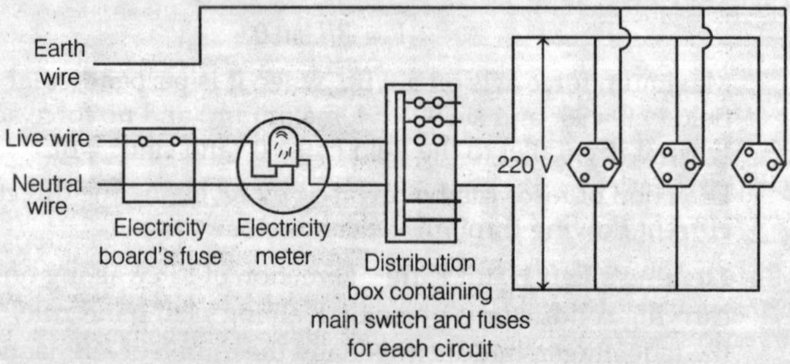

▲ Schematic diagram of the common domestic circuits

Intext Questions

On Page 196

Question 1 Why does a compass needle get deflected when brought near a bar magnet?

Sol. A compass needle is a small magnet itself. It has a north pole and a south pole. When north pole and south pole of the bar magnets are closer to those of compass needle, they attract or repel as per the properties of poles.

On Page 200

Question 1 Draw magnetic field lines around a bar magnet.

Sol.

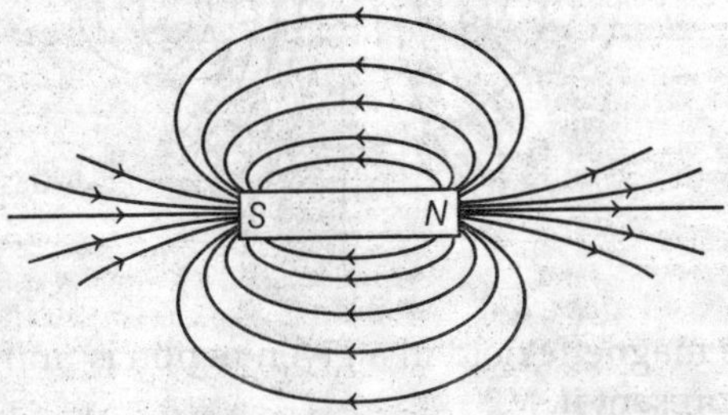

Question 2 List the properties of magnetic lines of force.

Sol. Following are the properties of magnetic lines of force

(i) These are close continuous curves originating at north pole and moving to south pole.

(ii) The strength of magnetic field is stronger when magnetic field lines are closer.

(iii) No two magnetic lines of force intersect each other.

(iv) Magnetic lines of force give the direction in which north pole of the compass needle would point at that place.

Question 3 Why do not two magnetic lines of force intersect each other?

Sol. The direction of magnetic field is taken as the direction in which the north pole of a compass needle moves when placed in that field. If two field lines cross each other, it would mean that a compass needle points towards two directions at the point of intersection, which is not possible.

On Page 201-202

Question 1 Consider a circular loop of wire lying in the plane of table. Let the current pass through the loop clockwise. Apply the right hand rule to find out the direction of the magnetic field inside and outside the loop.

Sol. Applying right hand rule, the magnetic field inside the loop is in vertically downward direction and outside the loop, it is in vertically upward direction.

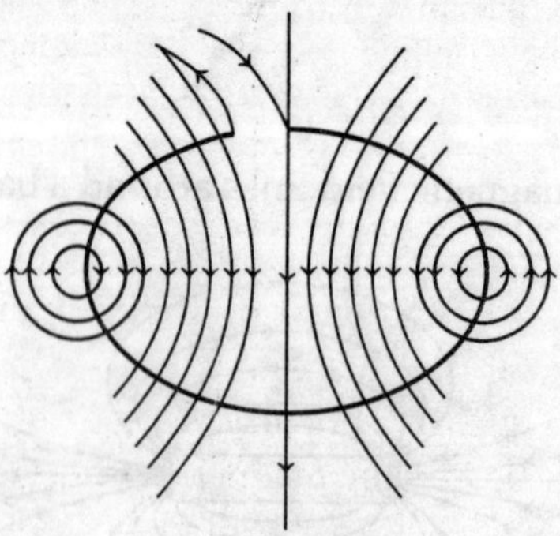

Question 2 The magnetic field in a given region is uniform. Draw a diagram to represent it.

Sol. In a uniform magnetic field, the magnetic field lines of force are parallel and equidistant from each other.

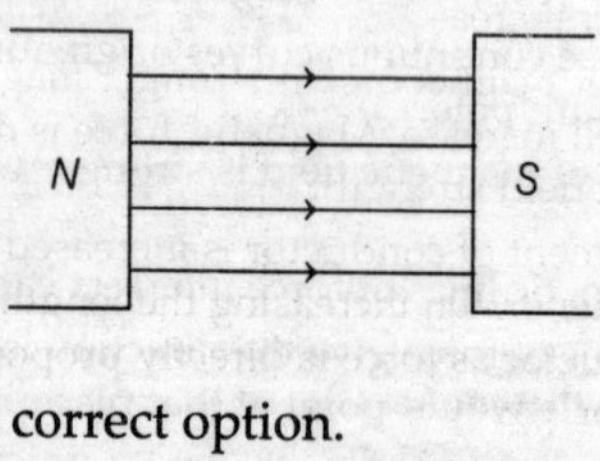

Question 3 Choose the correct option.

The magnetic field inside a long straight solenoid carrying current is

(a) zero

(b) decreases as we move towards its end

(c) increases as we move towards its end

(d) the same at all points

Sol. (d) Magnetic field inside a solenoid is same at all the points.

On Page 203-204

Question 1 Which of the following properties of a proton can change while it moves freely in a magnetic field?

(a) Mass
(b) Momentum
(c) Velocity
(d) Both (c) and (b)

Sol. (d) Velocity is a vector quantity, means it has both magnitude and direction. While the speed remains unchanged, the direction of the protons motion continuously changes as it moves in a circular or helical path. This changes in direction results is a change in the protons velocity.

Momentum (($p = mv$) depends on both the mass and the velocity. Since the direction of the protons velocity changes, its momentum also changes.

Question 2 In activity 12.7, how do we think the displacement of rod *AB* will be affected if

(i) current in rod *AB* is increased
(ii) a stronger horse shoe magnet is used
(iii) length of rod *AB* is increased?

Sol. In activity 12.7, the force acting on a current carrying conductor, when placed in a magnetic field is illustrated.

(i) When current in rod *AB* is increased, the displacement of rod is increased, as force acting on rod is directly proportional to the current flowing through it. On increasing the current force on the conductor increases.

(ii) A stronger magnet means stronger magnetic field. The displacement of rod will increase. Magnetic, force is directly proportional to the magnetic field strength.

(iii) Displacement of conductor is increased with an increase in length of the conductor. On increasing the length more force will be acted on the conductor as force is directly proportional to the length of the conductor.

Mistake Alert In this type of problem, always remember that the force depends on the length in the field, not on any other dimension.

Question 3 A positively charged particle (alpha particle) projected towards west is deflected towards north by a magnetic field. The direction of magnetic field is

(a) towards south
(b) towards east
(c) downward
(d) upward

Sol. (d) The positive charge particle is moving toward west *i.e.*, the direction of current is towards west (current flows in the direction of the motion of positive charge).

The particle is deflected towards north so, the direction of force is toward north. Thus, from Fleming's left hand rule, the direction of magnetic field is in upward direction.

On Page 205

Question 1 Name two safety measures commonly used in electric circuits and appliances.

Sol. (i) Earth wire (earthing) and (ii) fuse are two safety measures commonly used in electric circuits and appliances.

Question 2 An electric oven of 2 kW power rating is operated in a domestic electric circuit (220 V) that has a current rating of 5 A. What result do you except? Explain.

Sol. When a high power rating appliance is operated in a 5A current rating circuit, a large amount of heat is produced in the circuit.

This leads to possible melting of insulation cover of wires and hence a short-circuit. If a fuse is used in the circuit, the fuse wire melts and the circuit is broken.

Question 3 What precautions should be taken to avoid the overloading of domestic electric circuits?

Sol. To avoid overloading, following precautions must be taken

(i) Never connect too many appliances in a single socket.
(ii) Fuse should be used in the circuits.
(iii) Wires should be checked from time-to-time and those wires whose insulation is worn, should be replaced immediately.

Exercises

Question 1 Which of the following correctly describes the magnetic field near a long straight wire?

(a) The field consists of straight lines perpendicular to the wire.
(b) The field consists of straight lines parallel to the wire.
(c) The field consists of radial lines originating from the wire.
(d) The field consists of concentric circles centred on the wire.

Sol. (d) The magnetic field lines due to a straight current carrying wire are concentric circles, *i.e.*, the field consists of concentric circles centered on the wire.

Question 2 At the time of short circuit, the current in the circuit

(a) reduces substantially
(b) does not change
(c) increases heavily
(d) vary continuously

Sol. (c) Increases heavily.

During a short circuit, the circuits resistance becomes very low or nearly zero because there is an unintended direct path across the power source. According to Ohm's law $\left(I = \frac{V}{R}\right)$, when resistance R decreases the voltage remains the same, while the current in the circuit increases drastically. This high current can cause damage to the circuit components.

Question 3 State whether the following statements are true or false.

(a) The field at the centre of a long circular coil carrying current will be parallel straight lines.
(b) A wire with a green insulation is usually the live wire of an electric supply.

Sol. (a) True,

(b) False, the wire with a green insulation is the earth wire not the live wire.

Question 4 List two methods of producing magnetic fields.

Sol. Following are the methods of producing magnetic field

(a) Passing electric current through a straight conductor/circuit.
(b) Passing electric current through a circular loop.

Question 5 When is the force experienced by a current carrying conductor placed in magnetic field largest?

Sol. Force acting on current carrying conductor,

$$F = Bli \sin \theta,$$

F will be maximum when $\sin \theta$ is maximum.

$$(\sin \theta)_{max} = 1 = \sin 90°$$

$$\therefore \quad \theta = 90°$$

i.e., conductor is perpendicular to the field.

Question 6 Imagine that you are sitting in a chamber with your back to one wall. An electron beam, moving horizontally from back wall towards the front wall, is deflected by a strong magnetic field to your right side. What is the direction of magnetic field?

◎ **Thinking Process** The direction of the deflection of charged particles depends on the direction of the magnetic field and the velocity of the particles.

Sol. The direction of current is from front wall to back wall (opposite to the direction of motion of electron), direction of force is towards right. So, using Fleming's left hand rule, direction of force would be upwards.

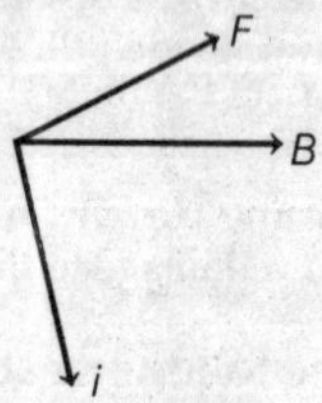

Question 7 State the rule to determine the direction of a

(i) magnetic field produced around a straight conductor carrying current.

(ii) force experienced by a current carrying straight conductor placed in a magnetic field.

(iii) current induced in a coil due to its rotation in magnetic field.

Sol. (i) **Ampere's right hand thumb rule** If current is passing through a conductor in the direction of thumb of the right hand, then the direction of magnetic field is given by that of curvature of fingers.

(ii) **Fleming's left hand rule** If the index finger, middle finger and thumb of left hand are stretched mutually perpendicular and index finger points in the direction of magnetic field, middle finger points in the direction of flow of electric current, then thumb points in the direction of force acting on the conductor.

(iii) **Fleming's right hand rule** If the index finger, middle finger and thumb of right hand are stretched mutually perpendicular and index finger points in direction of magnetic field, thumb points in the direction of motion of conductor, then middle finger points in the direction of induced current.

Mistake Alert Induced current only occurs when there is relative motion between the coil and the magnetic field, not when they are stationary.

Question 8 When does an electric short circuit occur?

Sol. When the insulation of wires is damaged or there is a fault in the appliance, due to which the live wire and neutral wire come in direct contact, the current in the circuit increases abruptly. This is called short-circuiting.

Question 9 What is the function of an earth wire? Why is it necessary to earth metallic appliances?

Sol. The earth wire is connected to a metallic plate deep inside the earth. In this way, the metallic body of the appliance is connected to the earth, which provides a low resistance conducting path for electric current. Hence, any leakage of current to the metallic body of appliance keeps its potential to that of the earth. The user might not get a severe electric shock on touching such an appliance.

DIKSHA APP Questions

☐ Short Answer Type

Q.1 The given magnet is divided into three parts *A*, *B* and *C*. Name the part when the strength of magnetic field is (i) maximum (ii) minimum. How will the density of magnetic field lines differ at these parts?

A	*B*	*C*

Sol. (i) Maximum strength at '*A*' and '*C*'.

(ii) Minimum strength at '*B*'.

At '*A*' and '*C*', magnetic field lines are crowded whereas field lines are spread out at '*B*'.

☐ Long Answer Type

Q.1 (i) Cable of microwave oven has three wires inside which have insulation of different colours black, green and red. Mention the significance of each colour and potential difference between red and black.

(ii) Design an activity with the help of two nails, very thin aluminium sheet, a 12 V battery and a key to illustrate how fuse works.

Sol. (i) Black wire is neutral wire (–). It is at zero volt. Red wire is live wire (+) at 220 V. Green wire is earth wire for safety. 220 V is the potential difference between black and red wire.

(ii) Set the apparatus as shown in the diagram. Switch on the current by pressing the key. Now pass the electric current through the circuit for sometime and observe what happens. Now, increase the electric current and observe what happens.

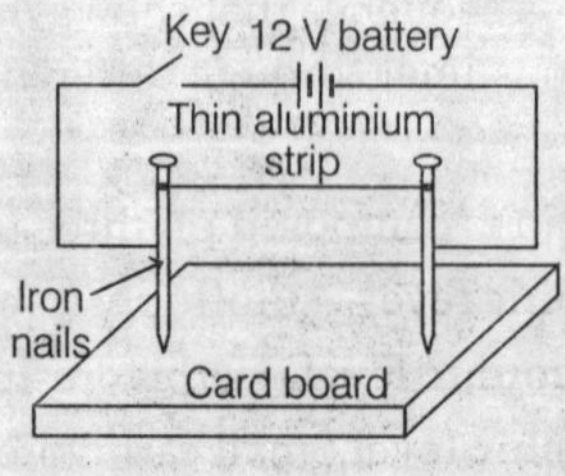

Observation The current below which aluminium strip does not melt is safe. The current at which aluminium strip melts is high current which should be avoided.

Our Environment

CHAPTER 13

Important Points

01 Our environment includes everything around us whether living or non-living.

02 All the living organisms in an environment together with the non living components forms an ecosystem.

03 An ecosystem is made up of two main components, *i.e.*, biotic and abiotic

04 In an ecosystem, the biotic factors may be classified as producers, consumers and decomposers depending on their mode of nutrition.

05 **Producers** or **autotrophs** (green plants) are capable of producing food with the help of inorganic substances and solar energy, *i.e.*, photosynthesis.

06 **Consumers** or **heterotrophic** on the producers either directly or indirectly for food.

07 **Decomposers** breakdown the dead bodies of all living organisms.

08 **Food chain** is a sequence that shows the flow of erergy from produces to consumer through different trophic levels in an ecosystem.

09 Each food chain is composed of three to five trophic levels.

(i) **First trophic level** Autotrophs/producers

(ii) **Second trophic level** Herbivores/primary consumers

(iii) **Third trophic level** Small carnivores/secondary consumers

(iv) **Fourth trophic level** Large carnivores/tertiary consumers.

10 In an ecosystem, there is flow of energy between various trophic levels.

11 Producers or autotrophs convert solar energy into chemical energy, which is then utilised by the consumers and decomposers as food.

12 About 1% of solar energy falling on leaves is utilised by the plants in photosynthesis to produce food.

13 A large amount of energy loss occurs when the organisms of the higher trophic level feeds on the lower trophic level organisms.

14 There is only **10% flow of energy** from one trophic level to the next higher level. Due to this energy loss, only 4 or 5 trophic levels are present in each food chain.

15 This flow of energy is unidirectional in the ecosystem and cannot be utilised by the previous trophic levels.

16 Sometimes, the non-biodegradable chemicals like pesticides and insecticides enter the food chains in land and aquatic ecosystems and then accumulate gradually at each trophic level. This is known as **biological magnification**.

17 **Food webs,** consisting of several interconnected food chains.

18 Humans are an integral part of the environment. Many of their activities can cause several environmental problems like ozone layer depletion and waste disposal.

19 Ozone (O_3), is composed of three oxygen atoms. It is a toxic chemical formed by the combination of free oxygen atom with molecular oxygen.

20 At higher level of atmosphere, the ozone shields the surface of earth from the entry of solar ultraviolet radiations.

21 The amount of ozone in the atmosphere began to drop sharply in the 1980s. This decrease is linked with the use of chemicals like chlorofluorocarbons (CFCs) which are used as refrigerant and in fire extinguishers.

22 In 1987, the United Nations Environment Programme (UNEP) made an agreement to freeze the CFCs production at 1986 levels.

23 The wastes generated by the various humans activities can be divided into two main categories
(i) **Biodegradable waste** (ii) **Non-biodegradable waste**

24 The enzymes present in the body of decomposers are capable of breaking down the biodegradable substances, but not the non-biodegradable materials.

25 The non-biodegradable materials like plastic and synthetic pesticides persist in the environment for a long duration and may harm other biotic factors.

26 There should be effective waste disposal methods so that our environment can be protected from its damaging and harmful effects.

Intext Questions

On Page 212

Question 1 What are trophic levels? Give an example of a food chain and state the different trophic levels in it.

Sol. The various links or steps in a food chain at which the transfer of food and energy takes place are called trophic levels. The producers form the first trophic level as they manufacture food. The primary consumers form the second trophic level, the secondary consumers form the third and the tertiary consumers form the fourth trophic level.

In the above figure, grass is the producer which is eaten by the grasshopper known as primary consumer then the grasshopper is eaten by shrew, secondary consumer and lastly shrew eaten up by owl, tertiary consumer.

Question 2 What is the role of decomposers in the ecosystem?

Sol. Organisms that feed on dead plants and animals are called decomposers, *e.g.*, bacteria, fungi, etc. The decomposers following roles in ecosystem.

(i) They help in recycling of materials, replenishment of the soil's nutrients, etc.

(ii) They clean the surroundings by decomposing dead organisms the organic wastes.

On Page 214

Question 1 Why are some substances biodegradable and some non-biodegradable?

Sol. Certain substances are termed biodegradable because they can be broken down into simpler substances by enzymatic actions of decomposers decomposers. Examples include organic waste like food scraps and paper. Non-biodegradable substances, such as plastics, cannot be easily broken down by enzymes and thus persist in the environment without decomposing.

Question 2 Give any two ways in which biodegradable substances would affect the environment.

Sol. The biodegradable substance can have several positive effects on the environment such as.

(i) Biodegradable substances act as a medium to return back the nutrients to the environment.

(ii) Biodegradable substances decompose naturally reducing accumulation of waste in landfills and preventing long-term environmental pollution.

Question 3 Give any two ways in which non-biodegradable substances would affect the environment.

Sol. Two ways in which biodegradable substance affect the environment are as follows

(i) They make the environment poisonous and unfit for survival.

(ii) They block the transfer of energy and minerals in the ecosystem.

On Page 216

Question 1 What is ozone and how does it affect any ecosystem?

Sol. Ozone is a tri-atomic molecule, i.e., made up of three atoms of oxygen joined together. Its molecular formula is O_3. It can affect any ecosystem in the following ways

(i) It protects against ultraviolet rays if, present in stratosphere.

(ii) Ozone dissipates the energy of UV rays by undergoing dissociation followed by reassociation.

$$2O_3 \longrightarrow 3O_2 + \text{Energy}$$

Question 2 How can you help in reducing the problem of waste disposal? Give any two methods.

Sol. (i) Using biodegradable materials (ii) Using recyclable materials.

Exercises

Question 1 Which of the following groups contain only biodegradable items?

(a) Grass, flowers and leather
(b) Grass, wood and plastic
(c) Fruit-peels, cake and lime-juice
(d) Cake, wood and grass

Sol. (c) Substances that are broken down by the biological processes are said to be biodegradable, *e.g.*, fruit, cake, lime-juice, wood, grass, cake, etc.

Question 2 Which of the following constitute a food-chain?

(a) Grass, wheat and mango (b) Grass, goat and human
(c) Goat, cow and elephant (d) Grass, fish and goat

Sol. (b) Each step of food chain form a trophic level. Producers (grass) form the first trophic level, herbivore (goat) the second and carnivore (human) the third trophic level.

Question 3 Which of the following are environment-friendly practices?

(a) Carrying cloth-bags to put purchases in while shopping
(b) Switching off unnecessary light and fans
(c) Walking to school instead of getting your mother to drop you on her scooter
(d) All of the above

Sol. (d) Cloth-bags are biodegradable, switching off unnecessary light and fans and limited use of petrol/diesel cause less pollution hence, environment friendly practices.

Question 4 What will happen if we kill all the organisms in one trophic level?

Sol. If all the organisms in one trophic level are removed, the lower trophic levels will likely to experience a population increase due to the absence of their predators or consumers. Conversely, the higher trophic levels will struggle to survive or may become extinct due to a lack of food resources. This disruption affects the flow of energy through the ecosystem, leading to imbalances and potentially causing widespread ecological damage

Question 5 Will the impact of removing all the organisms in a trophic level be different for different trophic levels? Can the organisms of any trophic level be removed without causing any damage to the ecosystem?

Sol. Yes, the impact of removing all organisms from a trophic level will vary depending on the level removed. The lower trophic levels, which typically have more individuals, play crucial roles in sustaining the 'ecosystem. Removing producers (the lowest trophic level) would disrupt the entire food chain, as all higher levels depend on them for energy. Removing organisms from higher trophic levels might initially lead to an increase in the population of organisms at lower levels, but it can also disrupt ecological balance.

No, removal of all organisms of trophic level will disturb the ecosystem as each trophic level plays an important role in maintaining the balance of the ecosystem.

Question 6 What is biological magnification? Will the levels of this magnification be different at different levels of the ecosystem?

Sol. Biological magnification refers to the process by which chemicals or toxins becomes more concentrated as they move up the food chain. These substances accumulate in the tissues of organisms at higher trophic levels because they are not broken down or excreted. The levels of magnification are different at each trophic level; higher trophic levels experience greater magnification due to the accumulation of toxins from the organisms they consume.

Question 7 What are the problems caused by the non-biodegradable wastes that we generate?

Sol. Non-biodegradable wastes persist in the environment for longer periods, leading to pollution of soil, water and air. These wastes can make environment toxic and unfit for survival. Additionally, the disposal of non biodegradable wastes is challenging and contributes to issues such as landfills overflow and chemical contamination.

Question 8 If all the waste we generate is biodegradable, will this have no impact on the environment?

Sol. Even if all waste were biodegradable, it could still impact the environment. While biodegradable waste does not accumulate indefinitely, large quantities can lead to problems such a air pollution due to the release of gases during decomposition. Additionally, excessive amount of biodegradable waste can distupt ecosystems and nutrient cycles, leading to issues like eutrophication in aquatic environments.

Question 9 Why is damage to the ozone layer a cause for concern? What steps are being taken to limit this damage?

Sol. The thinning of ozone layer present in stratosphere is called depletion of ozone layer. Due to depletion of ozone layer, harmful ultraviolet radiations will reach the surface of Earth, which may lead to skin diseases and cancer.

To reduce the depletion of ozone layer, the use of chlorofluorocarbons has been minimised.

DIKSHA APP Questions

Multiple Choice Questions

Q.1 Accumulation of non-biodegradable pesticides in the food chain in increasing amount at each higher trophic level is known as

(a) eutrophication (b) pollution
(c) bio-magnification (d) accumulation

Sol. (c) Bio-magnification refers to the increasing concentration of non-biodegradable pesticides at each trophic level in the food chain.

Q.2 In the given food chain, suppose the amount of energy at fourth trophic level is 5 kJ,what will be the energy available at the producer level?

Grass $\rightarrow$ Grasshopper $\rightarrow$ Frog $\rightarrow$ Snake $\rightarrow$ Hawk

(a) 5 kJ (b) 50 kJ (c) 500 kJ (d) 5000 kJ

Sol. (d) Using the 10% energy rule, if the energy at the fourth trophic level is 5 kJ, then the energy at the producers would be 5000 kJ.

Q.3 Which one of the following is an artificial ecosystem?

(a) Pond (b) Crop field (c) Lake (d) Forest

Sol. (b) A crop field is an artificial ecosystem because it is created and maintained by humans for agricultural purposes.

Q.4 Which of the following is not an example of abiotic factors?

(a) Light (b) Plants
(c) Heat (d) Temperature

Sol. (b) Plants are biotic factors because they are living organisms.

Q.5 Non - biodegradable materials are those

(a) which do not pollute environment
(b) which are not harmful
(c) which persist in environment and cause pollution
(d) plants are non - biodegradable material

Sol. (c) Non-biodegradable materials are substances that do not break down naturally and persist in the environment, leading to pollution.

Q.6 Following are the examples of bio degradable materials:

(a) D.D.Tand detergents (b) Plastics and melamine crockery

(c) D.D.Tand plants (d) All organic waste materials

Sol. (d) Biodegradable materials are those that can be broken down by natural processes, such as organic waste (e.g., food scraps, leaves, and plant matter).

Q.7 Tropic level in an ecosystem represents :-

(a) oxygen level (b) water level

(c) Energy level (d) salt level

Sol. (c) Trophic levels in an ecosystem represent the different energy levels in a food chain, starting with producers at the base and moving up to consumers.

Q.8 Which of the following is a logical sequence of food chain?

(a) Producer → consumer → decomposer

(b) Producer → decomposer → consumer

(c) Consumer → producer → decomposer

(d) Decomposer → producer → consumer

Sol. (a) The logical sequence of a food chain is Producer → Consumer → Decomposer, where producers make their own food, consumers eat producers or other consumers, and decomposers break down dead organisms to recycle nutrients.

□ Short Answer Type

Q.1 We often observe domestic waste decomposing in the by lanes of residential colonies. Suggest ways to make people realise that the improper disposal of waste is harmful to the environment.

Sol. Some of the ways to make people realise that the improper disposal of waste is harmful to the environment are as follows.

(i) Organising street plays

(ii) Encouraging the peoples to reuse and recycle the products.

(iii) Increasing awareness about the spread of the disease from the grabage heaps

(iv) Providing information related to minimising waste.

Q.2 (a) Why is it necessary to conserve our environment?

(b) State the importance of green and blue dust-bins in the safe disposal of the household waste.

(c) List two values exhibited by your classmate who is an active member of eco-club of your school. .

Sol. (a) It is necessary to conserve our environment because

(i) It helps in protecting the ozone layer.

(ii) It helps in maintaining animal and human food chains.

(iii) It provides us with many useful products such as medicines and wood.

(b) The importance of green and blue dust bins in the safe disposal of the household waste are as follows

(i) Green contain the waste that are biodegradable. The biodegradable waste are broken down into similar units and can be used as manures, fertilizers, compost biogas. The waste in green bin is safe as the waste is nontoxic. It also serve as breeding ground for mosquito. Material that can be put in a green bin in clude fruits, vegetables, flowers papers etc.

(ii) Blue bin contain non-biodegradable waste. The material present in blue bin can harm the environment by causing pollution when not disposed properly. Material that can be put in a blue bin include plastic, metal, chemicals etc.

(c) Two values exhibited by the classmate who is an active member of eco-club of our school are as follows :

(i) Creating environmental awareness among students and society.

(ii) Working hard on prevention of environmental degradation of surroundings.

Q.3 We do not clean ponds or lakes, but an aquarium needs to be cleaned. Why?

Sol. Ponds and lakes are natural ecosystem and they have self-cleaning mechanism driven by food chain and other environmental factors. But, an aquarium being an artificial eco-system do not have such mechanism. Therefore, aquarium need regular cleaning.

Q.4 Accumulation of harmful chemicals in our bodies can be avoided. Explain how this can be achieved?

Sol. Accumulation of harmful chemicals in our bodies can be avoided by following ways.

(i) By drinking plenty of water

(ii) By eating healthy food

(iii) By performing excerise

(iv) By not taking stress

Q.5 What are the problem caused by the notn biodegradable wastes that we generate?

Sol. The problems caused by non-biodegradable wastes are as follows

(i) They cause biomagnification. (ii) They increase pollution.

(iii) They kill useful microorganisms.

Q.6 Why is damage to the ozone layer a cause for concern? What steps are being taken to limit this damage?

Sol. The damage to the ozone layer is a concern because it allows more harmful UV rays to reach the Earth's surface, leading to increased risps of skin cancer, ageing and corneal cataracts.

To limit the damage to the ozone layer, the release of CFCs into the atmo sphere must be reduced. CFCs used in refrigerants and fire extinguishers should be replaced with environmentally safe alternatives. Also, the release of CFCs through industrial activities should be controlled

Q.7 Give difference between food chain and food web.

Sol. The diffeence between food chain and food web are as follows

Food chain	Food web
It refers to a natural system by which energy is transmitted from one organism to another.	It consists of a number of interconnected food chains.
Members of higher trophic level feed upon a single type of organisms	Members of higher trophic level feed upon many organisms.
Example- Carrots ---> rabbit --> snake --> eagle.	Example- A hawk might eat a mouse, a squirrel, a frog or some other animal. The snake may eat a beetle, a caterpillar, or some other animal

Q.8 How will you convince people that plastics are harmful to the environment?What alternatives of polythene bags do we have, which are environmental friendly?How can school inculcate environmental values in students?

Sol. One can convince people that plastics are harmful to the environment by highlighting that cows and others animals eat polythene which is very dangerous and often fatal and coloured polythene is very harmful for vegetables and fruits. Alternatives of polythene bags are prayer bags, jute bags, bags of biodegradable materials are eco-friendly School can inculcate environmental values in students by teaching students to protect environment. They should - make paper bags and distribute to small shopkeepers regularly and slowly their habits will change.

Q.9 What is eco system ?List two main components. How does ozone, effect any ecosystem? Give one example each from your daily life where domestic waste can be effectively reused and recycled.

Sol. An **ecosystem** is a community of living organisms interacting with their environment. **The two main components** of an ecosystem are biotic (living organisms) and abiotic (non-living factors)

Ozone's effect Ozone protects ecosystems by blocking harmful UV rays; depletion increases UV exposure, harming plants and animals.

Examples of effectively reusing and recycling domestic waste from daily life are as follows:

- **Reusing** Empty glass jars can be repurposed as storage containers for food, spices, or small household items.
- **Recycling** Paper waste, such as old newspapers or magazines, can be collected and sent to a recycling center to be turned into new paper products.

Q.10 Construct an aquatic food chain showing five tropic levels.

Sol.

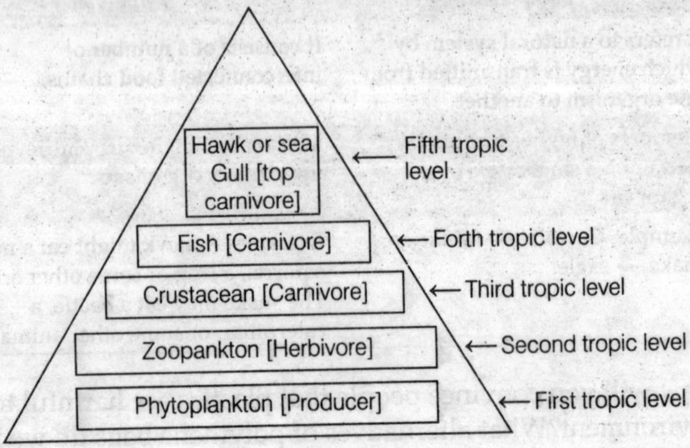